Reading Texts on Sovereignty

TEXTUAL MOMENTS IN THE HISTORY OF POLITICAL THOUGHT

Series Editors

J. C. Davis, Emeritus Professor of History, University of East Anglia, UK

John Morrow, Professor of Political Studies, University of Auckland, New Zealand

Textual Moments provides accessible, short readings of key texts in selected fields of political thought, encouraging close reading informed by cutting-edge scholarship. The unique short essay format of the series ensures that volumes cover a range of texts in roughly chronological order. The essays in each volume aim to open up a reading of the text and its significance in the political discourse in question and in the history of political thought more widely. Key moments in the textual history of a particular genre of political discourse are made accessible, appealing and instructive to students, scholars and general readers.

Published

Utopian Moments: Reading Utopian Texts, Miguel Avilés and J. C. Davis

Censorship Moments: Reading Texts in the History of Censorship and Freedom of Expression, Geoff Kemp

Revolutionary Moments: Reading Revolutionary Texts, Rachel Hammersley

Patriarchal Moments: Reading Patriarchal Texts, Cesare Cuttica and Gaby Mahlberg

Feminist Moments: Reading Feminist Texts, Susan Bruce and Katherine Smits

Liberal Moments: Reading Liberal Texts, Ewa Atanassow and Alan S. Kahan

Democratic Moments: Reading Democratic Texts, Xavier Márquez

Revolutionary Moments: Reading Revolutionary Texts, Rachel Hammersley

Conservative Moments: Reading Conservative Texts, Mark Garnett

Reading Texts on Sovereignty

Textual Moments in the History of Political Thought

Edited by Stella Achilleos and Antonis Balasopoulos

BLOOMSBURY ACADEMIC
LONDON · NEW YORK · OXFORD · NEW DELHI · SYDNEY

BLOOMSBURY ACADEMIC
Bloomsbury Publishing Plc
50 Bedford Square, London, WC1B 3DP, UK
1385 Broadway, New York, NY 10018, USA
29 Earlsfort Terrace, Dublin 2, Ireland

BLOOMSBURY, BLOOMSBURY ACADEMIC and the Diana logo are trademarks
of Bloomsbury Publishing Plc

First published in Great Britain 2021

Series design by Burge Agency
Cover image: © Max Krasnov/Shutterstock

A catalogue record for this book is available from the British Library.

A catalog record for this book is available from the Library of Congress.

ISBN: HB: 978-1-3500-9970-8
       PB: 978-1-3500-9969-2
       ePDF: 978-1-3500-9971-5
       eBook: 978-1-3500-9972-2

Typeset by RefineCatch Limited, Bungay, Suffolk

To find out more about our authors and books visit www.bloomsbury.com
and sign up for our newsletters.

CONTENTS

CONTRIBUTORS

Stella Achilleos is Associate Professor of Early Modern Studies at the Department of English Studies, University of Cyprus. She has published widely within her areas of expertise and her current research projects include a book-length study on violence and utopia in the early modern period.

Jed W. Atkins is the E. Blake Byrne Associate Professor of Classical Studies and Associate Professor of Political Science at Duke University. He is the author of *Cicero on Politics and the Limits of Reason* (Cambridge, 2013) and *Roman Political Thought* (Cambridge, 2018). He is coediting the forthcoming *Cambridge Companion to Cicero's Philosophy*.

Antonis Balasopoulos is Associate Professor in Comparative Literature at the Department of English Studies, University of Cyprus. Much of his published work concentrates on the literary, philosophical and political ramifications of the concept of Utopia. He has also edited or coedited four volumes and special issues. His book of collected essays, *Figures of Utopia: Literature, Politics, Philosophy*, is under preparation.

Marco Barducci (PhD, FRHistS) is currently Honorary Fellow in the Institute of Medieval and Early Modern Studies at Durham University. He is the author, among others, of *Hugo Grotius and the Century of Revolution, 1613–1718* (Oxford, 2017) and of *Order and Conflict. Anthony Ascham and English Political Thought, 1648–50* (Manchester, 2015).

Glenn Burgess is Professor of Early Modern History at the University of Hull. He is the author of *The Politics of the Ancient Constitution: An Introduction to English Political Thought 1603–1642* (1992); *Absolute Monarchy and the Stuart Constitution* (1996); *British Political Thought 1500–1660* (2009); and many articles, essays and edited collections.

Massimo Campanini was Associate Professor of Islamic Studies at the University of Naples L' Orientale. His most recent monographs included *Al-Ghazali and the Divine* (Routledge, 2019) and *Pensare nell'Islam* (Jaca Book, 2019).

Kate Langdon Forhan PhD is Professor Emeritus of Political Science at the University of Southern Maine. She has written multiple works on medieval political thought, including *The Political Theory of Christine de Pizan* (2002). Forhan also served as professor, dean, and provost at universities in the United States and France.

Dean Hammer is the John W. Wetzel Professor of Classics and Professor of Government at Franklin and Marshall College (USA). He is the author of *The Puritan Tradition, The Iliad as Politics: The Performance of Political Thought, Roman Political Thought and the Modern Theoretical Imagination, Roman Political Thought: From Cicero to Augustine*, and an edited volume, *A Companion to Greek Democracy and the Roman Republic*.

Kazutaka Inamura is Associate Professor of Political Philosophy at Waseda University. He published *Justice and Reciprocity in Aristotle's Political Philosophy* with Cambridge University Press. He is working on teleology, biology, and methodology in Aristotle's political thought and interested in the receptions of Aristotle in modern times.

Geoff Kemp is Senior Lecturer in Politics at the University of Auckland. Recent publications include the introduction to Locke's writings on liberty of the press in *John Locke: Literary and Historical Writings* (2019), and "Locke the Censor, Locke the Anti-Censor" in *Politics, Religion and Ideas in Seventeenth- and Eighteenth-Century Britain* (2019). He edited *Censorship Moments: Reading Texts in the History of Censorship and Freedom of Expression* (2014) in the present series.

Shmuel Lederman teaches at the University of Haifa and at the Open University of Israel. He is the author of *Hannah Arendt and Participatory Democracy: A People's Utopia* (2019), as well as numerous articles on Hannah Arendt's political thought.

Carine Lounissi is Associate Professor of American History at the University of Rouen-Normandie (France). She has published two books on Thomas Paine, the latest being *Thomas Paine and the French Revolution* (Palgrave, 2018). Her current project concerns the reception of the American Revolution in France in the 1770s and 1780s.

James Martel is a Professor of Political Science at San Francisco State University. He is the author, most recently of *Unburied Bodies: Subversive Corpses and the Authority of the Dead* (Amherst College Press, 2018) and *The Misinterpellated Subject* (Duke University Press, 2017). He is currently working on a new book entitled *Disappointing Vision: Anarchist Prophecy and the Power of Collective Sight*.

Michael Mendle, now retired, was Professor of History in the University of Alabama. He has written on political thought, the pamphlet culture, and the impact of effective shorthand upon the public life of the seventeenth century.

Sara Miglietti is Senior Lecturer at London's Warburg Institute and specializes in Renaissance philosophy and intellectual history. She is the editor of Jean Bodin's *Methodus* (2013) and coeditor of *Governing the Environment in the Early Modern World* (2017) and has published extensively on various aspects of early modern political thought.

John Morrow is Professor of Political Studies and Deputy Vice-chancellor (Academic) at the University of Auckland, New Zealand. His publications include *Coleridge's Political Thought* (1990), (with Mark Francis) *A History of Nineteenth-Century English Political Thought* (1994), *Thomas Carlyle* (2006) and *History of Western Political Thought* (third edition, 2019).

Mika Ojakangas is Professor of Political Thought at the University of Jyväskylä, Finland. He is the author of eighty articles and seven books. His most recently published books are *The Voice of Conscience: A Political Genealogy of Western Ethical Experience* (Bloomsbury 2013) and *On the Greek Origins of Biopolitics: A Reinterpretation of the History of Biopower* (Routledge 2016).

Yuri Pines 尤銳 is Professor of Chinese History, Hebrew University of Jerusalem. His monographs include *The* Book of Lord Shang: *Apologetics of State Power in Early China* (2017); *The Everlasting Empire: The Political Culture of Ancient China and Its Imperial Legacy* (2012); and *Envisioning Eternal Empire: Chinese Political Thought of the Warring States Era* (2009).

Carlo Salzani is Gastwissenschaftler (guest scholar) at the Messerli Research Institute, Vienna (Austria). He has published widely on Robert Musil, Walter Benjamin, Franz Kafka, Giorgio Agamben, and the animal question.

Vasileios Syros is a Docent in Political History and the History of Political Thought at the Universities of Helsinki and Jyväskylä (Finland) and a Senior Research Fellow at The Medici Archive Project (Florence, Italy). His teaching and research interests converge at the intersection of the history of Christian/ Latin, Jewish, and Islamic political thought. His current research focuses on plagues and good government in early modern Europe.

David Lay Williams is Professor of Political Science at DePaul University. He is the author of *Rousseau's Platonic Enlightenment* (2007) and *Rousseau's "Social Contract": An Introduction* (2014), as well as numerous essays. He is presently completing a book project on economic inequality in Western political thought.

Carl E. Young is an Assistant Professor of Classics at Hillsdale College. He is the author of various articles on Greek political thought and its reception in the Renaissance.

Michael Zuckert is Nancy Dreux Professor of Political Science Emeritus at University of Notre Dame (USA). He is currently Visiting Professor at the School for Civic and Economic Thought and Leadership at Arizona State University. He has taught and written in the areas of Modern Political Philosophy, American constitutionalism and American Political Thought. He was founding editor of the journal *American Political Thought*.

SERIES EDITORS' FOREWORD

At the heart of the serious study of the history of political thought, as expressed through both canonical and non-canonical works of all kinds, has been the question (to which we all too readily assume an answer), "How shall I read this text?" Answers have varied greatly over time. Once the political works of the past—especially those of Classical Greece and Rome—were read with an eye to their immediate application to the present. And, until comparatively recently, the canonical works of political philosophy were selected and read as expressions of perennial, abiding truths about politics, social morality, and justice. The problem with this approach was that it made little or no concession to historically changing contexts, and meant that the "truths" we identified were all too often *our* truths. A marxisant sociology of knowledge struggled to break free from the "eternal verities" of political thought by exploring the ways in which past societies shaped their own forms of political expression in distinctive yet commonly grounded conceptions of their own image. The problem remained that the perception of what shaped past societies was all too often driven by the demands of a current political agenda. In both cases, present concerns shaped the narrative history of political thought off which the reading of texts fed. The last half century has seen another powerful and influential attempt to break free from a present-centered history of political thought by locating texts as speech acts or moves within a contemporary context of linguistic usage. Here the frequently perceived problem has been (a by-no-means inevitable) narrowing of focus to canonical texts, while the study of other forms of political expression in images, speech, performance and gesture—in all forms of political culture—has burgeoned independently.

We have, then, a variety of ways of approaching past texts and the interplay of text and context. The series "Textual Moments in the History of Political Thought" (in which *Sovereign Moments* is the ninth title) is designed to encourage fresh readings of thematically selected texts. Each chapter identifies a key textual moment or passage and exposes it to a reading by an acknowledged expert. The aim is fresh insight, accessibility, and the encouragement to read, in a more informed way for oneself.

If by sovereignty we mean the cluster questions relating to final, determining authority within a given political entity, then decisions about sovereignty would seem central to both political theorizing and contemporary political claims. The answers to the question as to whose decision finally authorizes, or declares illegitimate, our responses to the situations confronting us contributes not only to the shaping of our civic existence but also goes much of the way to identifying the kind of polis to which we belong or aspire.

Is that authority to be found in what we have come to think of as the nation state (however defined) or some cultural, ethnic or religious subdivision of that state? Is it to be found in such supra-national organizations as we have been able to construct and sustain? Or, more nebulously, might it be sought in the realm of natural/human rights? As this collection shows, the conversations engaging with these issues have a long history but retain their urgency and freshness. The essays in this volume discuss a range of textual moments in which the idea of sovereignty plays a decisive role. The coverage is extensive in both temporal and geographical terms. The book opens with chapters on texts from ancient Chinese, Greek, and Roman sources and extends through the medieval, early modern, and modern worlds to conclude with studies of thinkers from the second half of the twentieth century. The essay on Lord Shang, an important fourth-century Chinese figure, and that on the tenth-century Islamic philosopher Al-Fārābī, the founder of social and political philosophy in that tradition who engaged with the works of ancient Greek writers, provide comparative insights into the treatment of an idea which is usually identified with western political thought. Understandably, however, given the conscious attention to sovereignty within that tradition, major figures from it are very well represented in the volume.

The authors engage with a range of implications of the conception of sovereignty which focus on supreme and final human power in the state, and they also explore the importance attached to justifying such power by reference to its effectiveness in advancing political objectives in specific historical contexts. These accounts consider sovereignty in relation to arguments about the sources of legitimate power, the basis of political obligation, the necessity for social and political stability and the constitutional and other institutional requirements needed to give effect to them. These matters primarily concern sovereignty in relation to the internal life of states but some of the essays in the volume also consider accounts of it that focus on its implications for the relationships between states.

So, issues of sovereignty continue to appear inescapable but, to engage with these conversations about them, we must read with skill and awareness of context.

J. C. Davis
John Morrow

ACKNOWLEDGMENTS

Conceptualizing, planning and editing this volume has been a long and arduous, but also a highly stimulating and enriching process. We would not have been able to cope with the many—in some cases routine, in others exceptional—challenges we faced without the unstinting encouragement, support, experience and guidance of the General Editors of the series, J. C. Davis and John Morrow, to whom we owe a great and abiding debt of gratitude.

We would likewise like to thank our authors for their patience with the rigors of the editorial process, but more importantly, for their commitment to the volume in the midst of difficult and challenging times for all humanity; and extend our special thanks to those who undertook to contribute to the volume under far greater strains on time than we had originally envisaged.

Further, we are grateful to our institution, the University of Cyprus: more broadly, for its varied support of our research endeavors and, more specifically, for granting a one-semester sabbatical leave to one of us that contributed to the completion of this book.

Our editing of the book was marked by the eruption of a pandemic that exposed us to the pressures of living in quarantine and of finding a balance between the demanding task of completing this project and the challenging realities of home-schooling and constant childcare. Therefore, our warmest and most enduring gratitude goes to our respective families and children for all their love, patience, and understanding during these testing times.

Around the time of submitting the final manuscript to the press, we were sadly informed that one of the contributors to this volume, Prof. Massimo Campanini, a prominent scholar of medieval Islam, passed away. Grieved by his loss to the scholarly community, we would like to dedicate this volume to his loving memory.

Stella Achilleos
Antonis Balasopoulos

Introduction

Stella Achilleos and Antonis Balasopoulos

This volume examines a political concept the definition of which may at first glance appear to be simple: deriving from the Latin term *superanus* (via the French *souveraineté*), sovereignty in its political sense refers to a supreme type of power that admits nothing above itself. Yet, while suggesting its analytical centrality, the countless attempts made in the history of political thought to redefine the concept also point to its intriguing elusiveness. Considered in its most general and abstract form, sovereignty appears to withdraw into the nebulous realm that Tacitus, in his *Annals*, designated as "*arcana imperii*" (Book II, chapter 36)—the secrets of imperial power or, more broadly, the state. Indeed, as a concept inevitably entangled with the questions of the origin and foundation of authority and power, sovereignty has long appeared to resist both analysis and definition in a manner that endows it with a theological aura: "supremacy is supremacy is supremacy," as Michael Zuckert suggests, in his discussion in the present volume, regarding the "inexorable logic" through which the question was resolved during the complex debates on sovereignty in the era of the American Revolution; it is the logic of "a truth that no reasoning and no evidence could shake" (see below, p. 122). Writing in the late sixteenth century, Montaigne would make a similar claim regarding the power of tautology when it comes to sovereignty while referring to the inaccessible origin of the legitimacy of law and the legal system: "the laws maintain their credit not because they are just, but because they are laws. This is the mystical basis of their authority. They have no other" ("On Experience," *Essays*, 353). Reference to the legitimacy of sovereignty itself has often been marked by this type of tautological mysticism. In its most abstract theoretical formulations, sovereignty has also been haunted by the specter of nothingness: as Georges Bataille darkly proclaimed in his twentieth-century definition of the term (in his *The Accursed Share*), sovereignty *is* nothing. For though, in his view, sovereignty is the property of a *subject*, it is also a force that, in its presupposition of absolute freedom from any external determination, including action, calculation, and utility of any sort, ruptures subjectivity itself: sovereignty is thus "the power to rise, indifferent to death, above the laws which ensure the maintenance of life [. . .] the sovereignty to which man constantly aspires has never even been accessible [. . .] Never can we *be* sovereign" (*Literature and Evil,* 155, 166, 194).

From another standpoint, however—and the one that by and large dominates the history of its reception—sovereignty is not simply a frustratingly elusive theoretical abstraction but a practical or expedient concept closely interlinked with the existence, nature and objectives of a state. In this respect, sovereignty is *effective* power, power that proves itself in practice by producing concrete political results. If it involves a "speech act"—a proclamation of supremacy such as that analyzed by Dean Hammer in his discussion of Augustus' *Res gestae* in this volume—such an act has to remain plausible. As Neil Walker has put it, the claim to sovereignty is only authentically such when it becomes an institutional fact, whose credibility and plausibility must be proven through the internalization by social actors of a complex set of rules that derive from it and in turn provide verification for the sovereign claim (*Sovereignty in Transition,* 7).

The fact that sovereignty proper cannot be upheld unless it grounds itself in solid practices and institutional formations as well as in its discursive expressions points to one of the most central tenets of the concept: that sovereign is as sovereign does. One of the main targets of this volume is to explore the theoretical and practical implications of this tenet. The essays which are included here therefore engage with some of the key questions that arise in relation to various of sovereignty's conceptual and political manifestations. In doing so, the chapters in this volume invite us to reflect on how the various reconfigurations of the concept of sovereignty dramatize the inherent tensions between "subjective" and "objective," theoretical and practical, conceptual and institutional, fundamentally ahistorical and historicist approaches to the subject. Likewise, while the volume largely concentrates on the conceptual and political ramifications of internal sovereignty, some of the chapters also call attention to the important divide between "internal" and "external" views—sovereignty when considered from within the state, on the one hand, and sovereignty when considered as an aspect of inter-state relations and thus of the international state order, on the other.

The issues raised in this volume involve, for instance, such key questions as the relation between sovereignty and constitutionality. To take one such question: what is the relation between sovereignty and the different constitutional forms through which it may be expressed (monarchy, oligarchy, democracy, aristocracy, and various mixed models)? What is the nature of sovereign will and how is it expressed through different types of sovereignty, such as (absolutist) monarchical or popular sovereignty? Such issues are especially prominent, for example, in Kazutaka Inamura's chapter on Aristotle and the philosopher's idea of the sovereign (το κύριον) in relation to different types of constitution; Jed W. Atkins and Carl E. Young's chapter on Polybius and the compound constitution; Michael Mendle's chapter on the constitutional debates in the revolutionary context of mid-seventeenth-century England; David Lay Williams' chapter on Jean-Jacques Rousseau's take on sovereignty and the general will; and Carine Lounissi's chapter on Thomas Paine and the concept of popular sovereignty. At the same time, these chapters engage with a broader set of interrelated issues, such as the relation between sovereignty and the rule of law—a question of central significance that many of the chapters in this volume address.

Further, the volume could not but include discussion of some of the key features frequently attributed to sovereignty, such as that of sovereignty's indivisibility, first advanced by Jean Bodin in his seminal work *Les Six Livres de la République*. While Bodin's theory of sovereignty comes under scrutiny in Sara Miglietti's chapter on the author, his idea of sovereignty's indivisibility is further taken up, within different contexts, in Stella Achilleos' chapter on Shakespeare and Antonis Balasopoulos' chapter on Lenin. Other chapters also examine some of the most central questions concerning the concept of sovereignty, such as: the relation between political sovereignty and natural or divine law, and the extent to which the former might be seen as limited by the latter (a central point of consideration in Massimo Campanini's chapter on Al-Fārābī and in Geoff Kemp's chapter on John Locke); the question of sovereignty and political obligation (which is the main focus of John Morrow's chapter on T. H. Green's critique of John Austin); the relation between sovereignty and subjects' rights, especially as this pertains to the questions of disobedience and resistance (an idea explored in Marco Barducci's chapter on Hugo Grotius, absolutism, contractualism, and resistance); the relation between sovereignty and the practice of political counsel (an issue addressed in Kate Langdon Forhan's chapter on Christine de Pizan and the problem of sovereignty in fifteenth-century France).

All of the chapters in the volume, each from its own perspective, open up questions about the relation between sovereignty and stability. For many of the theorists discussed here, sovereignty provides the condition for the existence of social order and security. For Hobbes, whose contractual theory of sovereignty (which is discussed in Glenn Burgess' contribution to this volume) holds a prominent position in this tradition, the establishment of the figure of the sovereign offers the only possible opportunity to escape from the horrors of the perpetual war of all against all that defines his view of the state of nature. However, for theorists standing on the other side of the fence in this matter (a perspective that is, as suggested by Shmuel Lederman's, Carlo Salzani's and James Martel's chapters, more prominent in the twentieth century), sovereignty does not in any way guarantee the escape from violence. Take Derrida, for instance: for him, as James Martel highlights in his contribution, "even as it purports to be the solution to violence, [. . .] sovereignty is more often the source of rather than the solution to bloodshed" (see below, p. 180).

This dreadful possibility that is ultimately inherent in sovereignty is no doubt hinted at in the dictum "sovereign is as sovereign does": for sovereignty's capacity to define itself in this manner also insinuates its capacity for arbitrary action, as that is made possible by its position above the law or, to recall Schmitt, by the position of the sovereign as the one who decides on the state of exception. This is what Schmitt refers to as "the infinite, incomprehensible abyss of the force of the *pouvoir constituant*" from which "new forms emerge incessantly, which it can destroy at any time and in which its power is never limited for good" (*Dictatorship*, 127). As Mika Ojakangas notes in his chapter, "this unlimited power lays down the foundations of the constitution—without becoming subject to the constitution once it is established" (see below, p. 158). In this respect, sovereignty comes to be structured on the basis of an endlessly opposing set of possibilities that involve the positions of nomos and anomia (or the order of law and the anomia of the exception), and that constantly threaten to dissolve sovereignty itself into nothing. This characterization cannot but serve to highlight the actual fragility of sovereignty, which is constantly on the verge of nullifying itself by setting itself against its own devices and purpose of existence. In all their figurative force, the words spoken by the Fool to Lear in Shakespeare's play aptly reflect on the position of sovereignty itself: "thou art an O without a figure [. . .] thou art nothing" (*King Lear* 1.4.183–5). Some of the most central questions raised in this volume spring from the aporia of this nothingness and they include not only the seminal issue of stability, but also such significant questions as those of political and civil rights. As many chapters in the volume ask: is sovereignty ultimately a threat to rights or the only foundation thereof?

At the same time that it sets out to address the various questions highlighted above (and other interrelated ones), this volume also aims to situate the interrogation of sovereignty's conceptual and political manifestations within different historical contexts, starting with some of the earliest engagements with the concept in both a non-Western and a European context (the first two chapters, by Yuri Pines and Kazutaka Inamura, being devoted to texts from fourth-century BCE China and Greece respectively). The periodization of the concept (or, the attempt thereof) is in itself immensely useful in inviting us to reflect on how different ideas about sovereignty have developed and unfolded over time. As a reading of the first two chapters of this volume suggests, sovereignty in its earliest incarnations seems largely a question of the "art of government" and its moral and practical prerequisites rather than an analytical exposition of concrete prerogatives or, relatedly, an examination of institutional limits to power. The spheres of law on the one hand, and politics on the other, are not yet sufficiently separate to introduce the tensions and complications we

frequently observe in the era of political modernity, particularly the era after
the Peace of Westphalia (1648), with which a number of commentators have
fully identified the provenance of the concept of sovereignty. Yet if the
Athenian city-state, in the context of which Plato and Aristotle undertook
the earliest western explorations of the nature and the pre-requisites of
supreme power over others, was very different from the European states of
early modernity, the Chinese context with which this volume begins is, as
Yuri Pines puts it, already one of "highly centralized and profoundly
bureaucratized territorial states" (see below, p. 10); and even in the ancient
Greek context, as Kazutaka Inamura illustrates with regard to the case of
Aristotle, unaccountability to any power superior than the sovereign's own,
and hence the idea of the sovereign as "uncontrolled controller" (see below,
p. 18)—a feature crucial to early modern theories of sovereignty—is already
in place.

   Of course, significant differences remain: the modern division between
"state," on the one hand, and "civil society," on the other, is as yet
unimaginable, as are the complex systems of mediations and balances or the
regulating instrument of a written Constitution, the quandaries of balancing
central power and individual rights, protections and freedoms, or an
understanding of the role of the state that would exceed the limits of the
roles of imposing taxation and deciding on peace and war. To the extent that
the question of sovereignty revolves around the identification of *who* is
sovereign in terms of qualities and prerogatives, the ancient debates remain
primarily *subjective* rather than juridical or institutional in any developed
sense, and accordingly testify to the subjection of questions of law, legitimacy,
and legality to those of *de facto* political power, as is the case with the more
"absolutist" versions of the theory of sovereignty that follow during the era
of the Roman Empire and in the late medieval and early modern periods.

   Still, Polybius' *Histories* in the second century BCE provide early testimony
to the fact that, as Jo-Anne Pemberton has argued, the concept of sovereignty
contains an essentially "democratic thrust" (*Sovereignty: Interpretations*, 3)
notwithstanding its apparent connection with personal and absolute rule.
For in inevitably articulating the conditions of the legitimacy of rule, the
theory of sovereignty makes such rule an explicit matter for reflection: even
the most intransigent "orthodoxy" in such matters is only one step away
from "heterodoxy," from contestation and dissensus. Thus, in Jed W. Atkins
and Carl E. Young's analysis, Polybius already shifts attention away from the
qualifications and prerogatives of sovereignty and toward the problems
besetting the attainment of a stable constitution, which he saw as feasible to
the degree that it incorporated distinct yet equal powers that check and
balance each other, as Montesquieu and the drafters of the US Constitution
would envision sovereignty several centuries later. As Michael Mendle's
chapter on Henry Parker's *Observations* and the response to it by King
Charles I's spokesmen on the eve of the English Civil War shows, on the other
hand, dispute over "the boundaries of the political and the regal channels"

(see below, p. 92) could, given the right combination of circumstances, erupt into full-scale military confrontation for supreme power.

Indeed, for all its appearance as a theory that aims to put questions of the grounds of legitimacy and the prerogatives of supreme authority to rest, the theory of sovereignty attained some of its most important moments of development and evolution in periods of great political turbulence and instability, and largely as a response to them: Lord Shang's thought on sovereign power, with whom the volume begins, is one of the many—and heavily conflicting—ideological outcrops of the Warring States period in China, from 453–221 BCE. Plato and Aristotle both reflected on the art of rule and the nature of supreme authority in a highly volatile world, marked by civil strife and "revolution" (in the classical sense) between forms of political constitution. Marsilius of Padua, as Vasileios Syros shows in the context of the early fourteenth century, set as his "avowed goal" the identification and elimination of the "exceptional cause of civil strife that infested various societies across Christian Europe," namely "the Papacy's claim to both temporal and spiritual power" (see below, pp. 49–50). Christine de Pizan's reflections on sovereignty—which she avoids naming as such—in fifteenth-century France arise in a time "of war and chaos," which is why they focus on "the recovery of peace and good rule at a time in which all traditional forms of political authority had been delegitimized" (see below, p. 59). Bodin's foundational *République* was first published, as Sara Miglietti points out, at "a moment of deep crisis for the kingdom of France, shattered by gruesome civil wars that pitted Catholics against Huguenots for over thirty years" (see below, p. 66). Hobbes' equally, if not more, theoretically momentous *Leviathan*, was, as is well-known, published in the wake of the English Civil War, and with the clear aim of providing the theoretical grounds for a new solidification of supreme authority after the earthquakes of a revolutionary decade; and Shakespeare's references to sovereignty, as Stella Achilleos underlines, evoke a complex set of conflicts and transitions in English history, which include the fifteenth-century Wars of the Roses, the events of Henry VIII's split from the Roman Catholic Church, the subsequent struggles of the Reformation and Counter-Reformation, the debates over the issue of succession in the final years of Elizabeth I, and the political tensions that marked James I's first few years on the English throne. From the late eighteenth century onward, of course, sovereignty becomes a theory of either the legitimacy of political revolution (implicitly in Rousseau, world historically in Paine and, in the early twentieth century, Lenin), or of the grounds and nature of legitimate supreme authority in the post-revolutionary state (the objective of the debates following the American Revolution).

After the convulsions of war and revolution of the first half of the twentieth century, the long tension between sovereignty as a concept pertaining to the orderly world of constituted power—institutions, checks and balances, jurisdictional limits, civic freedoms—and as one that reveals its essence only in the violent outbursts of constituent power—the "dictatorial" concentration of authority, the fundamentally extra-legal nature of sovereign power, its essentially aporetic position with regard to the distinction between politics and law—seems to abate, as parliamentary democracy becomes the now more-or-less practically uncontested horizon of the organization of political life, at least in the great majority of states. In this sense, Carl Schmitt's anti-parliamentary decisionism is the last stage of the long evolution of modern sovereignty theory from the late Middle Ages onward; yet in discounting earlier, nineteenth-century and early twentieth-century theories of an essentially Lockean, liberal democratic order, Schmitt also pushed thought to a return to the old questions of the *essence* of sovereign power, which, like a number of his epigones, he viewed as essentially violent and arbitrary rather than as derived from purely rational desiderata. For all their differences from Schmitt and from each other, Arendt, Foucault, Derrida, and Agamben all share a fascination with the opaque, violent, and even inhuman logic of sovereignty. They also tend to offer us meta-commentaries on its potency and its risks rather than new conceptions of sovereign legitimacy. In a sense, the relatively unprecedented pacification of at least European society after World War II weakened the self-evidence of Hobbesian conceptions of sovereignty as a necessary bulwark against potential social chaos, at the same time that it encouraged focus on what we might call the "absolutist unconscious" of *all* sovereignty against the relatively placating liberal vision of a rationally and legally constrained version of supremacy: the Schmittian "state of exception" and what it reveals about the dark nature of authentically sovereign (and for Schmitt authentically political) power has seemed to haunt most of the post-World War II engagements with the subject.

The mostly pessimistic tone of a late-stage theory that frequently points to how ethically impossible it is to live *with* sovereignty at the same time that it tends to either confess or evade the equally impossible nature of living *without* it, should also be seen in the light of another and parallel development towards relative social pacification and stabilization in the post-war period. At the same time that parliamentary democracy becomes for the first time in history a stable and almost global norm, there arise the first efforts at inter-state governance, in their first form in the League of Nations, then with the United Nations, then with the European Union: these have been frequently seen in relation to the search for peace and an end at least to inter-imperialist rivalry, but they have also been understood as corresponding with the new tasks of governance imposed by the globalization of capital and the concurrent formation of transnational institutions intended to coordinate global competition and to regulate global capital flows. A new tension—now between the more or less stabilized form of national parliamentary democracy and the demands and pressures exerted by these institutions—seems to have largely replaced early twentieth-century frictions between the democratic state and anti-parliamentarian and anti-statist ideas and movements.

References

Bataille, Georges, *The Accursed Share*, vols 2 and 3, trans. Robert Hurley (New York: Zone Books, 1993).

Bataille, Georges, *Literature and Evil*, trans. Alastair Hamilton (London: Penguin, 2012).

Montaigne, Michel de, *Essays*, trans. J. M. Cohen (London: Penguin, 1993).

Pemberton, Jo-Anne, *Sovereignty: Interpretations* (London: Palgrave Macmillan, 2009).

Schmitt, Carl, *Dictatorship*, trans. Michael Hoelzland and Graham Ward (Cambridge: Polity Press, 2013).

Shakespeare, William, "King Lear," in *The Arden Shakespeare Complete Works*, rev. ed., ed. Richard Proudfoot, Ann Thompson and David Scott Kastan (London and New York: Bloomsbury, 2011).

Tacitus, *The Annals: The Reigns of Tiberius, Claudius and Nero*, trans. J. C. Yardley (Oxford: Oxford UP, 2008).

Walker, Neil, "Late Sovereignty in the European Union," in *Sovereignty in Transition*, ed. Neil Walker (Oxford: Hart Publishing, 2006), 3–32.

1

The *Book of Lord Shang* on the Origins of the State

Yuri Pines

In antiquity, the people resided together and dwelled herdlike in turmoil; hence, they were in need of superiors. So All-under-Heaven are happy having superiors and consider this orderly rule. Now, if you have a sovereign but no laws, it is as harmful as having no sovereign; if you have laws but are unable to overcome [those] who wreak havoc, it is as if you have no laws. Although All-under-Heaven have no peace without a ruler, they delight in flouting his laws: hence, the entire generation is in a state of confusion.[1]

How did the state come into existence? Is it essential to human society, or is it a product of certain social circumstances? Why do the people relinquish their freedoms for the sake of external coercive apparatus? How do the foundations of the state in the past reflect—if at all—on its desirable mode of functioning in the present? The rise of the modern state in the West triggered heated debates about these questions. For many thinkers of European modernity—from Thomas Hobbes to Jean-Jacques Rousseau, to Friedrich Engels—the question of the origins of the organized political community mattered a lot and had a direct bearing on their views of the contemporaneous state and its possible trajectory.

Unbeknownst to modern European theorists, similar debates about the origins of the state and of the ruler's power were launched twenty centuries earlier, on the opposite side of Eurasia. Chinese thinkers of the Warring States period (453–221 BCE) lived under conditions that bear a certain degree of resemblance to those of early modern Europe. Their age witnessed rapid and radical transition from the loose aristocratic polities of the preceding Bronze Age (*ca.* 1500–400 BCE) to highly centralized and profoundly bureaucratized territorial states, each of which tried, to paraphrase Eric Hobsbawm, to reach "down to the humblest inhabitant of the least of its villages."[2] And much like in early modern Europe, the rise of the new state aroused a plethora of positive and negative emotions and generated heated debates, which included, among other things, putting forward conflicting perspectives about the state's origins.[3]

Among the debaters of that extraordinarily vibrant age, dubbed the age of the "Hundred Schools of Thought," the towering figure of Shang Yang (a.k.a. Gongsun Yang or Lord Shang, d. 338 BCE) is particularly important. Shang Yang was renowned not so much as a thinker but as an extraordinarily successful—and hugely controversial—political reformer. He reshaped the political, social, and to a certain extent also economic and military structure of the state of Qin, turning it into the most assertive, arguably most oppressive, and undoubtedly politically and militarily most successful state of the Warring States period. The *Book of Lord Shang*, attributed to him (but penned in part by his later followers) summarizes the major arguments in favor of his reforms. It defends the radical overhaul of existent institutions, dismisses the moralizing discourse of Shang Yang's opponents as politically irrelevant, or, worse, subversive, and provides justification for the maintenance of a powerful state apparatus that imposes total control over subjects' lives.[4] This is the immediate context of chapter 7, "Opening the Blocked" ("Kai sai"), from which the above extract is cited. This chapter is an ideological centerpiece of the *Book of Lord Shang*. It provides one of the most sophisticated justifications of the absolute power of the state in the entire corpus of China's political texts.

The first section of the chapter deals with the genesis of the state. It starts with the following depiction:

> When Heaven and Earth were formed, the people were born. At that time, the people knew their mothers but not their fathers; their way was one of attachment to relatives and of selfishness. Attachment to relatives results in particularity; selfishness results in malignity. The people multiplied, and as they were engaged in particularity and malignity, there was turmoil. At that time, the people began seeking victories and forcefully seizing [each other's property]. (7.1)

From the first phrases we can see the distinctiveness of Shang Yang's approach. During the Warring States period there were two major attitudes to the "state of nature" that preceded the formation of the state. The majority view represented most vividly by Mozi (*ca.* 460–390 BCE) depicted primeval society as plagued by intrinsic turmoil. Like Hobbes, Mozi considered pre-political society as a bestial situation of war of all against all, the only remedy to which was the establishment of the state. In contrast, a minority view, most vividly evident in some chapters of the *Zhuangzi* (probably penned slightly later than the *Book of Lord Shang*), argued that the "state of nature" was an era of harmony and peace. According to this view, the creators of organized society were villains who destroyed the primeval idyll.[5] The "Opening the Blocked" chapter combines both approaches. Turmoil is not intrinsic to a stateless society. Whereas the matriarchal (or promiscuous) situation in which "the people knew their mothers but not their fathers" is not enviable, it is not deplorable either; after all, the "attachment to relatives" characteristic of that age was considered by many thinkers—most notably the followers of Confucius (Kongzi, 551–479 BCE)—as a normative state of affairs. However, primeval society could not sustain itself for long because of population pressure. When "the people multiplied," the intrinsic selfishness of human beings began endangering the social order. As the weaknesses of stateless society became evident, it had to be reformed:

> Seeking victories results in struggles; forceful seizure results in quarrels. When there are quarrels but no proper [norms], no one attains his natural life span. Therefore, the worthies established impartiality and propriety and instituted selflessness; the people began rejoicing in benevolence. At that time, attachment to relatives declined, and elevation of the worthy was established. In general, the benevolent are devoted to the love of benefit, whereas the worthy view overcoming one another as the [proper] Way.[6] The people multiplied yet lacked regulations; for a long time they viewed overcoming one another as the [proper] Way, and hence there again was turmoil. (7.1)

The kin-based order, which fostered selfishness, proved inadequate in coping with population pressure and the resultant struggles; hence, unidentified "worthies" intervened, replacing that order with the incipient stratified society based on the "elevation of the worthy." It was at this stage that morality was first taught to the populace, apparently calming the struggles and putting an end to the forceful mutual seizure of property of the earlier age. We witness, then, profound social, ideological, and political change. However, morality and social stratification alone could not resolve the fundamental problem of human selfishness, which brought about renewed competition for material wealth and social prestige. Hence, the new cycle of population increase resulted in a new deterioration of the social order, which required a more radical overhaul of society:

> Therefore, the sages took responsibility. They created distinctions among lands, property, men, and women. When distinctions were fixed but regulations were still lacking, this was unacceptable; hence, they established prohibitions. When prohibitions were established but none supervised [their implementation], this was unacceptable; hence, they established officials. When officials were instituted but not unified, this was unacceptable; hence, they established the ruler. When the ruler was

established, the elevation of the worthy declined, and the esteem of nobility was established. (7.1)

As the morality-based society proved to be inadequate in coping with its internal contradictions, a new form of sociopolitical system had to come into existence. This new system—the state—was generated by unidentified "sages" (i.e. the people on a higher intellectual level than mere "worthies"). Yet the sages did not create the state as a single act of genius intervention. Rather, its formation was a result of a lengthy process of increasing political complexity and social change. Overall, society evolved from an egalitarian, promiscuous, kin-based order to an incipient stratified order and then to a mature political organization based on property distinctions, prohibitions, and officials. This process was crowned with the establishment of a ruler, and it is only then that we can speak of a fully formed state. This is an extraordinarily sophisticated and dynamic model.

The above narrative differs from most other stories of state formation insofar as the ruler's role is concerned. In *Mozi*, for instance, the formation of the state was a top-down process. First the universal ruler—Son of Heaven—was established; then he created territorial distinctions in the realm and appointed local officials. In *Zhuangzi*, as well, the procedure was top-down; in this case, however, the state was the product of the power-hungry sages who were also its earliest rulers. In the "Opening the Blocked" chapter, in contrast, the ruler is the last to appear. He crowns the state formation rather than initiates it.

And yet, the ruler's role is crucial. "Unifying" the officials is the *sine qua non* for creating a properly functioning state. And it is not just unifying the officials. It is unifying the realm, first in a single state and then, as the text hints elsewhere (7.3), in All-under-Heaven. The unification of the entire known world was the common cherished goal of political thinkers of the Warring States period, the only way to ensure lasting universal peace.[7] The author of the "Opening the Blocked" chapter shared this goal, but he reminds us that unity—first in a single state and then in the entire subcelestial realm—requires the unifier. By the very fact of his singularity, the ruler ensures the proper functioning of the political system. He is not the system's creator but its pivot. This is the rationale for concentrating all imaginable power in the sovereign's hands.

The author avoids eulogizing the state excessively. From his point of view, it is conceivable that during a lengthy prestate period there were no rulers, yet this situation was not necessarily unmanageable. However, once population pressure had generated social tensions, overall adjustment of the sociopolitical system became necessary, and the formation of the state became inevitable. Although moral education could, for a certain period of time, moderate the intrinsic selfishness of human beings, it could not fundamentally alter it, especially when demographic growth brought about increased contention. Competition among the worthies became as unmanageable as the earlier contention among ordinary individuals. The narrative implies that morality simply became a veneer for the pursuit of selfish struggles. The sages' response was to preserve order through the creation of an effective political system that should not eradicate selfishness but only prevent it from damaging social life. They thus focused on the implementation of effective laws, regulations and prohibitions rather than on education. This is precisely what the *Book of Lord Shang* consistently considers the best remedy for social turmoil. The author summarizes:

> In the early ages, [the people] were attached to relatives and were devoted to themselves; in the middle ages, they elevated the worthy and rejoiced in benevolence; in the recent age, they esteem nobility and respect officials. When they elevated the worthy, they used the Way to overcome each other; but the establishment of the ruler caused the worthies to become useless. Being attached to relatives, they considered selfishness as the Way; but the establishment of impartiality and propriety caused selfishness no longer to be practiced. In these three cases, it is not that their affairs are opposite; it is that the Way of the people is base and what they value changes. When the affairs of the world change, one should implement a different Way. (7.1)

The fundamental presupposition of Shang Yang's theory is that everything is changeable. There are no immutable social norms, no immutable moral values. Everything—from kinship ties, to ethical norms, to political institutions—is bound to change once there is change in objective circumstances (such as population increase and the resultant struggle for insufficient resources). The ideas of Shang Yang's rivals—be they Confucians who advocated "attachment to relatives" or followers of Mozi who promulgated the "elevation of the worthy"—are not necessarily wrong. To the contrary, their ideas were relevant in certain historical circumstances. But in the current age of "esteem of nobility and respect of officials" what matters is power, and power alone.

This understanding is the backdrop for the subsequent discussion in the "Opening the Blocked" chapter. In different eras, distinct socio-political arrangements are viable; but in the current age, it is vital to realize that political power is based on coercion. "When the people are ignorant, one can become monarch through knowledge; when the generation is knowledgeable, one can become monarch through force" (7.2). This is the rationale for the author's two most controversial suggestions. The first is to commit all state resources (material, human, and even intellectual) to resolute war, which would end with the establishment of the new universal dynasty in All-under-Heaven—the only way for universal peace. The second is to impose merciless punishments on even slight offences so as to nip evildoing in the bud. Both recommendations appalled many of Shang Yang's contemporaries (as they appall most readers today), and he was well aware of it. Yet both are logically related to his view of the state's origins. In the current age of permanent warfare when "every state of ten thousand chariots [i.e. a large state] is engaged in [offensive] war, whereas every state of one thousand chariots [i.e. a medium-sized state] is engaged in defense" (7.3), the ways of peace and righteousness are blocked. Similarly, lenience toward law-breakers is not true righteousness—to the contrary, it generates turmoil and harms the people. The resolute employment of force both domestically and externally is the only way to peace and tranquility. The author defends the imposition of harsh penal laws as follows:

> If you instruct them through righteousness, the people indulge themselves; when the people indulge, there is turmoil; when there is turmoil, the people will be hurt by what they detest. What I call "punishments" is the root of righteousness, whereas what our generation calls righteousness is the way of violence . . . Thus, by killing and punishing, I return to virtue, whereas [what is called] righteousness corresponds to violence. (7.4–7.5)

This passage epitomizes Shang Yang's dialectical view of politics. He agrees with the moralizing thinkers (like the followers of Confucius and Mozi) that the ultimate goal of policy makers is to rule by "virtue" (de), which in the Chinese context means primarily reliance on moral and non-coercive methods of control. However, he never elaborates how this future "rule by virtue" will look, and whether or not it will require another radical modification of the sociopolitical order. What matters is the here and now: the road toward the goal of "returning to virtue" requires the employment of harsh and unpopular means of "killing and punishing." In the current age of "extra crafty" (7.2) people, one cannot ensure order through mere reasoning and hortatory proclamations. The absolute power of the state apparatus is the only means to make the people comply. And the ensuing compliance, in turn, is the only means to ensure the people's well-being. Recall the statement from the epigraph: "Although All-under-Heaven have no peace without a ruler, they delight in flouting his laws: hence, the entire generation is in a state of confusion." The people are the ultimate beneficiaries of the powerful state, but their selfishness prevents them from realizing that and causes them to flout the laws. In this situation, coercion is the only way to let the people enjoy a peaceful and tranquil life. The author explains in the final lines of the chapter:

> To benefit the people of All-under-Heaven nothing is better than orderly rule, and in orderly rule nothing is more secure than establishing the ruler. The Way of establishing the ruler is nowhere broader than in relying on laws; in the task of relying on laws, nothing is more urgent than eradicating depravity; the root of eradicating depravity is nowhere deeper than in making punishments stern. Hence, the True Monarch prohibits through rewards and encourages through punishments; he pursues

transgressions and not goodness; he relies on punishments to eradicate punishments. (7.6)

The sophistication of Shang Yang's political thought is presented here at its best. First, ever since the demise of primeval kin-based or incipiently stratified order, society cannot function without a clearly pronounced hierarchical order headed by a ruler. Second, whereas the ruler is the pivot of the sociopolitical order, he cannot engender this order alone: he must rely on the legal system and especially on stern punishments, which will make his rule really effective. Third, although in principle the people "are happy" to be guarded by the ruler, they are intrinsically inclined to flout the laws; hence, unless they are overawed by stern punishments, they will damage the very order on which their peace and prosperity depends. The ruler-centered political system is a social must, and it has to be actively protected from members of society whose selfishness and narrowmindedness lead them to repeated transgressions. This is the rationale of Shang Yang's political model.

The final section cited above poses a curious question of the relation between the ruler and the law. Whereas in the "Opening the Blocked" chapter the law refers clearly to the ruler's tool, *viz.* the means to safeguard his position through overawing the subjects, this does not necessarily imply that the ruler stands above it. To the contrary, *fa* 法 which is translated above as "law," but which may refer also to more broadly understood impersonal standards, methods, and models to be followed, should normatively guide and even constrain the ruler. This emphasis on *fa* gained Shang Yang and his associates the name "the School of *fa*," which is translated, somewhat problematically, as "the School of Law" or "Legalists."[8] So does the ruler stand above the law or beneath it?

The answer is equivocal. On the one hand, from other chapters of the *Book of Lord Shang* it is clear that the ruler should subordinate his personal likes and dislikes to superior standards or laws (*fa*), which should never be violated (see, e.g. *Book of Lord Shang* 14.4; 23.3–4). On the other hand, laws are neither eternal nor unchangeable. As the discussion above clarified, they are the product of certain historical conditions, and under new circumstances they should be radically altered. The exclusive right to alter the laws is that of the sovereign alone. In his position as the locus of political authority, the ruler has the right to change the law when appropriate. And yet, this should never be a whimsical change. Any twisting of laws for the sake of the ruler's selfish needs would invalidate the laws and undermine the very political system that is supposed to safeguard the ruler's absolute authority.

In the final account, the *Book of Lord Shang* does not solve the contradiction between the ruler's superiority over the law in his position as an absolute sovereign and his subordination to the law as a normal (and possibly erring) human being. Shang Yang did not envision any institutional constraints on the ruler's authority, since those would dramatically impair the sovereign's power. The only means to correct an erring sovereign was through mild suasion. This was not enough, however, to solve the tension between the need to concentrate all the power in the hands of a single monarch and the tacit understanding that this monarch is prone to be a fallible individual. This tension remained the perennial weakness of China's monarchist ideology for millennia to come.[9]

Notes

This research was supported by the Israel Science Foundation (grant No. 568/19) and by the Michael William Lipson Chair in Chinese Studies.

1   *The Book of Lord Shang* 7.6. All citations from this text (*Shangjunshu*) follow Yuri Pines, trans. and ed., *The Book of Lord Shang: Apologetics of State Power in Early China* (New York: Columbia University Press, 2017), indicating the chapter and the section's number.

2   Eric J. Hobsbawm, *Nations and Nationalism since 1780: Programme, Myth Reality*, 2nd ed. (Cambridge: Cambridge University Press, 2000), 80.

3   For comparing modern European and early Chinese theories of the origin of the state, see Yuri Pines and Gideon Shelach, "'Using the Past to Serve the Present': Comparative Perspectives on Chinese and Western Theories of the Origins of the State," in *Genesis and Regeneration: Essays on Conceptions of Origins*, ed. Shaul Shaked (Jerusalem: The Israel Academy of Science and Humanities, 2005), 127–63.

4   For a detailed study of this text, see Pines, *The Book of Lord Shang*.

5   For Mozi's and *Zhuangzi*'s views, see Pines and Shelach, "Using the Past," 131–3 and 140–2.

6   The Way ("*Dao*") is considered in early China as the summa of proper moral and political principles.

7   See Yuri Pines, *The Everlasting Empire: The Political Culture of Ancient China and Its Imperial Legacy* (Princeton, NJ: Princeton University Press, 2012), 11–43.

8   For the problematic of this designation compare Paul R. Goldin, "Persistent Misconceptions about Chinese 'Legalism,'" *Journal of Chinese Philosophy* 38, no. 1 (2011): 64–80 and Yuri Pines, "Legalism in Chinese Philosophy," in *Stanford Encyclopedia of Philosophy*, ed. Edward N. Zalta et al. *http://plato. stanford.edu/entries/chinese-legalism/* (First published 2014).

9   See more on this topic in Yuri Pines, *The Everlasting Empire*, 44–75.

2

Aristotle on Sovereignty

Kazutaka Inamura

A constitution [or politeia] may be defined as "the organization of a city [or polis], in respect of its offices generally, but especially in respect of that particular office which is sovereign in all issues." The civic body is everywhere the sovereign of the city; in fact the civic body is the constitution itself. In democratic cities, for example, the people [dēmos] is sovereign: in oligarchies, on the other hand, the few [or oligoi] have that position; and this difference in the sovereign bodies is the reason why we say that the two types of constitution differ—as we may equally apply the same reasoning to other types besides these.[1]

The term "constitution" [politeia] signifies the same thing as the term "civic body" [politeuma]. The civic body in every city [polis] is the sovereign [to kurion]; and the sovereign must necessarily be either One, or Few, or Many. On this basis we may say that when the One, or the Few, or the Many rule with a view to the common interest, the constitutions under which they do so must necessarily be right constitutions. On the other hand, the constitutions directed to the personal interest of the One, or the Few, or the Masses, must necessarily be perversions.[2]

Some political theorists consider it problematic to use the term "sovereignty" to describe aspects of ancient Greek political thought. The concept of sovereignty was formulated by sixteenth- and seventeenth-century political theorists, Jean Bodin and Thomas Hobbes, and fully developed as popular sovereignty distinct from the government, by Jean-Jacques Rousseau. Josiah Ober argues that sovereignty is of limited utility in explaining ancient Athenian democracy, because it refers to the unitary state power held by "a monarch" or "representative assembly."[3] Arlene Saxonhouse asserts that the crucial point at issue in ancient democracy had little to do with the translation of the general will into the policy of the state but with engagement in politics—who speaks in the assembly and who works as a public official.[4] Using the concept of "sovereignty" in the analysis of Greek political thought may result in anachronism.

In recent literature, however, Kinch Hoekstra and Melissa Lane have suggested that the elements of sovereignty may be traced in classical thought. Hoekstra draws our attention to the feature of unaccountability. In the theoretical framework of "absolute sovereignty" as formulated by early modern thinkers in Greek terms, the actions of the sovereign ruler are unaccountable to anyone except God. In fifth-century BCE Athens, the *demos* or people were also understood to be the uncontrolled controllers.[5] Lane refers to Aristotle's argument about the assembly's control of officeholders in his *Politics* [hereafter, *Pol.*] 3.11. The sovereign people controlled the entire state by electing the highest public officials and holding them accountable for their work. The people themselves were held to no higher accountability.[6]

The origins of political concepts such as "sovereignty," "rights," "democracy," or "currency" can be found by tracing the historical evolution of these ideas and identifying features in ancient thought which are similar to the core concepts of modern political theory. In the process, we can also note the differences between the ancient and modern formulations of each concept. As becomes clear, it is not productive to compare ancient and modern thought without taking into account the full framework of political theory. Some aspects of "sovereignty" are essentially related to other theoretical terms such as "citizen," "constitution," and "ruling." Present-day political theorists and historians need to identify the conceptual relations between such terms.

It is not necessarily the best practice to refer to the Greek term "sovereign" (κύριος) in order to identify the idea of sovereignty. Aristotle might have had the same idea as political theorists of later generations, even if he did not use the term. It is thus necessary to examine the conceptual connections of the term "sovereignty." Understanding the meaning and usage of the word is only a small step toward exploring the concept of sovereignty.

The Greek term "κύριος" means "having power or authority over."[7] For example, as Aristotle notoriously states, a woman has the deliberative part of the soul, but her soul lacks authority (ἄκυρος), while the deliberative faculty is entirely missing from a slave (*Pol.* 1.13. 1260a12–13). According to this perspective, even if a woman has the potential to exercise the deliberative capacity, she does not have mastery over the soul. The deliberative part is sovereign in the soul when the emotional self is fully developed and abides by reason. In the context of human action, this means that people can control their actions and decide whether and how to act. Their action is voluntary because they are not forced to act by others (*Nicomachean Ethics* 3.5. 1114a31–b1; 1114b30–32). Thus, Aristotle uses the term "sovereign" to express a human's control of action: "a human is, alone among animals, a starting point of certain actions; we would not say that any of the other creatures acts. The starting points that are of this sort—those that originate movements—are termed 'authoritative [sovereign],' most rightly so in the case of those things whose results cannot be otherwise, as perhaps where god is the starting point" (*Eudemian Ethics* 2.6. 1222b19–23).[8] The sovereign human is the starting point or ruling (ἀρχή) of action. Aristotle's sovereignty means the controlling power that necessarily initiates the process of purposive action.

When this understanding is applied to a political system, it means "having authority or ruling power over a state." The first passage quoted at the beginning of this essay defines a constitution as an organization of the state's office that is sovereign in all issues. The term "sovereign" is introduced in the context of how to classify various constitutions. Constitution (πολιτεία) in Greek is not the codified set of laws antecedent to the government,[9] but is identical to the civic body (πολίτευμα). By the civic body, the passage means "the people" in democracy and "the few" in oligarchy. Democracy is a political system whose governing civic body consists of the people while oligarchy is a system in which the few take the most authoritative office of the state. Thus, the difference in the civic body serves to identify which constitution the state establishes. Who rules the state is the defining criterion in Aristotle's typology of constitutions.

According to this criterion, in the second passage quoted at the beginning of this essay, Aristotle considers the possible number of sovereign rulers: one, few, and many. Next, he treats the beneficiary of governance as another criterion for classification. When the sovereign rulers look after the common benefit among free individuals, their political system is a right constitution. When they are concerned with their private interests only, their political system is deviant. Thus, Aristotle classifies kingship, aristocracy, and polity as right constitutions, and tyranny, oligarchy, and democracy as deviant from the former (*Pol.* 3.7. 1279a25–b10).

Aristotle also raises the issue of sovereignty in his *Politics* 3.10. Here, he addresses the question of who must be made sovereign—the masses, the rich, decent people, the best person or a tyrant. First, he criticizes majoritarian democracy, where the poor are made sovereign and they divide up the property of the rich among themselves. Although the poor masses may be convinced of the righteousness of their claim, Aristotle opposes their logic because it is detrimental to the state. Aristotle also opposes the idea of conferring sovereignty on special individuals, because when authority is always held by such individuals the commoners are deprived of honors and public offices. Thus, when ancient Greeks discuss issues about sovereignty, they focus on who holds the position of decision making and public administration. They do not debate the right to offer a framework of government. They dispute who exercises the political authority and who makes political decisions about everything relating to the state.

This feature is one important difference between Aristotle's and modern notions of sovereignty. According to Richard Tuck, although there are several differences between Jean Bodin, Thomas Hobbes, and Jean-Jacques Rousseau, their modern notions involve an essential line of demarcation between sovereignty and government. The sovereign authority has the right to reign, while the government actually exercises political power and manages the everyday affairs of the state. Even if the sovereign monarch cannot rule the state due to physical inability, he or she still retains the rights to reign, as when he or she sleeps. Furthermore, the sovereign authority is absolute, that is, it is never restricted by any external authority or divided between different branches of government.[10] In the passages quoted at the beginning of this essay, however, Aristotle does not proclaim these features. He instead considers who exercises political power rather than who holds the rights to form the government. He also explores who is the beneficiary of political governance. These are the criteria for his constitutional typology and political analysis.

Aristotle draws attention to the characteristics of sovereign rulers to develop his typology of constitutions. In *Politics* 3.8 (1279b20–24) and 4.4 (1290a30–b3), he presents two hypothetical situations: one in which the majority were rich and sovereign in the state, and another in which the poor were fewer in number than the rich but were stronger and sovereign in the constitution. According to the "number-of-rulers" criterion (elaborated in the second passage quoted at the start of this chapter), the former is a democracy and the latter is an oligarchy. However, Aristotle proposes to classify constitutions in terms of real causes or reasons—wealth and freedom (1279b39–1280a6, 1290a40–b3). This is because the citizens claim political authority on the basis of these reasons, whereas the number of rulers in the state is an incidental feature. In reality, the few happen to be rich and the many happen to be poor; however, these facts are not the defining criteria for organizing the constitution. Thus, Aristotle defines democracy and oligarchy as systems, wherein the sovereign members, respectively, are free individuals and the rich.[11]

This "who-rules" criterion is also used in further divisions among constitutions. Aristotle classifies various constitutions within his famous six-fold scheme. For example, Aristotle lists four or five subtypes of democracy (*Pol.* 4.4. 1291b30–1292a38; 4.6. 1292b22–1293a10; and 6.4. 1318b1–1319b32); in the first subtype, relatively rich people form the government body, and in the last subtype, anyone (or even illegitimate citizens) can participate in government. Each subtype incrementally broadens the scope of popular participation.[12]

In Aristotle's view, the character of the governing class determines the characteristics of their constitution (cf. *Pol.* 7.13. 1332a33–34). In other words, the most influential part of a state determines the nature of its whole. This is because the governing body organizes the state to achieve its purposes, such as freedom and wealth. In a democracy, people claim political authority based on their status as free and introduce democratic features in order to secure their freedom; thus, freedom serves as the ultimate goal in a democratic setting.

Aristotle's argument in *Politics* 3.11 is key to considering whether he develops a notion of popular sovereignty. Melissa Lane draws attention to this argument to assert that Aristotle holds the view of popular sovereignty as the people's control of officeholders.[13] Marsilius of Padua originally referred to Aristotle's *Politics* 3.11 to justify his claim that the political authority for legislation should reside in the universal body of the citizens.[14] Here, Aristotle examines the view that the masses should be more sovereign than the few good (1281a40–42). His proposal is to allow the masses to participate in the assembly or popular court, but not to hold the highest office. This is because the mass sometimes possess greater merit in virtue and practical wisdom as a group than the few, even if they are not eminent individually (1281a42–b31).

This allocation of political power to the masses can be considered as a primitive version of popular sovereignty, but Aristotle uses a different rationale for popular participation. First, he permits popular participation because if the masses were excluded from public offices, they would be antagonistic towards their state (*Pol.* 3.11. 1281b28–31), rather than because he holds that the people have a legitimate right to enjoy freedom and to control the state according to their will. Second, he does not maintain that the masses should have a unitary power that cannot be divided among different types of people. Instead, he allocates different types of political powers to different people according to the proper fit between their role and ability. He restricts the power of the popular assembly to the election and assessment of public officials. Third, it is uncertain whether he would name such a constitution a democracy. Rather, it appears to be a mixed constitution of democracy and aristocracy, based on the "number-of-rulers" criterion, because both the masses and the good minority have a fair share in the constitution.

Furthermore, the constitution envisaged in *Politics* 3.11 may be classified as an aristocracy. Aristotle maintains that "in reality there are three elements which may claim an equal share in the mixed form of constitution: free birth, wealth, and merit [virtue] [. . .] Obviously, therefore, we ought always to use the term 'constitutional government' [polity] for a mixture of only two elements, where these elements are the rich and the poor; and we ought to confine the name 'aristocracy' to a mixture of three, which is really more of an aristocracy than any other form so called, except the first and true form" (*Pol.* 4.8. 1294a19–25; cf. 4.7. 1293b7–21; 5.7. 1307a5–12). When the masses take up public offices based on their virtue, Aristotle calls the constitution an aristocracy. This is because in Aristotle's typology, constitutions are classified on the basis of their reason for participating in political authority. In *Politics* 3.11, Aristotle does not consider freedom to be the basis on which the masses are integrated into the political process. Thus, his allocation of deliberative and judicial powers to the masses is not an expression of popular sovereignty, wherein the masses control officeholders according to their will, but of an aristocratic governance, where virtue is the only criterion for claiming and exercising political authority.[15]

According to Bodin, the state can be a monarchy and be governed as a democracy or aristocracy. It is also possible for a democratic state to be governed as an aristocracy; in which case, the masses hold the sovereignty, and public offices are assigned only to noblemen.[16] According to Rousseau, the state can be governed by a monarch when it is decided by the will of the sovereign people, i.e., by the votes in the assembly of the entire people.[17] Aristotle, however, does not define the constitution in these manners. When the sovereign people actually influence the government or exercise the power to choose the administrative government, Aristotle would classify it as a mixed constitution of democracy and aristocracy. If the sovereign people have the right to form the government but remain inert and do not exercise their power, then it would be an aristocracy or monarchy. In Aristotle's philosophy, actuality rather than potentiality is important for analyzing power relations in politics. The two passages quoted at the start of this chapter express this realist attitude towards examining constitutions. The class of the sovereign rulers and the beneficiary of their governance are two criteria in Aristotle's classification of constitutions. He uses the concept of sovereignty to apply the former criterion for analyzing who actually exercises political power in a state.

Notes

1   Aristotle, *Politics*, 3.6. 1278b7–15. As to the text of the *Politics*, I have followed *Aristotelis Politica*, ed. W. D. Ross (Oxford: Oxford University Press, 1957), unless stated otherwise. About translations, I have used Aristotle, *Politics*, trans. Ernest Barker and rev. R. F. Stalley (Oxford: Oxford University Press, 1995), with their original translations preserved. The Greek term "sovereign" (κύριος) can be translated into "having authority." The translation of the term "polis" into "city" may pose problems. Its translation can be "city-state" or "state." For a discussion of the concept "polis," see Mogens Herman Hansen, *Polis: An Introduction to the Ancient Greek City-State* (Oxford: Oxford University Press, 2006).

2   Aristotle, *Politics*, 3.7. 1279a25–31. Subsequent references to Aristotle's *Politics* will be cited parenthetically in the text.

3   Josiah Ober, *The Athenian Revolution: Essays on Ancient Greek Democracy and Political Theory* (Princeton: Princeton University Press, 1996), 120–2.

4   Arlene W. Saxonhouse, *Athenian Democracy: Modern Mythmakers and Ancient Theorists* (Notre Dame: University of Notre Dame Press, 1996), 7, 33, 141, 145–6. See Mogens Herman Hansen, *The Athenian Democracy in the Age of Demosthenes: Structure, Principles, and Ideology*, trans. J. A. Crook (Norman: University of Oklahoma Press, 1999), 150–5, in which Hansen argues that the popular assembly in fourth-century BCE Athens was not sovereign because its powers were limited. For a discussion of an ambivalent position, see R. G. Mulgan, "Aristotle's Sovereign," *Political Studies* 18 (1970): 518–22.

5   Kinch Hoekstra, "Athenian Democracy and Popular Tyranny," in *Popular Sovereignty in Historical Perspective*, ed. Richard Bourke and Quentin Skinner (Cambridge: Cambridge University Press, 2016), 15–51.

6   Melissa Lane, "Popular Sovereignty as Control of Office-holders: Aristotle on Greek Democracy," in *Popular Sovereignty*, 52–72.

7   See the entry "κύριος" in *A Greek-English Lexicon*, ninth ed., compiled Henry George Liddell and Robert Scott (Oxford: Clarendon Press, 1996).

8   Aristotle, *Eudemian Ethics*, trans. and ed. Brad Inwood and Raphael Woolf (Cambridge: Cambridge University Press, 2013), 25.

9   In a modern political theory, a constitution creates a government. For this view, see Thomas Paine, *Rights of Man*, ed. with an introduction by Henry Collins, Penguin Classics (London: Penguin Books, 1969), Part First, 93.

10 For a description of modern sovereignty, see Richard Tuck, "Democratic Sovereignty and Democratic Government: The Sleeping Sovereign," in *Popular Sovereignty*, 115–41 and Richard Tuck, *The Sleeping Sovereign: The Invention of Modern Democracy* (Cambridge: Cambridge University Press, 2015).

11 For a discussion of his typology in this paragraph and the three subsequent paragraphs, see Kazutaka Inamura, "Scientific Classification and Essentialism in the Aristotelian Typology of Constitutions," *History of Political Thought* 40 (2019): 196–218.

12 As to subtypes of oligarchy, see *Pol.* 4.5. 1292a39–b2, 4.6. 1293a12–34, 6.6. 1320b18–1321a4; as to subtypes of aristocracy, *Pol.* 4.7. 1293a35–b21; as to subtypes of tyranny, *Pol.* 4.10. 1295a1–24.

13 Lane, "Popular Sovereignty," 59–62. In the scholarly literature, this argument is called "the wisdom of the multitude." Another important argument is Aristotle's description of the deliberative body of a state in *Politics* 4.14, because the text (1299a1–2) describes it as sovereign in the constitution. However, even in this chapter, Aristotle discusses various methods for separating the deliberative authorities. The text might be an addition by an editor of a later generation.

14 Marsilius of Padua, *The Defender of the Peace*, ed. Annabel Brett (Cambridge: Cambridge University Press, 2005), Discourse I, Ch. 12, Sec. 4, 76–7. For a discussion of Marsilius of Padua's treatment of the concept of sovereignty, see the relevant chapter in this volume.

15 For a discussion of the criterion of aristocracy, see Kazutaka Inamura, *Justice and Reciprocity in Aristotle's Political Philosophy* (Cambridge: Cambridge University Press, 2015), 84–5. Although this book classifies the constitution

conceived of in *Politics* 3.11 as a mixed constitution, the current chapter classifies it as an aristocracy with serious regard to his classificatory criterion.

16 Jean Bodin, *The Six Bookes of a Commonwealth*, ed. Kenneth Douglas McRae (Cambridge, MA: Harvard University Press, 1962), 199–200, 249. See also Tuck, "Democratic Sovereignty," 121 for reference.

17 Jean-Jacques Rousseau, "Of the Social Contract," in *The Social Contract and Other Later Political Writings*, ed. Victor Gourevitch (Cambridge: Cambridge University Press, 1997), Bk. 3, Ch. 16–18, 116–20.

3

Divided Sovereignty

Polybius and the Compound Constitution

Jed W. Atkins and Carl E. Young

After all this, someone might reasonably wonder what role there is left for the people in this system of government, when the Senate is responsible for all the particulars I have mentioned, and most importantly manages all the state's revenues and expenses, and the consuls have plenipotentiary power in the run-up to war and when out fighting campaigns. But the people do have a part to play, and a very important one at that, because they control rewards and punishments. There is no other provision within the constitution for these functions, but without them human life itself has no coherence, let alone governments and constitutions. For when the difference between better and worse is ignored, or when it is recognized but poorly managed, no business that is taken in hand turns out well. How could it, if the bad are honoured no less than the good? So the people assess many of the cases where the penalty for the offence is a substantial fine, especially where the accused have held the highest offices, and all such cases where the penalty is death; and they assign offices to those who deserve them, which, in a political context, is the greatest possible reward for virtue. Then they are responsible for assessing legislation; most importantly, it is

*they who decide whether or not to go to war; and they also either
ratify or abrogate alliances, truces, and treaties. And again, all this
means that it would be plausible to suggest that the people's role is
paramount, and that the constitution is a democracy.*[1]

A cavalry commander from the Greek city of Megalopolis, Polybius was
taken to Rome as a hostage in 167 BCE. During his stay, he associated with
some of Rome's leading political families. As a result, he had the opportunity
to observe Rome's political system, which he credited with enabling Rome
to become the undisputed master of the Mediterranean World (1.1; 6.2).
Book 6 of his *Histories* describes the Roman constitution and explains why
it was so successful. Several aspects of Polybius' account have had an
enduring influence in the history of political thought. For example, his
theory that constitutional change followed a cyclical pattern (*anakyklôsis*)
was adopted by Machiavelli in his *Discourses on Livy* (1.2). His account of
the Roman constitution as a "mixed" or—perhaps better—"compound"
constitution that separated and balanced ruling powers was further
developed in the eighteenth century by Montesquieu and the American
founding fathers.[2] The following chapter will describe the main features of
Polybius' theory and highlight its distinctive characteristics through
comparisons with the accounts of Plato and John Locke. These comparisons
illustrate the important philosophical presuppositions that differentiate
conceptions of sovereignty. We argue that Polybius innovates through his
analysis of separate, independent, and sovereign constitutional powers, but
that his theory lacks the notion of popular sovereignty commonly embraced
by modern liberal theorists.

At the outset, we must note two important pieces of terminology. First, the
word "constitution" in modern English translations renders one of two Greek
words, *politeuma* and *politeia*. In Polybius' account, *politeuma* indicates the
form of political community characterized by its supreme governing power. As
for *politeia*, as elsewhere in Greek political thought, the term includes both the
formal institutional aspects of a political system and its political culture.
In addition to the basic governing offices and assemblies of the Roman
constitution, Polybius discusses institutions such as the Roman army, funeral
addresses, and religion; civic virtues such as patriotism and honor; and political
emotions such as fear. Second, Polybius does not use a single word that
corresponds to "sovereignty." If we understand the basic concept of
"sovereignty" as indicating the supreme ruling authority within a political
community,[3] candidates for signifying the concept in Polybius include a variety
of Greek terms: power (*dynamis*), authority (*exousia*), rule (*archê*), and
mastery/master or control (*kyrios*). To indicate the supreme ruling authority,
Polybius modifies these terms with adjectives such as "plenipotentiary" or
"paramount" (*autokratôr*), "great" (*megas*), or "sole" (*monos*).

In book 6, Polybius classifies the Roman constitution according to the traditional Greek schema of rule by one, few, and many. Of these, his analysis of "rule by the many" is the most consequential for the discussion of "sovereignty"; in fact, some scholars have found in Polybius' account evidence of "popular sovereignty" at Rome. The key passage is found at 6.14 in the passage extracted at the beginning of this chapter. The part within the constitution left to "the people" is "a very important one" because "they control rewards and punishments" (6.14.3–4). In other words, "the people" are "sovereign" (*monos . . . kyrios*) over the elections of magistrates, the judgments of the law courts, and the ratification of legislation. Here Polybius seems to describe the Roman republican idea of sovereignty, which resides in the fact that the people alone entrusted magistrates with their authoritative use of force. However, Polybius' account departs from the realities of Roman Republican practice.

Most importantly, Polybius' account misleadingly compares the Roman *populus* with *dêmos* in Greek democratic thought.[4] Accordingly, he ignores the complex nature of Roman popular assemblies, which were subject to significant limitations on popular power absent from Athenian democracy. For instance, under the Roman Republic, the people did not have the right to assemble themselves without the initiative of a magistrate or tribune. They voted in blocks weighted by class towards the wealthy and could only vote "yes" or "no" on legislation proposed by a magistrate. While it is true that only the people could pass legislation, this legislation could be annulled by a priest called an augur. Nor did the Roman system use the democratic device of sortition as a means to select members of the law courts, as the Athenians did. Finally, while the popular vote was necessary to confer *imperium* (the power to use coercive force) on magistrates, the election also had to be ratified by Rome's aristocratic body, the Senate. While the Senate's ratification was likely only a formality, its presence signified an important component of Roman republican ideology: the people were not the supreme authority. After all, the Romans represented their civic body as not simply the *populus Romanus* but *SPQR: Senatus Populusque Romanus.*[5]

Polybius overemphasizes the "democratic" nature of the Roman constitution in order to bring his account into line with his wider constitutional theory. The "people" (*dêmos*) make decisions about the good and bad, the just and unjust, and rewards and punishments, which are crucial for the "coherence," that is, the "stability" (*sunechontai*) of "governments," "constitutions," and even "human life" (6.14.4). Earlier in the book, Polybius provided an account of how these popular ethical conceptions arose, based on his understanding of human nature (6.6). Human beings are self-interested and motivated by fear of bodily harm. They also possess the moral imagination to empathize with those who suffer and to fashion a code of ethics that supports mutual assistance. This account of the honorable and dishonorable, just and unjust, derives from humanity's natural sense of rational self-interest.

For Polybius the moral validation of the people is what separates the good and bad forms of simple constitutions; it is what makes them "true" or "genuine" (*alêthinês*, 6.7.1). Rulers acquire this validation, and concomitantly the approval of the people, by ruling with a view to the common good and in accordance with the moral concepts that the people naturally work out for themselves. They lose the moral validation of the people, however, when they rule in their own interests—a behavior that eventually leads to revolution, and hence to constitutional change. Even a hereditary monarchy requires the support of "the people" (*hoi polloi*), who "maintain the supreme power (*archê*)" (6.7.2). As Polybius' account develops, it becomes clear that moral validation belongs to the citizen-body as a whole. "The general populace" (*to plêthos*)—this includes both the nobles and the many (6.7.5–6)—determines whether the ruler adheres to the common moral system (6.6.8, 8.1, 8.6, 9.1). The best way of maintaining the moral validation of the majority of the citizen-body is to ensure that those in office rule in the interest of the ruled. Given that those in power tend not to rule for the common good when security takes away their ability to see the interests of others, moral validation is best attained through a constitution that provides for equal powers. This includes popular power, which is required to check the actions of the other parts of the constitution and in turn must be checked by them. For Polybius is acutely aware of how easily the moral validation of the majority can turn into the partisan rule of the mob. In fact, his account of constitutional change takes advantage of the fact that the terms for "the people," *to plêthos* and *hoi polloi*, can indicate the citizen-body as a whole and the factional interests of the crowd.

Constitutional stability, therefore, requires that popular moral validation be adequately expressed in terms of constitutional power. The people should possess an adequate share of or "part" in the constitution along with monarchs and aristocrats. Polybius' reasoning follows his social psychology. If human beings are moved by fear and competitive self-interest, a stable constitution could emerge by incorporating distinct but equal powers that check and balance one another. Such a constitution does not eliminate self-interest but moderates its effects through the institutionalization of fear within the constitution, so that each part "fears" another equal part interfering with its powers. Similarly, in his account of the compound constitution, Polybius does not seek to eliminate conflict but makes it productive by linking the self-interested desire for honor and status to the promotion of the common good. Provided that constitutional powers are kept separate and equal, competition between the parts will check the factional aggrandizement of power that leads to political revolution, and thus will ensure a secure political community (6.15–18).[6]

The success of the Roman constitution in Polybius' view comes from the unparalleled degree to which it incorporates the distinct powers of rule by one, few, and many so that each part checks and balances the others. Each "part" of the constitution has the supreme authority or "sovereignty" within its sphere. For example, just as Polybius represents the people as "sovereign" (*kyrios*) over the election of magistracies and the law courts, so he also represents the consuls' *imperium* in war as an authority or power (*exousia, dynamis*) that is "almost unlimited" or "paramount" (*autokratôr*) within its sphere (6.12.5; 6.14.2). Consequently, the people must have enough power within the constitution to check the "monarchical" powers of the consuls (6.12) and the extensive authority of the senate, ranging over revenue, foreign policy, public crimes, and religion (6.13).

In order to understand better what Polybius' conception of "sovereignty" entails and what it does not, let us consider it alongside two other influential theories. The first is Plato's *Laws*, which offered the first extended discussion of a mixed constitution in the history of political thought. Polybius' account in the *Histories* reveals a critical awareness of Plato's political thought, and the *Laws* in particular (cf. *Histories* 6.45–47 and *Laws* 631b, 682e–683a, 712e). Nevertheless, we should stress that our purpose in comparing the two is not to make any claims about Polybius' reception of Plato, but to illuminate more clearly the specific characteristics of Polybius' account of sovereignty.

Plato's *Laws* foreshadows several aspects of Polybius' theory. Most significantly, it precedes Polybius in describing and endorsing a mixed constitution with checks or curbs on power that incorporates multiple simple constitutions (691d8–692b1). Similarly, for Plato good forms of constitutions require popular validation; Plato's mixed constitution is "a government of the willing, by the willing" (832c; cf. 700a, 723a, 739a–b).[7]

However, the differences between Plato and Polybius are significant. Whereas Polybius sought to make conflict productive, Plato tries to eliminate faction. The success of the mixed constitution at achieving this end separates it from the unmixed forms, which, since they privilege the dominance of one part of society over the rest, are in reality "factional states" (*stasiôteiai*), not constitutions (*politeiai*) (713a, 832c). In contrast to "factional states," Plato's mixed constitution achieves political friendship in the city by moderating the monarchic principle of authority and the democratic principle of freedom (693e). The result is an agreement between the constitutive parts of the city about who should rule and be ruled. The goal is not, as in the case of Polybius, to delimit constitutional powers and ensure that they have sufficient weight to check and balance one another. Thus, in Plato there is no separation of powers. This difference has serious implications for sovereignty. It follows that if there are no clearly demarcated powers, then there can be no particular sphere over which the people are "sovereign." According to Plato's Athenian Stranger, under a constitution where freedom is properly mixed, the "people were not sovereign (*kyrios*) over anything but in a manner of speaking were willingly enslaved to the laws" (700a).

Finally, it is worth noting that Plato's and Polybius' accounts disagree over the explanatory power of "political science." Whereas Polybius suggests that an accurate account of social psychology can lead to precise predictive power, Plato emphasizes that any rational account of politics must be limited by the gods, chance, and human nature. Polybius' account of nature focuses on human impulses and desires from which morality emerges, whereas Plato's account also extends to the natural law constituted by the right reason that orders the cosmos.

Given these contrasts with Plato, it is tempting to see Polybius' account of sovereignty as foreshadowing that in the modern constitutional tradition. Polybius' constitutional theory certainly foreshadows modern accounts as regards the idea of constitutional design as a predictive "science" and recognition of the great benefit of incorporating distinct and separate constitutional powers. Benjamin Straumann has argued that the legal or juridical nature of Polybius' notion of constitutional powers anticipates an essential element of modern constitutionalism.[8] We must be cautious of speaking of these powers in strictly legal terms; after all, the Roman constitution was comprised of customary practices (*mos/mores*) no less than rights (*iura*) and statutes (*lex/leges*), and while Polybius' thought was surely shaped by Roman experience, the theoretical terms he uses are Greek. In Greek constitutional thought, rights are present but not as significant as in Roman political thought influenced by Roman law. Nevertheless, it is noteworthy that the terms that Polybius uses to describe the "powers" of the different parts of the constitution (*dynamis* and especially *exousia*) are identical to those used to express "rights" in Roman law, where rights are conceived as the "power" by which one exercises a justified claim to a good or action. In fact, when the translators of Justinian's *Corpus Iuris Civilis* sought to render Roman law into Greek, they sometimes chose *exousia* to render the Roman idea of rights (*ius, potestas*). And one might reasonably wonder what it means for part of the constitution to possess a power (*exousia*) that is "paramount in its sphere" (*autokratôr*) if the possessor of this power does not have "the unquestionable right to command and be obeyed" by others within this sphere, a right that is crucial to the modern idea of legitimacy.[9] Hence, we may plausibly attribute to Polybius the notion of sovereign constitutional powers.

However, while Polybius foreshadows the later tradition through his discussion of sovereign constitutional powers, he does not embrace the notion of popular sovereignty promulgated by "most modern liberal democracies today," which "conceive[s] of sovereignty as exercised by the people ruling through a constitution."[10] This modern notion of sovereignty also entails a corresponding notion of political legitimacy. Polybius' theory, however, lacks the idea of the people as an independent body of rights holders necessary for legitimacy. Moreover, his constitutional theory does not completely distinguish between the people and the "state" as a separate abstract entity through which the people may rule.

First, consider the idea of legitimacy as it relates to sovereignty. The Lockean account of sovereignty posits the people as a body of rights holders with claims that legitimate government must respect inasmuch as its authority is derived from the consent of the governed. Polybius comes no closer to a notion of legitimacy based on contractarian consent than Plato. For both Plato and Polybius, good rule requires the willing acceptance of the ruled. Yet, neither conceives of people in a state of nature as "free, equal, and independent" rights holders.[11] In contrast to Locke, they conceive of freedom not as a natural right but as a hard-won achievement. A decent political order does not protect already-free individuals but provides the conditions through which people may become free (cf. *Laws* 694a–b, 699e–700a, 701a–e and *Histories* 6.72, 6.8.4, 6.9.5).

According to Polybius, the morality according to which the people measure political rule consists of morally appropriate actions and obligations (*kathêkon*); Polybius' stress is on duties, not rights (6.6.7). Nor does Polybius embrace Plato's idea of natural law as cosmic right reason prescribing the common good, which serves as the basis for the claim in the *Laws* that constitutions whose rule is not in the interest of the common good do not count as *politieiai* in any meaningful sense (713a, 715a). Because he lacks these concepts, Polybius argues that rule which harms the common good may be described as "bad" or "unjust," and will on his theory eventually lack the approval of the ruled. Nevertheless, however bad or unjust such a rule is, Polybius does not suggest that it is illegitimate or that the people have a "right" to rebel.

Second, modern constitutional theory conceives of constitutions as regulating the power of the state, an abstract entity separate from "the people" and irreducible to individual office holders.[12] Polybius' analysis of powers that attach to offices, assemblies, and courts sounds abstract due to lack of details, but we must remember that what is regulated by the Roman constitution *includes* the citizen-body itself. The constitution orders not just offices but the people's customs and religion; inasmuch as the democratic part of the constitution requires ordered assemblies of citizens, the constitution is not something that the people rule through so much as something of which they themselves are a constitutive part. Thus, there is no space in Polybius' thought for a "zone of non-coincidence" between an independent or sovereign people and an abstract state that governs on their behalf and hence is answerable to their will.[13]

In final assessment, Polybius' most important contribution to a notion of sovereignty stems from his account of the constitution of separable, independent powers, each "sovereign" within its own sphere. This idea is not found in Plato, and it does not correspond to the later Hobbesian or Bodinean notion of sovereignty as undivided.[14] Nor does Polybius' compound constitution accurately represent the historic procedures of the Republican constitution, where, as we saw with the example of the "democratic element," the authority in areas set aside to the people could be limited by other factors. Polybius' theory does not include the notion of "popular sovereignty," if by this we mean the notion that the people are an independent body of rights holders with claims that the state must acknowledge in order to be legitimate. For Polybius, popular sovereignty means that the citizen-body determines the specific moral code in accordance with which they will all live collectively, and by which political rule itself will be measured.

Notes

1   Polybius, *Histories* 6.14. All references to Polybius follow *Polybius: The Histories*, trans. Robin Waterfield (Oxford: Oxford University Press, 2010).

2   In Polybius' account, the constitutive parts of the constitution maintain their integrity and are not blended together.

3   Daniel Philpott, "Sovereignty," in *The Oxford Handbook of the History of Political Philosophy*, ed. George Klosko (Oxford: Oxford University Press, 2011), 561–72.

4   Paul Cartledge, *Democracy: A Life* (Oxford: Oxford University Press, 2016), 257.

5   See references in Jed W. Atkins, *Roman Political Thought* (Cambridge: Cambridge University Press, 2018), 15–22.

6   See Jed W. Atkins, *Cicero on Politics and the Limits of Reason* (Cambridge: Cambridge University Press, 2013), 85–93 and Atkins, *Roman Political Thought*, 22–4.

7   All references to Plato follow *Plato: Laws*, trans. Tom Griffith (Cambridge: Cambridge University Press, 2016).

8   Benjamin Straumann, *Crisis and Constitutionalism: Roman Political Thought from the Fall of the Republic to the Age of Revolution* (Oxford: Oxford University Press, 2016), 152–3.

9   Atkins, *Roman Political Thought*, 20. Atkins' quote summarizes the definition of sovereignty in Philpott, "Sovereignty."

10 Philpott, "Sovereignty," 563.

11 John Locke, *Second Treatise of Government*, Bk. II, Ch. VIII.

12 David Runciman, "The Concept of the State: The Sovereignty of a Fiction," in *States and Citizens: History, Theory, Prospects*, ed. Quentin Skinner and Bo Strath (Cambridge: Cambridge University Press, 2003), 28–38.

13 A. Brett, "The Development of the Idea of Citizens' Rights," in *States and Citizens*, 97–112.

14 For discussions of Hobbes' and Bodin's notions of sovereignty, see the relevant chapters in this volume.

4

Reading Sovereignty in Augustus' *Res gestae*

Dean Hammer

My name was incorporated into the hymn of the Salii by decree of the senate, and it was ratified by law that I should be permanently sacrosanct and that I should hold the tribunician power for as long as I live.[1]

In my sixth and seventh consulships, after I had put an end to civil wars, although by everyone's agreement I had power over everything, I transferred the state from my power into the control of the Roman senate and people. For this service, I was named Augustus by senatorial decree.[2]

When I was holding my thirteenth consulship, both the senate and the equestrian order and the people of Rome all together hailed me as father of the fatherland.[3]

Inscribed on two bronze pillars that were placed outside his mausoleum at the instruction of his will, Augustus' *Res gestae divi Augusti* eludes easy classification. Nicolet gives us some sense of the mix of genres reflected in the *Res gestae*: the inscriptions of Oriental kings that celebrated victories in the first person; the *cursus honorum* that listed positions and honors; and the *elogia*, which was a tradition of Roman dynasties.[4] Its status as a political document is similarly elusive since it seems more to record than justify. In fact, what Augustus records may be read in two different ways. In one, the *Res gestae* is approached for its insights into the constitutional provisions by which Augustus legitimated his authority;[5] in the other, it either reveals or disguises the extra-constitutional aspects of his rule.[6]

Lurking in the backdrop of these approaches are two quite different conceptions of sovereignty. One perspective, that of constitutional sovereignty, uses the *Res gestae* to identify formal institutional and legal continuities that authorize Augustus' power, as well as to shed light on the processes by which particular constitutional arrangements are legitimated. In the second interpretation, sovereignty lies in the power to will, whether by a collectivity or more effectively by an individual (as in Bodin), or decide (as developed by Schmitt and Agamben).[7] Moreover, Augustus' claims of formal authority are juxtaposed to the violations of the norms and legal provisions of the Republic that are excluded from or glossed over in the text. From this perspective, the real import of the *Res gestae* is a claim to authority that rests on Augustus' sacrosanct status and accomplishments. If one locates authority in law, the other locates it in awe. The tension between these readings of sovereignty becomes most apparent in arguments that try to have it both ways, identifying Augustus as emerging as the singular leader through his *auctoritas* and virtues "without infringing [on the] sovereignty of the senate and people of Rome,"[8] or as "the senate and people [giving] Augustus supreme power, and he [giving] most of it back."[9]

At issue here is the challenge of giving coherence to the *Res gestae* as an articulation of Augustus' authority. That requires a different reading of sovereignty, one less beholden to a concept that is more modern in its formulation. A beginning point is to return to the term that many, beginning with Bodin and extending into current scholarship, translate as sovereignty, and that is *maiestas*. In its usage, the term suggests a more complicated intertwining of law and awe than captured by notions of sovereignty. In the Republic, *maiestas* was connected to the Roman people in the phrase, *maiestas populi Romani*, which is a republicanized majesty by which the *populus Romanus* was conceived as indivisible, perpetual, and inviolable.[10] There are legal aspects: *maiestas* treaties and *maiestas* laws (technically, *maiestas minuta populi Romani*) required that subject territories and domestic officials recognize and act on behalf of the supremacy of the Roman people, conceived as a corporate entity. But these legal aspects are closely connected to the divine, generally, and Jupiter, specifically, as the protector and augmenter of the *res publica*, conceived as the *populus Romanus*.[11] The *maiestas populi Romani* is not reducible to law or a divinely authorized will, but is a discursive framework within which the collectivity is imagined, laws and institutions created, decisions made, and actions justified and from which there is no appeal. I will refer to this as *foundational authority* to avoid some of the conceptual confusion that arises from the language of sovereignty. In using this phrase, I am placing my argument in the context of scholarship that has sought to revise how we think about sovereignty. For Arendt, the perpetuity in and by which the act of foundation is carried out resides not in the existence of an "identical will" but of "an agreed purpose for which alone the promises are valid and binding," able to "dispose of the future as though it were the present."[12] The notion of foundational authority changes what we look for in asking about what authorizes Augustus' actions: neither a conformity to nor an usurpation of law, but an underlying discursive framework that organizes particular norms and practices that are remembered and transmitted through writing as well as through a range of social, religious, and political practices. My interest is to read Augustus' *Res gestae* within this discursive framework, as both structured by, and in turn structuring, an authorizing language he inherited from the Republic.

Reading the *Res gestae*

The importance of the authorizing language of the Republic is borne out by the attention paid by Augustus to his role as acting on behalf of, and authorized by, the *populus Romanus* (*RG* 1.4, 8.1, 13, 21.3, 26.1, 27.1, 30.1, 32.3, 34.1, 35.1); as maintaining in appearance, if not in actual fact, the legality and formal equality of magisterial *potestas* (*RG* 5–6); and as affirming ancestral ways (*RG* 6.1, 8.5, 13, 27.2). The derivation of power from office signals the importance of Augustus' gesture, as disingenuous as it may have been, of returning all the laws, provinces, and the army to the people during 28–27 BCE (*RG* 34.1). As has been noted frequently, Augustus could claim to represent the *maiestas populi Romani* in its derivative form by way of holding office. Augustus would have fallen under protection of the *maiestas* laws as a holder of the *proconsular imperium* and as possessor of tribunician sacrosanctity, granted originally in 36 BCE but given permanence as *tribunicia potestas* in 23 BCE (*RG* 4.4).[13]

The careful attention paid by Augustus to a framework that seems to authorize his actions suggests the limits of viewing Augustus' sovereignty as an act of unconstrained will.[14] But attempts to locate Augustus' power in a set of legal and constitutional considerations, as somehow an authority that is transferred to Augustus, miss how Augustus, in fact, plays upon while also transforming the foundational, authorizing framework of the *res publica*. Rather than there being a constitutional *transfer* of *maiestas*, in which the *princeps* acts as an agent of the people, one sees, instead, a *transformation* in the meaning of *maiestas*. Whatever the authorizing gestures described by Augustus, there is a more fundamental transformation in the republican authorizing framework. The inviolability of a fictive entity, the *populus Romanus*, is now relocated in the inviolability of a real individual. Moreover, the *princeps* does not possess inviolability because he is acting as an agent of that entity, as would have been the case in the Republic, but because he is endowed with a divine quality of supremacy that is to be recognized unconditionally by the people (*RG* 10.1) and other states (*RG* 25.2). The *Res gestae* traces, and culminates in, the two fullest expressions of the effort by Augustus to appropriate from the corporate body of the people, and assimilate into his body, the *maiestas* of Jupiter as the preserver of the Roman people and the father of the gods: the identification of his sanctity with his permanent and living divinity as *Augustus*; and the association of the form of Jupiter's authority with Augustus' role as the *pater patriae*.

Augustus waits until the penultimate section of the *Res gestae* to mention the title, *Augustus*, that was given to him in 27 BCE (*RG* 34.2). The reference is out of place chronologically, but serves as a crystallization of Augustus' sanctity. Ovid notes that "Augustus alone bears a name that ranks with Jove supreme" because of the association of the name with the dedication of temples by priests, augury and the power of augmentation (Ov. *Fast.* 1.608, 1.610–12; also Cass. Dio 53.16.8). Although not mentioned in the *Res gestae*, but no doubt remembered by the Roman audience, an early expression of Augustus' power of augmentation appears in the *ludi saeculares* in 17 BCE, a festival involving sacrifices and games celebrating the new age. The *ludi saeculares* has republican roots, originally called the *ludi Terintini*. Augustus recites an archaic prayer on behalf of the *maiestas* of the Roman people (*CIL* 32323.93), but also includes himself and his family (*CIL* 32323.98–99). The prayer emphasizes his role in the extension of the "*maiestas* of the Empire" as the bringer of peace. One also reads in Horace of the blessing of Pax Augusta by which the "prestige of *maiestas* of the Empire was extended" (Horace *Ode* 4.15.14–15; also *Carm. saec.*). This is alluded to in the *Res gestae* through Augustus' mention of the consecration of the Altar of Augustan Peace (*RG* 12.2), and the closing of the gates of the Temple of Janus to indicate peace across the empire on three occasions (*RG* 13). Although the first day of the *ludi saeculares* consists of a sacrifice to Jupiter Optimus Maximus, the second and third days consist of sacrifices to Juno, Apollo, and Diana who, along with Mars, become Augustus' patron gods and replace many of Jupiter's functions.[15]

Jupiter is not forgotten; instead, Augustus appropriates into his own person Jupiter's *maiestas* that was once conferred on the *populus Romanus*. Augustus could maintain this association of the sacrosanctity of his body with holding the tribunician power (*tribunicia potestas*) (*RG* 4.4). But the sacred elements do not reside in the office (punctuated by the fact that Augustus did not hold the office) but in his body being made inviolable or sacrosanct in perpetuity (*RG* 10.1; also Cass. Dio 53.17.9; *Dig.* 48.4.1.1). Augustus also notes his inclusion in the Salian Hymns of the priests of Mars, a priesthood that dated their origins to Numa, making him like Hercules and an equal of the gods (*RG* 10.1; Cass. Dio 51.20.1). And in his election to the *pontifex maximus*, Augustus adds to the *sacrosanctitus* of his tribunician power the *sanctitus*, or inviolability, of the priesthood bestowed by inauguration. Augustus would claim his role in overseeing the sacred rites of the state as a right of inheritance from Caesar (originating with Aeneas and his care of the *penates*), now extended over the whole of Italy (*RG* 10.2).[16]

One Augustan innovation is a different type of *vota* in which prayers and offerings were made (by consuls, priests, and citizens of different towns) to Jupiter to protect the state by protecting the health of Augustus' actual body (*RG* 9; Hor. *Ode* 1.12.49–54; Plin. *Pan.* 94).[17] The investment of *maiestas* in the body of the *princeps* underlies Augustus' expansion of the *lex maiestatis* from a republican concept used to give expression to the inviolability of the corporate body to one about the inviolability of the individual body of the single ruler. When Ulpian notes how crimes of *maiestas* may resemble sacrilege (*Dig.* 48.4.1.pro), he is reflecting both a continuity and a modification of *maiestas*, from a derivative relationship to a sacred quality possessed by the *princeps*.

Even in treaties, in which the *maiestas populi Romani* had its longest running expression in the Republic, there is a difference during Augustus' own reign about the source of authority. Although a treaty with Mytilene in 25 BCE likely retained conventional elements of *maiestas* treaties, by the time he writes his *Res gestae*, Augustus states, "The whole of Italy of its own free will swore allegiance to me," as later did the other provinces (*RG* 25.2). If one sees the worship by subject territories of the deified *Urbs Roma*, one now observes a veneration of the *maiestas* of the single body of the *princeps*.

Just as the *Res gestae* moves toward the culminating expression of the assimilation of Jupiter's divinity into Augustus' personal *maiestas*, so it ends with Augustus' appropriation of a form of Jupiter's authority when Augustus is given the title of *pater patriae* in 2 BCE, at first through popular acclamation and then through the senate (*RG* 35.1). The title establishes an assumption of Jupiter's role as father of the gods, and his corollary role as father of the *populus Romanus*, making Augustus father of the state (Cass. Dio 53.18.3; Ov. *Trist.* 2.37–40; Ov. *Fast.* 2.131–32). Some suggestion of the importance of this title is made by Ovid, who writes that being the *pater patriae* means that "Caesar is the state" (*res est publica Caesar*) (Ov. *Trist.* 4.4.13–15). Bauman has suggested that one implication of this oath is that it provides a legal basis for the extension of *maiestas* to his household.[18] But it signals a more fundamental change in the relationship of the *princeps* to the *populus Romanus* by making the state an extension of that household in which the *princeps* is not the representative of the people or their agent, but their master (e.g. Dio Cass, 53.17.3). In 30 BCE, the senate decreed that a libation be offered to his *genius*, or personal spirit, at all banquets, placing in the public realm a household ritual dedicated to the health of the *paterfamilias* (*RG* 9.2).[19] In *Res gestae*, Augustus employs this language of the *paterfamilias*, referring to the funds he provides to the plebs and the state out of his own patrimony and largesse (*RG* 15: to plebs; 17: adds to public treasury; 18: for grain). It is as though Augustus and subsequent *principes* reverse the legendary transfer of *maiestas* from the gods to the kings and then to the people, investing themselves with a much earlier version of *maiestas*. In fact, this transfer is heightened by Augustus' identification of himself with Romulus, seen, for example, in the fact that he considered adopting the name Romulus in 27 BCE (Suet. *Aug.* 7.2), locating his house where Romulus had lived (Cass. Dio 53.16.5), comparing his own youth to Romulus' (*RG* 1.1; Dion. Hal. 2.56.7), and adopting the name of *pater* which was first given to Romulus (Livy 1.16).

I think there is too little evidence to conclude with any certainty that Augustus is articulating a "new philosophy of empire,"[20] any more than references to the *maiestas populi Romani* in the Republic reflect a theorized notion of the *res publica*. But there is also more going on in the *Res gestae* than premising his authority on an extension of republican *auctoritas*. I think we can read the *Res gestae* as part of a discursive transformation in the authorizing framework of the Republic. Augustus and subsequent *principes* could have it both ways. In a culture that thrived on legalisms, Augustus could claim to be returning law to Rome, a notion on which the *Res gestae* begins and ends (*RG* 1.1; 34.1–3). In a state that for centuries had defined itself as the *senatus populusque Romanus*—the initials SPQR inscribed on coins, public documents, and monuments—Augustus could claim to be acting on behalf of, and at the request of, both (*RG* 1; 4; 5; 6; 9; 10; 11; 12; 13; 26.1; 32.3; 34; 35). And in the complicated legal and customary arrangement of official power in the Republic that, more than anything else, resisted kingship, Augustus could both claim particular formal powers and resist others (*RG* 6.1; 7; 8.5; 10.1–2; 34.1). But Augustus also transforms the fictive entity of the *populus Romanus*, both appropriating the *maiestas* of Jupiter and, relatedly, the *paterfamilias* of the state. In a sense, Augustus appropriated a much earlier version of *maiestas*, a divine quality that was unconditional, inviolable, and was to be recognized by the people.[21] Augustus unites in his person law and awe, or for the Greeks as they wrote about Augustus, *hegemonia* and *theiotês*. The *maiestas populi Romani* had already provided the blueprint for the indivisibility, perpetuity, and inviolability of the fictional body of the *populus Romanus*. Augustus' authority rested on his appropriation of that foundational authority into his own body.

Notes

1   *Res Gestae* 10.1. All references to *Res Gestae* follow Alison Cooley, *Res Gestae Divi Augusti: Text, Translation, and Commentary* (Cambridge: Cambridge University Press, 2009).

2   Ibid., 34.1–2.

3   Ibid., 35.1.

4   Claude Nicolet, *Space, Geography, and Politics in the Early Roman Empire* (Ann Arbor: University of Michigan Press, 1991), 20. Helpful commentaries are provided by P. A. Brunt and J. M. Moore, *Res Gestae Divi Augusti: The Achievements of the Divine Augustus* (London: Oxford University Press, 1967); John Scheid, *Res gestae divi Augusti* (Paris: Les Belles Lettres, 2007); and Cooley, *Res Gestae*, whose text I follow.

5   Theodor Mommsen, *Römisches Staatsrecht* (Leipzig: Verlag von S. Hirzl, 1887–1888), 2.2, 748; F. E. Adcock, "The Achievement of Augustus," in *The Cambridge Ancient History*, ed. Stanley Arthur Cook, F. E. Adcock, and M. P. Charlesworth (Cambridge: Cambridge University Press, 1934); E. T. Salmon, "The Evolution of Augustus' Principate," *Historia: Zeitschrift für Alte Geschichte* 5 (1956): 456–78; E. S. Ramage, *The Nature and Purpose of Augustus' "Res Gestae"* (Stuttgart: Steiner, 1989).

6   Ronald Syme, *The Roman Revolution* (Oxford: Oxford University Press, 2002), 523; Karl Galinsky, *Augustan Culture: An Interpretive Introduction* (Princeton, N.J.: Princeton University Press, 1996), 12; Giorgio Agamben, *Homo Sacer. Sovereign Power and Bare Life* (Stanford, Calif.: Stanford University Press, 1998); Michèle Lowrie, "Sovereignty before the Law: Agamben and the Roman Republic," *Law and Humanities* 1 (2007): 55; Michèle Lowrie, "Auctoritas and Representation: Augustus' Res gestae," in *Writing, Performance, and Authority in Augustan Rome*, ed. Michèle Lowrie (Oxford: Oxford University Press, 2009), 284.

7   For discussions of Bodin, Schmitt, and Agamben on sovereignty, see the relevant chapters in this volume. See also the relevant chapter on Arendt, who is cited below.

8   Cooley, *Res Gestae*, 36, drawing on Hans-Joachim Diesner, "Augustus und sein Tatenbericht," *Klio* 67 (1985): 41.

9   William Turpin, "Res Gestae 34.1 and the Settlement of 27 BC," *The Classical Quarterly* 44 (1994): 427–37 (430); also Brian Campbell, *The Romans and their World: A Short Introduction* (New Haven: Yale University Press, 2011), 100.

10   Dean Hammer, "Thinking about Sovereignty: Is there a Fictional State in the Roman Republic?," in *Proceedings of the British Academy*, ed. Christopher Smith (London: British Academy, forthcoming). See discussions in Hans Georg Gundel, "Der Begriff Maiestas im politischen Denken der römischen Republick," *Historia* 12 (1963): 283–320; Richard A. Bauman, *The Crimen Maiestatis in the Roman Republic and Augustan Principate* (Johannesburg: Witwatersrand University Press, 1967); Jean-Louis Ferrary, "Les origines de la loi de majesté à Rome," *Comptes rendus des séances de l'Académie des Inscriptions et Belles-Lettres* (1983): 556–72; Yan Thomas, "L'institution de la Majesté," *Revue de synthèse* 112 (1991): 331–86; Nicholas Greenwood Onuf, *The Republican Legacy in International Thought* (Cambridge: Cambridge University Press, 1998); Clifford Ando, *Law, Language, and Empire in the Roman Tradition* (Philadelphia: University of Pennsylvania Press, 2011); Valentina Arena, *Libertas and the Practice of Politics in the Late Roman Republic* (Cambridge: Cambridge University Press, 2012).

11   See, for example, Hor. *Carm.* 1.12–19; Ov. *Met.* 2.62; Ov. *Fast.* 5.126; Macrob. *Sat.* 1.12.17.

12   Hannah Arendt, *The Human Condition* (Chicago: University of Chicago Press, 1998), 245; also Pavlos Eleftheriadis, "Law and Sovereignty," *Law and Philosophy* 29 (2010): 535–69 (569); Neil MacCormick, *Questioning Sovereignty: Law, State, and Nation in the European Commonwealth* (Oxford: Oxford University Press, 1999), 129, 109, 141.

13 Brunt and Moore, *Res Gestae*, 10–1.

14 Jean Bodin, *On Sovereignty: Four Chapters from the Six Books of the Commonwealth*, ed. Julian H. Franklin (Cambridge: Cambridge University Press, 1992), 1.8, 27, notes that taking an oath "to keep the laws and customs of the land" weakens "sovereign majesty."

15 J. Rufus Fears, "The Cult of Jupiter and Roman Imperial Ideology," in *Aufstieg und Niedergang der römischen Welt*, ed. Wolfgang Haase (Berlin: Gruyter, 1981), 13–14, 60; also John F. Miller, *Apollo, Augustus, and the Poets* (Cambridge: Cambridge University Press, 2009).

16 See Trevor S. Luke, *Ushering in a New Republic: Theologies of Arrival at Rome in the First Century BCE* (Ann Arbor: University of Michigan Press, 2014), 240.

17 Fears, "Cult," 64, 98–9.

18 Bauman, *Crimen*, 228.

19 J. S. Richardson, *Augustan Rome 44 BC to AD 14: The Restoration of the Republic and the Establishment of the Empire* (Edinburgh: Edinburgh University Press, 2012), 208; John Pollini, *From Republic to Empire: Rhetoric, Religion, and Power in the Visual Culture of ancient Rome* (Norman: University of Oklahoma Press, 2012), 330–2.

20 Ramage, *Nature*, 57.

21 Georges Dumézil, "Maiestas et Gravitas: De quelques Différences entre les Romains et les Austronésiens," *Revue de philologie, de littérature et d'histoire anciennes* 26 (1952): 7–28 (18).

5

Al-Fārābī

The Sovereignty of the Philosopher-King

Massimo Campanini

The ruler may be a first ruler, and he may be a secondary ruler. The secondary ruler is the one who is ruled by one human being while he rules another human being. [. . .]
The first ruler without qualification is the one who does not need— not in anything at all—to be ruled by another human being. Rather, he has already attained the sciences and cognitions in actuality and has no need of a human being to guide him in anything. He has the ability for excellent apprehension of each and every particular thing that ought to be done, and the faculty for excellently guiding everyone other than himself to all that he has instructed them in; the ability to use everyone as a means to do a particular thing pertaining to that action he is intent on; and the ability to determine, define, and direct the activities toward happiness. That comes about only in an inhabitant having a great, extraordinary nature when his soul has joined with the Active Intellect. He obtains that only by having first attained the passive intellect, then, after that, having attained the intellect called "acquired." Through attaining the acquired [intellect] there comes about the conjunction with the Active Intellect that was mentioned in the book On the Soul.

This human being is the king in truth according to the ancients, and he is the one of whom it ought to be said that he receives revelation.

[. . .]

The people who are governed by the rulership of this ruler are the virtuous, good and happy people. If they are a nation, then that is the virtuous nation.[1]

If a contemporary Western scholar, aware of the debates about sovereignty between, say, Hobbes and Locke, were to read this passage alone, isolated from its context, he/she would remain quite perplexed. At first glance, al-Fārābī's text seems to have no connection at all with modern or contemporary issues of politics and government.[2] For it displays clear metaphysical concerns.

Actually, al-Fārābī (*ca.* 870–950 AD), adduces the following example:

Truth → politics → happiness

that is, glossing the formula, he argues that metaphysical truth is the foundation of political action and political action's aim is to achieve happiness. On the other hand, metaphysical truth is grounded upon knowledge and happiness is first of all mental. Truth is what the being is (τὸ ὂν ἐστιν) and Truth/true is first of all God, the First Being who exists by Itself. Al-Fārābī writes that "It is said of Him that He is True (*yuqāl lahu annahu haqq*) [. . .] and this for two reasons simultaneously: because His existence is the most perfect of all the existences, and because, since He is intelligible, the one who grasps Him by intellect as existent incidentally grasps through Him also [all] that is existent."[3] On these bases, the present chapter is devoted to the elucidation of this paradigm examining its implications for the idea of sovereignty, which is therefore completely different from Hobbes' or Locke's.

In a passage worthy of consideration from the *Book of Political Regimes* (*Kitāb al-siyāsa al-madanīya*), al-Fārābī declares that the principles of existents, the right rulership consequent to knowledge and finally the happiness consequent to knowledge and right rulership, are conceived, or comprehended (*intellecta*), or imagined. Conceived signifies that the principles exist in the soul as they exist in reality. Imagined means that the principles impress in the soul their representations or imitations. Comprehended refers to a higher level of understanding, abstracted from materiality. Most human beings have no capacity to understand and conceive correctly the knowledge of supreme objects such as the Agent Intellect and the supreme rulership. Therefore, they need to imagine the principles of existents and their degrees; and they need to be solicited to grasp them in a way different from pure reason, that is through imitation. Religion (*milla*) involves the rooting of these imitative images in the soul of common people. The learned scholars on their part grasp the principles through conceptualization, while a third level is that of the naïve believers who are satisfied simply with imagination.[4]

This theory implies the distinction between two kinds of assent: a philosophical and a religious one. Apart from the thorny issue of the relation between reason and revelation, which I do not want to deal with here, the problem involves the necessity of classifying the sciences. Al-Fārābī devoted a whole book to the classification of sciences (the *Ihsā' al-'ulūm*) which is important because, by following the correct path in achieving knowledge, the philosopher will be able to get full mastery of knowledge and consequently to achieve a more perfect realization of himself/herself—prerequisites of right rulership and happiness. The epistemological and methodological aim of the organization of sciences is to make the existent beings intelligible, helping the human intellect to perfect itself by elevating it up to the level of the acquired intellect (*'aql mustafād*). The acquired intellect is the one connecting itself with the Agent Intellect, the first of the separate Intelligences. According to al-Fārābī, then, logic is the *organon* at the basis of knowledge; metaphysics is the architectonic science, so to speak. It is what Aristotle in *Metaphysics* Γ 2, 1003b15 defines as "science studying beings-qua-beings"; politics is the supreme science, at the top of the pyramid. The practical aim of the *ihsā' al-'ulūm* is to provide the ruler with the instruments useful to manage the state and lead humans to achieve happiness, which is the goal of politics.

The ruler of the virtuous city, the *imām*-prophet-philosopher-king, knows the truth because he is "a man whose passive intellect is perfected through the acquisition of all the intelligibles, so that he becomes intellect in act and intelligible in act and, insofar as intelligible, he becomes [identical to] what he understands [by intellect] (*wa sāra al-ma'qūl minhu huwa alladhī ya'qul*)."[5] Therefore, the ruler of the virtuous city is tantamount to God, the First Being, because "the relation of the First Cause (*al-sabab al-awwal*) with the other existent beings is tantamount to the relation of the king (*malik*) of the virtuous city with all the other parts (*ajzā'*) of the city itself [that is the other citizens]."[6]

Fortified by these almost divine endowments, the ruler governs the city. However, politics is not simply *siyāsa*, that is, "management of people." It is more properly *tartīb* and *tadbīr*, that is, *arrangement* and *regime*. *Tartīb* and *tadbīr* hint at a well-knitted structure, *nizām*. "The function of the city's governor—that is, the king—," al-Fārābī writes, "is to govern cities so as to tie the parts of the city to one another and to give it consonance."[7]

The perfect order of the world is mirrored in the perfect order of the city; and as the First Being (*al-Awwal*), God, keeps the universe stable and orderly, so the first ruler (*al-ra'īs al-awwal*), the *imām*-prophet-philosopher-king of the excellent city, keeps political society in a similar condition.

The exercise of sovereignty and authority, according to al-Fārābī, allows the *imām*-prophet-philosopher-king to put in practice Truth. On the other hand, the universe's order displays itself in knowledge. As perfect science cannot but be true, knowledge—the connective element of the two previous propositions—is relational. This is the reason why al-Fārābī does not discuss the institutions of the virtuous city themselves, but examines the *ideas of the inhabitants of the virtuous city* (this is the title of al-Fārābī's most famous work). The virtuous city's inhabitants live in harmonious relation one with the other. And because the political order is the realization of perfect knowledge and the apex of perfect knowledge is metaphysics, obviously it is necessary to set up the political order starting from metaphysics, whose subject is the First Being, God.

Al-Fārābī's idea of rulership is not historical in so far as he speaks of a political system projected in the heaven of a *realized* utopia. In Islam utopia has a precise model in the past: the Islamic state of the Prophet in Medina or, for the Shi'is, the Prophet's Medina and the golden age of the *imām*s.[8] Therefore, in order to grasp his theory, an intriguing issue is whether al-Fārābī was a Shi'i or not. I will try to suggest an answer starting from the hierarchical structure of government as described in the *Fuṣūl muntaza'a* or *Selected Aphorisms*.

In Aphorism 58 al-Fārābī describes four kinds of excellent and virtuous *politeiae*, which must be compared with Plato's *Republic*, allegedly the main source, along with Plato's *Laws*, of al-Fārābī's political thought.[9] They are— hierarchically organized in order of perfection:

1 First of all the monarchy of the *ra'īs al-awwal*, the First ruler who corresponds to the *imām*-prophet-philosopher-king of the *Madīna al-fāḍila*, the virtuous city.

2 At the second level there is the aristocratic government (*ri'āsa al-akhiyār wa dhawī al-faḍā'il*, literally "the rulership of the best and the most virtuous"), wherein the functions and the abilities of the *imam* are divided among a number of different leaders.

3 Then there is the government of that king or *ra'īs* who manages power in agreement with the religious Law (*malik al-sunna*) and performs the revealed juridical norms (*sharā'i'*).

4 Finally, there is the regime of an assembly that governs in agreement with the Law, but whose leader is not a single man but an assembly of different kings (*rua'sā' al-sunna*).[10]

If we take into account together Plato's and Aristotle's political theories, the four levels would correspond respectively to the government of: (1) the philosopher-king; (2) aristocracy; (3) natural monarchy; (4) democracy. Looking more closely at the scheme, however, we realize that the first two levels embody the speculative and rational dimension of power's management; while the second two levels embody the legal and juridical dimension of power's management.[11] Moreover, the philosopher-king of al-Fārābī enjoys a fundamental quality the philosopher-king of Plato does not have: the quality of being a prophet. There is a transition from a government inspired by philosophy to the best government inspired by religion (i.e. (Shi'i) Islam).[12] Therefore, if we wish to read al-Fārābī's hierarchy of powers not in a Greek way, but in an Islamic way, we realize that the four levels correspond roughly: (1) to the supreme level of the (Shi'i) *imāms*; (2) to the prophetical level, the prophets being the conveyors of that Truth which only the *imāms* are able to interpret thoroughly; (3) to the level of that *'ālim* (scholar or *faqīh*— in Ruhollāh Khomeynī's terms the *velāyat-e faqīh*, the "vice-regency of the jurist") who governs supported by an assembly of *"ulamā"*; (4) to the assembly of *ulamā*. If we wish even more to emphasize the religious commitment of al-Fārābī, we could say that the *ulamā* carry on the legacy of the prophets, because their government is grounded on customary law, and the prophets allegedly brought the Law to the people. From another perspective again: the speculative monarchy is that of the *imāms*; law and jurisprudence are the basis of the prophets' (*rusul*) government; the plurality of rulers of the fourth level reproduces the *ulamā*'s *corpus*. Certainly, we can suggest that the rule of Law is needed when the institution of the *imām*'s rulership and/or of a philosophical regime is no more possible or viable. In the *Book of the Ideas of the Inhabitants of the Virtuous City*, al-Fārābī simply places the Supreme Legislator (the *imām*-prophet-philosopher-king) at the top of the government, and posits, immediately below, the rulership of the *imāms* who succeed one another after the First Ruler and Legislator.[13] Considering this analysis, it is reasonable to suppose that al-Fārābī was Shi'i.[14] And his theory of sovereignty must be collocated in this framework.

A last point: in *Fusūl muntaza'a*'s Aphorism 93, discussing the situation of the virtuous in corrupt and deviant cities, al-Fārābī sketches the famous theory of the "plants" (*nawābit*).[15] They are the "irregulars" living inside the perfect city. The issue is controversial and in order to understand it better we can recall the Muslim Spanish philosopher Ibn Bājja/Avempace, although he lived much later than al-Fārābī, dying in 1039.

According to Avempace the "plants" are the virtuous people— philosophers—hidden within the wicked political regime: they are "solitary" (*mutawahhidūn*) and their intellectual web, the web of their perfected minds, allows them to cooperate for the imperfect city's emendation.[16] Their presence within an otherwise deviant polity is therefore positive. On the contrary, according to al-Fārābī, the "plants" are the dissidents, weeds to be eradicated.[17] Their presence in the perfect city is negative. Al-Fārābī argues that "happiness is obtained only by removing evils from cities and from nations—not just the voluntary ones, but also the natural ones."[18]

In Aphorism 93, using an extremely meaningful Qur'anic term, *hijra*, the emigration of the Prophet Muhammad from Mecca to Medina, al-Fārābī says that "the virtuous person is forbidden to reside in the corrupt regimes, and it is obligatory for him to emigrate (*hijra*) to the virtuous city if any exists in actuality in his time."[19] Al-Fārābī seems here to be very close to Avempace, although in the *Book of the Ideas of the Inhabitants of the*

Virtuous City he apparently argues that happiness is attainable also in the wicked cities.

In any case, al-Fārābī seems to anticipate Michel Foucault in envisaging a bio-political control of society: the right and just ideas must be imposed, even by force, and control over the political system involves also the control over the citizens' bodies. Al-Fārābī's political regime seems therefore authoritarian, tantamount to the "illiberal society" Karl Popper charged Plato (and al-Fārābī was platonic in political philosophy) with having theorized. However, if a regime is perfect, it would be stupid and foolish to rebel. Who can dissent from the truth? Only a madman. In the perfect regime freedom to contest the status quo cannot exist, because all people are happy and satisfied with what they have. This is the unavoidable conclusion of a political philosophy—al-Fārābī's philosophy—grounded upon the metaphysical concept of hierarchy: everything occupies its own place in the perfect system—be it the cosmos, the human body or the political regime—and turning upside down this order is foolish. Sovereignty's aim is to keep this perfect order safe and durable. The power of the *imām*-prophet-philosopher-king is therefore irresistible, also because it is religiously characterized: as *imām* he is a legislator; as prophet he leads people through suasion and education; as philosopher he theorizes Truth and wisdom; as king he is the army's commander. Obviously, in this case we are very far from Foucault: the system does not produce resistance; it is perfect, closed in on itself, and immutable.

Notes

1   Al-Fārābī, *The Political Regime* in *Alfarabi. The Political Writings*, vol. 2, trans., annot., and intro. Charles E. Butterworth (Ithaca and London: Cornell University Press, 2015), §§ 79–80, 68–9.

2   For a long time, the interpretation of al-Fārābī's politics has been dominated by Muhsin Mahdi and his disciples. I recall only Muhsin Mahdi, *Alfarabi and the Foundation of Islamic Political Philosophy* (Chicago: Chicago University Press, 2001); and Miriam Galston, *Politics and Excellence: The Political Philosophy of Alfarabi* (Princeton: Princeton University Press, 1990). I tried to propose a different key of interpretation in a number of papers, among which are Massimo Campanini, "Alfarabi and the Foundation of Political Theology in Islam," in *Islam, the State and Political Authority: Medieval Issues and Modern Concerns*, ed. Asma Afsaruddin (New York: Palgrave Macmillan, 2011)—but see the answer by Charles E. Butterworth, "Alfarabi's Goal: Political Philosophy, not Political Theology" in the same volume; Mokdad Arfa Mensia provided a substantial contribution with *Al-Fārābī. Falsafat al-Dīn wa 'Ulūm al-Islām (F. Philosophy of Religion and the Sciences of Islam)* (Beirut: Dār al-Mudār al-Islāmī, 2011) and "Al-Fārābī et la science des Usūl al-fiqh," *Arabic Sciences and Philosophy* 27 (2017): 139–63, stressing that, in al-Fārābī's perspective, the Islamic science of *fiqh* (jurisprudence) is necessary for the

virtuous city's ruler, provided that the principles of jurisprudence (*usūl al-fiqh*) are replete with philosophical contents. Finally, I would mention Pierre Vallat, *Farabi et l'écoled'Alexandrie. Des premises de la connaissance à la philosophiepolitique* (Paris: Vrin, 2004), who criticizes the Straussian approach of Muhsin Mahdi, but at the same time emphasizes the civil character of religion in al-Fārābī, due mostly to the impact of the import of the Greek heritage within this thought.

3   Al-Fārābī, *Kitāb ārā' ahl al-madīna al-fādila* (*Book of the Ideas of the Inhabitants of the Virtuous City*), my translation in al-Fārābī, *La cittàvirtuosa* (Milano: Rizzoli, 1996), 77. See obviously the edition of Richard Walzer, *Alfarabi on the Perfect State* (Oxford: Clarendon Press, 1985), 75.

4   Al-Fārābī, *The Political Regime*, §§ 88–91, 74–5.

5   Al-Fārābī, *Kitābārā' ahl al-madīna al-fādila,* my translation in *La città virtuosa,* cit., 217. Walzer's translation, 241.

6   Ibid., 213. Walzer's translation, 237.

7   Al-Fārābī, *The Political Regime*, § 88, 73.

8   I have discussed at length the issue of retrospective utopia in a number of articles and books. See M. Campanini, "The Utopian Dimension of a (Possible?) Islamic Philosophy of History," in *Utopia in the Present: Cultural Politics and Challenge,* ed. C. Gualtieri (Bern: Peter Lang, 2018), 43–56.

9   Richard Walzer was a staunch supporter of this interpretation, but, for example in his commentary to *Kitāb ārā' ahl al-madīna al-fādila,* he goes so far as to attempt to find a Platonic or at least Greek source even for the commas of al-Fārābī's text: an evident exaggeration hampering a correct perception of the philosopher's aims.

10   Al-Fārābī, *Selected Aphorisms,* in *Alfarabi: The Political Writings,* vol. 1, trans., annot., and intro. Charles E. Butterworth (Ithaca and London: Cornell University Press, 2001), 37–8.

11   There is no reason to separate neatly the two levels as Leo Strauss seems to recommend in relation to al-Fārābī's Commentary to Plato's *Law.*

12   See also Hans Daiber, *The Ruler as Philosopher: A New Interpretation of al-Fārābī's View* (Amsterdam-Oxford-New York: North Holland Publication Co., 1986).

13   Al-Fārābī, *Kitāb ārā' ahl al-madīna al-fādila,* my translation in *La città virtuosa,* cit., 221–5. Walzer's translation, 247–53.

14   Cfr. Patricia Crone, *Medieval Islamic Political Thought* (Edinburgh: Edinburgh University Press, 2004), chapter 14 and note 69 in the chapter.

15   See Ilai Alon, "Fārābī's Funny Flora. Al-Nawābit as 'Opposition'," *Arabica* 37, no. 1 (1990): 56–90.

16   See Ibn Baǧǧa, *La conduite de l'isolé et deux autres épîtres,* trans. and comment. C. Genequand, with the Arabic text (Paris: Vrin, 2010).

17   Al-Fārābī, *The Political Regime*, §§ 122–126, 90–4.

18   Ibid., § 88, 73.

19   Al-Fārābī, *Selected Aphorisms,* 60–1.

6

Marsilius of Padua on Sovereignty

Vasileios Syros

The legislator, or the primary and proper efficient cause of the law, is the people or the entire body of the citizens, or its "weightier part" (valencior pars)—through their vote or volition, which is expressed in debates taking place in the general assembly of the citizens commanding or determining what must be implemented or omitted with regard to human civil acts, under pain or punishment. The "weightier part" can be defined according to the quality and quantity of the members of the political community over which a law is made. The entire body of the citizens or its weightier part is the legislator regardless of whether it creates the laws directly by itself or assigns the task of making laws to one person or multiple persons, who are not and cannot be the legislator in the absolute sense, but only in a relative sense and for a specific period, in accordance with the authority of the primary legislator.[1]

The foregoing passage from Marsilius of Padua's (1270/90–1342) *Defensor pacis* (*The Defender of Peace*, 1324) conveys the core of one of the most significant contributions to medieval discourse on the question of sovereignty. Unlike other works of medieval political theory, the *Defensor pacis* is not a mirror of princes or a conventional piece of advice literature intended to proffer political advice to the prospective ruler. Its avowed goal is to identify and eliminate the exceptional cause of civil strife (I.i.2–3, 7; I.xix) that infested various societies across Christian Europe, especially Italy (i.e. the Papacy's claim to both temporal and spiritual power). More broadly, though, Marsilius, in *Dictio* I, proposes a model of political organization which, despite the specificities of the different parts of the world, can ensure political and societal stability and tranquility.

The *Defensor pacis* departs from the medieval tradition in two important respects: (a) in medieval political writing kingship is almost universally considered to be the best form of rule and a precondition for an orderly society.[2] Marsilius does not share the emphasis on the primacy of kingship; instead, he advocates a scheme of social and political arrangements that rests upon the body of the citizens as the only true and legitimate source of political authority and can provide the foundation for different types of healthy, or, in Marsilius' lexicon, well-tempered government, such as monarchy, aristocracy, and polity (I.viii.2–4); (b) concomitantly, while the majority of medieval authors are concerned with the persona and qualifications of the ruler as the guarantor of the social order, the focus in the *Defensor pacis* lies on the procedures that can facilitate the evolution of a properly functioning polity, generate a system of laws conducive to the common benefit, and produce a ruler or government composed of multiple persons that seek to promote the public good and act within the law.

As paradoxical as it may sound, Marsilius' justification of the role of the *legislator humanus* (a term defined in the extract above) brings him close to the definition of sovereignty in Jean Bodin's *Les six livres de la République* (*The Six Books of the Commonwealth*, 1576) as the absolute and perpetual power of a commonwealth:[3] both thinkers converge in the notion that sovereign authority is absolute, unconditional, undivided, and inalienable; but they differ on the primary locus of sovereignty, which Bodin envisions as a powerful monarch, while allowing that it might exist in other forms of government (although they are not likely to be equally effective). At the same time, Bodin's theory appears to be less centripetal than is often assumed. For both Bodin and Marsilius are acutely aware of the need for delegation and they carefully distinguish between sovereignty as a theoretical construct and the mechanisms whereby it is manifested and implemented with the aid of various magistrates and officeholders.

Albeit not a conventional commentary on Aristotle, the *Defensor pacis*, especially *Dictio* I, is replete with quotations from and references to various works of the ancient Greek thinker, notably the *Politics*.[4] Marsilius uses Aristotle's political philosophy to corroborate his own arguments, and on several occasions he reworks and modifies Aristotle's ideas to support his own doctrines. One of the most startling differences between Aristotle and Marsilius concerns their respective notions of the legislator: Aristotle is committed to the vision of the lawgiver, such as Solon (Athens) and Lycurgus (Sparta), who, equipped with sagacity and foresight, lays down a constitution (i.e. a set of general rules, for the function of a city). Marsilius, on the other hand, employs the term "legislator" to designate the body of the citizens, which involves a multiplicity of individuals who morph into a unified whole when making laws and appointing the government.[5]

Marsilius' theory about the *legislator humanus* rests on the notion that the best laws are those promulgated for the benefit of the entire community. Marsilius deduces from this that what the entire body of the citizens wishes and aspires to, both intellectually and emotionally, can be evaluated with greater certainty regarding its truth and the degree to which it conforms to the public good. For every whole, or at least every corporeal whole, is greater in size than any part of it considered separately, flaws, defects, and lacunas in the laws are more likely to be noticed by a greater number of people than any of its segments. Moreover, the entire body of the citizens is more able to measure the utility and validity of the laws since no one seeks to deliberately harm himself. Thus, anyone will be in a position to determine whether a law is designed with an eye to the interests of one or few persons and can protest (I.xii.5).

The second argument which Marsilius brings forward to uphold the supreme authority of the *legislator humanus* is related to the enactment of the laws: the entire body of the citizens has the capabilities and resources to assure the implementation of the laws; it possesses the coercive force to restrain and punish malefactors and offenders; and a law is more likely to be observed by the citizens as long as they feel empowered because they have been part of the process of lawmaking and have endorsed the laws. If, on the other hand, one or a group of persons possessed the authority to issue and impose laws on the entire body of the citizens, they would devolve into despots. Their laws, despite their potential merits, would spark a backlash and would be accepted with hesitation or rejected by the rest of the citizens, who would hold grudges, thinking that they had been ignored or excluded (I.xii.6, 8).

One of the central tenets of Marsilius' thinking is that the laws constitute one of the means to attain a materially sufficient life, which is one of the principal objectives of the political community. This line of reasoning is premised on the Aristotelian dictum that all humans, unless impeded, are by nature inclined to form and live in associations so as to procure adequate material resources for themselves (I.iv.2; I.xiii.2). Marsilius also invokes the Stoic principle, mediated by Cicero's *De officiis* (*On Duties*), that human actions are dictated by the tendency to secure what is conducive to human life and safety and to avoid what can be harmful (I.iv.1–3, 5; I.i.4).[6] Humans thus create and opt to live in political communities in order to achieve and enjoy what contributes to material sufficiency and avoid what can cause harm. Therefore, all matters pertaining to the common weal, including the laws, should be the subject of collective deliberation (I.xii.7). In line with the Aristotelian worldview and the assumption that nature never does anything in vain, Marsilius contends that the portion of the citizenry that desires the preservation of the political community must surpass the segment that does not; the opposite would indicate an egregious natural anomaly and the futility of natural desire (I.xiii.2). Marsilius maintains that all or at least the majority of the citizens are of sound mind and reason and are actuated by a right desire for the means, such as the laws, which are associated with the endurance of the political community. Although not every citizen has the skills, expertise, experience, or leisure to undertake the discovery of the laws (I.xii.2), all the citizens have the ability to judge what has been discovered and presented to them for approval and can discern if any amendments are necessary (I.xiii.2).

Marsilius' treatment of the question about whether a small group of individuals, however stellar their credentials and track record might be, should have the prerogative to pass laws for the entire community is colored by his polemic against papal efforts to control both temporal and spiritual affairs and establish what one could call a theocracy. But at a more fundamental level, Marsilius articulates a theory about the sovereignty of the collected citizenry that draws inspiration from Aristotle's conception of collective wisdom, as formulated in Book III of the *Politics*. According to Aristotle, although every person is not an expert, when various individuals come together, each one of them contributes their share of wisdom and knowledge. The knowledge accrued through this process outweighs the judgment of the experts.[7] Marsilius argues, following Aristotle, that many individuals, when engaging in collective deliberation, are able to pronounce a correct judgment about the quality of a work of art, a building, or a ship, without necessarily being able to conceive or produce them (I.xiii.3). Consequently, although some of the less learned are less qualified to appraise a law or some other affair as compared to the experts, their number could rise to such an extent that they could judge equally well or even better than the learned (I.xiii.4).

Marsilius parallels legislation to the development of the sciences and the arts: he affirms that an assessment made by one individual or even all the people of a specific period, however intelligent or knowledgeable they might be, is inadequate and incomplete as compared with the knowledge accumulated over time by multiple generations, who are able to complement and refine what has been discovered earlier (I.xi.3; I.xiii.7). Marsilius therefore deems it expedient for the entire body of the citizens to entrust a number of persons who are prudent and experienced with the preparation of the laws or statutes. As soon as the drafts of the laws have been designed and passed through preliminary scrutiny, they should be presented to the assembly of all the citizens for ratification so that each citizen will have the opportunity to deliberate, recommend changes, and decide whether to approve or reject them (I.xiii.8).

In addition to being in charge of legislation, the *legislator humanus* elects, appoints, monitors, and, if necessary, can correct or remove the ruler/ government (I.xv.3–14; I.xviii.1–7). In contrast with medieval advice literature and Renaissance specimens of that genre, such as Machiavelli's *Prince*, the *Defensor pacis* deemphasizes the importance of the ruler's personal attributes for effective leadership. True, Marsilius does highlight how sound knowledge of the laws, prudence, moral virtue, especially justice, and strong and genuine dedication to the political community are relevant to salutary government (I.xiv.1–7, 9–10; Ixv.1) and the ruler's capacity to serve as the guardian of justice (I.iv.4). But his main concern is to spell out the ways in which the ruler can fulfill his mandate for the sake of the common utility and in accordance with the laws. Utilizing Neoplatonic teachings about the hierarchy of causes, Marsilius proclaims the *legislator humanus* to be the primary or proper efficient cause that grants the ruler, who acts as the secondary (instrumental or executive) cause, the authority to establish and differentiate the other parts of the political community according to the form (i.e. the law), stipulated by the *legislator humanus*. Marsilius is clearly more explicit than Aristotle on the necessity for representation and delegation of authority. At the core of his discussion of the topic lies the conviction that in a well-constituted community the ruler or rulers operate as a reliable and faithful representative/deputy of the entire body of the citizens. As such, all of their decisions and actions should be closely aligned with the consent, priorities, and preferences of the *legislator humanus* (I.xv.4).

To bring the relationship between the *legislator humanus* and the governing part into sharper relief, Marsilius points to the correspondences between the physical body and the body politic: the formation of the political community according to human reason is analogous to the evolution of a living organism in a manner consonant with the laws prevalent in nature. The *legislator humanus* acts as the equivalent of the heart and first creates the government; the government is akin to the heart and is nobler, more perfect, and more complete in its qualities and moral virtues than the other parts of the political community. Subsequently, the *legislator humanus* endows the government with a certain virtue that is universal in causality (i.e. the law), as well as with the authority or power to pronounce and carry out civil judgments in accordance with the laws and the common good. The authority bestowed upon the ruler and his coercive or armed instrumental power resemble the heat of the heart and the spirit, respectively. In order for the ruler to be able to pursue his duties and safeguard the longevity of the political community, his authority and power must be regulated by the laws (I.xv.5–7; I.x.1–2, 4). And just as the heart in a healthy physical organism never stops beating, the function of the ruler in a well-ordered community must never cease (I.xv.12–13).

Marsilius concedes that norms of political behavior, institutional procedures, and modes of deliberation about civil affairs may vary according to the characteristics, specific conditions, and needs of every community (I.xv.2; I.xvii.10). But, overall, he is insistent on the importance of a general template of political organization that posits the *legislator humanus* as the sole legitimate source of political authority. As optimistic, however, as Marsilius appears to be regarding the ability of the multitude to make correct decisions regarding civil affairs, his theory of sovereignty is a far cry from an advocacy of democracy in the modern sense: his definition of the *legislator humanus* does not favor mere majority rule; rather, it involves the criteria of quantity and quality concerning the make-up of the political community.[8] Like Aristotle and most medieval political theorists, Marsilius includes democracy among the degenerate types of regime (I.viii.2–3). A form of government in which the common folk would have the upper hand at the expense of the other parts of the community is incompatible with the Marsilian idea that balance and symmetry are constitutive features of an orderly political entity (I.iii.3). For the disproportionate growth of any segment of society in terms of quantity or quality (as was the case, in Marsilius' eyes, with the clergy in Christian Europe), can lead to convulsions, drastic political changes, or constitutional transformation (I.xv.10).

Marsilius' understanding of civic participation is much more exclusive than modern approaches to citizenship: in his view, a citizen is a person who participates in the government or deliberative or judicial function according to his rank and qualifications. As such, women, children, foreigners, and slaves are not part of the citizenry (I.xii.4). Last but not least, it is noteworthy that Marsilius differentiates the priestly, the military, and the judicial or deliberative parts, which are parts of the political community in the strict sense and comprise the honorable class (*honorabilitas*); from those in charge of the treasury and financial transactions, the craftsmen, and the farmers, who compose the common folk (*vulgus*) and can only be counted as parts of the political community in a broad sense, because they are just necessary (I.v.1). In keeping with this distinction, Marsilius recommends that the discovery of the laws can be performed with greater efficiency by the *prudentes*, i.e., those persons who have a modicum of leisure, are typically older, and have more experience in practical affairs, than by the mechanics, who invest all their time and energy into obtaining the necessities of life (I.xii.2; I.xvii.4).

The *Defensor pacis* provides an important prism through which to look at church–state relations and the role of civil religion. Another crucial facet of Marsilius' political theory that makes it so relevant to today's concerns is the discussion of the relationship between the body of the citizens and a small group of experts. Marsilius considers that the more leeway someone has to make laws, however competent, virtuous, and well-intentioned he might be, the greater the danger is that his judgments will be skewed and influenced by ignorance or perverted emotions. For Marsilius, every person yields at times to corrupt impulses, and, as evidenced by the decretals of the clergy, is likely to behave selfishly, privilege his own benefit over the common good, and act in a tyrannical manner (I.xi.4–7; I.xii.7–8; I.xiii.5; I.xviii.3). Through his attack on the Papacy, Marsilius foresaw one of the greatest challenges facing modern societies: the phenomenon of technocracy and the need to question the belief that ceding sovereignty to experts can be a panacea for political and social troubles.

Notes

1   Marsilius of Padua, *Defensor pacis*, I.xii.3, here and hereafter cited from
     Marsilius of Padua, *The Defensor Pacis*, trans. and intro. Alan Gewirth [=
     Marsilius of Padua, *The Defender of Peace*, vol. 2] (New York: Columbia
     University Press, 1956; repr. 2001). Subsequent references to the *Defensor
     pacis* will be made parenthetically in the text by discourse, chapter, and
     paragraph numbers. I have followed Gewirth's English translation, occasionally
     making minor amendments to render Marsilius' text more intelligible.

2   There are a few exceptions, such as Ptolemy of Lucca's (*ca.* 1240–1327) *De
     regimine principum* (*On the Government of Rulers*). Like Marsilius, Ptolemy
     was exposed to the republican methods of government that prevailed in the
     Italian cities. See, in general, Vasileios Syros, "Marsilius of Padua and Isaac
     Abravanel on Kingship: The Medieval Precedents of Modern Republicanism
     Revisited," *Medieval Encounters* 26, no. 3 (2020): 203–25; Antony Black,
     "Christianity and Republicanism: A Response to Nederman," *American
     Political Science Review* 92, no. 4 (1998): 919–21; idem, "Christianity and
     Republicanism: From St. Cyprian to Rousseau," *American Political Science
     Review* 91, no. 3 (1997): 647–56; Cary J. Nederman, "The Puzzling Case of
     Christianity and Republicanism: A Comment on Black," *American Political
     Science Review* 92, no. 4 (1998): 913–8. Compare Serena Ferente, "Popolo and
     Law: Late Medieval Sovereignty in Marsilius and the Jurists," in *Popular
     Sovereignty in Historical Perspective*, ed. Richard Bourke and Quentin Skinner
     (Cambridge: Cambridge University Press, 2016), 96–114; and Alan Gewirth,
     "Republicanism and Absolutism in the Thought of Marsilius of Padua,"
     Medioevo 5 (1979): 23–48.

3   Jean Bodin, *On Sovereignty: Four Chapters from the Six Books of the
     Commonwealth*, ed. and trans. Julian H. Franklin (Cambridge: Cambridge
     University Press, 1992), 1. On Bodin, see Sara Miglietti's chapter in this
     volume.

4   Consider also Kazutaka Inamura's chapter in this volume. Marsilius was
     working from medieval Latin translations of Aristotle's works rather than the
     Greek original. On the sources of Marsilius' political theory, see Vasileios
     Syros, *Marsilius of Padua at the Intersection of Ancient and Medieval
     Traditions of Political Thought* (Toronto: University of Toronto Press, 2012).

5   Vasileios Syros, "The Principle of the Sovereignty of the Multitude in the
     Works of Marsilius of Padua, Peter of Auvergne, and Some Other Aristotelian
     Commentators," in *The World of Marsilius of Padua*, ed. Gerson Moreno-
     Riaño (Tunhout: Brepols, 2006), 227–48.

6   The influence of Cicero's philosophy on Marsilius is examined in Cary J.
     Nederman, *The Bonds of Humanity: Cicero's Legacies in European Social and
     Political Thought, ca. 1100–ca. 1550* (University Park, PA: Pennsylvania State
     University Press, 2020), 108–22. More generally, see Vasileios Syros, "Founders
     and Kings Versus Orators: Medieval and Early Modern Views on the Origins
     of Social Life," *Viator* 42, no. 1 (2011): 383–408.

7   Consider also Jeremy Waldron, "The Wisdom of the Multitude: Some
     Reflections on Book 3, Chapter 11 of Aristotle's *Politics*," *Political Theory* 23,

no. 4 (1995): 563–84—repr. in *Aristotle's Politics: Critical Essays*, ed. Richard Kraut and Steven Skultety (Lanham, MD: Rowman & Littlefield, 2005), 145–65.

8   For further discussion, see, e.g., Takashi Shogimen, "Consent and Popular Sovereignty in Medieval Political Thought: Marsilius of Padua's *Defensor pacis*," in *Democratic Moments: Reading Democratic Texts*, ed. Xavier Márquez (London: Bloomsbury, 2018), 49–56; Filimon Peonidis "Marsilius of Padua as a Democratic Theorist," *Roda da Fortuna* 5 (2016): 106–24; Mary E. Sullivan, "Democracy and the *Defensor Pacis* Revisited: Marsiglio of Padua's Democratic Arguments," *Viator* 41, no. 2 (2010): 257–69; James H. Burns, "Majorities: An Exploration," *History of Political Thought* 24, no. 1 (2003): 66–85.

7

The King "Should Be" Sovereign

Christine de Pizan and the Problem of Sovereignty in Fifteenth-Century France

Kate Langdon Forhan

The three types of estate ought to be one polity like a living body, according to the words of Plutarch . . . There the prince and princes hold the place of the head in as much as they are or should be sovereign and from them ought to come specific ordinances just as from the mind of a person springs forth the external deeds that the limbs achieve. The knights and nobles take the place of the hands and arms because just as a person's arms have to be strong in order to endure labor, so they have the burden of defending the law of the prince and the polity. They are also comparable to the hands because, just as the hands push aside harmful things, so they ought to push all harmful and useless things aside. The rest of the people are like the belly, the feet, and the legs because just as the belly receives all that the head and limbs prepare for it, so, too, the activity of the prince and nobles must be directed to the common good, as will be

better explained further later. And just as the legs and feet
sustain the human body, so too, the laborers sustain all the
other estates.[1]

* * *

For just as the human body is not whole, but is defective and
deformed when it lacks any of its members, so the body politic
cannot be perfect, whole, and healthy if all the estates . . . are not
properly joined and united together. Consequently, they can help
each other, as each exercises its assigned task, solely for the
conservation of the whole community, just as the members of the
human body help to guide and nourish the whole body. And in so
far as one of them fails in this, the whole body feels it and is
deprived by it.[2]

The attempts by medieval jurists and philosophers to comprehend sovereignty and to elaborate its foundational relationship to law and custom strive either to negotiate the relationship between ecclesiastical and secular power, or secondly, to ground a king's legitimate sovereignty in something other than papal or imperial endorsement, or both. As Francesco Maiolo puts it, ". . . the fact that the medieval jurists did not use the equivalent for the English term *sovereignty* is neither evidence of the absence of sovereignty as phenomenon, nor of the lack of awareness of the important implications of it. The jurists employed the vocabulary which they thought would best fit."[3]

In this chapter, I will argue that that the phrase "would best fit" is one of the most distinctive hallmarks of the political ideas of Christine de Pizan (1364–*ca.* 1430). It is noteworthy that Christine de Pizan never uses the term "sovereignty" in any of her works. To discern a theory of sovereignty in her thought requires an examination of the constituent parts of a ruler's legitimate authority over his realm. Although the king may technically be a sovereign, she believes that it is an attenuated sovereignty, resting on the ruler's recognition of a complex social structure that both supports and constrains him. He is a "good king" like Charles "the Wise"[4] when he recognizes societal interdependence, accepts consultation, and acts prudently to serve the common good.

Christine de Pizan confronted the problem of political authority in a time of war and chaos. That the king was—"or should be"—sovereign, as she urges in the citation above, was a given. Her goal was to provide her readers, whether princes, nobles or others, with tools that could be used to buttress and sustain his political authority and legitimacy when the traditional supports of custom, law, patriarchy, and social class were inadequate. Her many works address practical advice for the recovery of peace and good rule at a time in which all traditional forms of political authority had been delegitimized. Christine de Pizan's contributions to political thought are therefore highly contextual, drawing on her deep and painful experience of political and social turmoil as well as her own consequent experience of personal and financial vulnerability. The contrast could not be greater between the dismal events in France between 1380 and 1430 and the orderly, idealized worlds Christine discovered in the influential works she valued, for example, John of Salisbury's *Policraticus*, Boethius' *Consolatio*, and Aristotle's *Nicomachean Ethics*.

By the late fourteenth and early fifteenth centuries, the legitimacy of the French monarchy was contested by the English claim to the crown of France by Edward III of England and his successors, and shaken due to the weaknesses of the disabled King Charles VI. The consequent conflict over the disputed monarchy was compounded by papal schism (1378–1417), civil war, increasing political and social violence, and successive waves of plague, labor shortages, and economic strain. The fragility of traditional sources of political authority directly undermined the king's legitimacy and thus royal sovereignty.

The citations above, from *The Book of the Body Politic* (1405–1407), illustrate Christine's use of the corporate metaphor both to understand sociopolitical roles and to provide a foundation for a claim to royal sovereignty. The wise king governs as the head of a body, where all members are essential to the well-being of the whole. This interdependence necessitates consultation with other members of the "body" as well as the exercise of prudence by everyone. This becomes a moral exhortation not only to the king, but to all members of the body politic, as indicated by the varied recipients of Christine's works. She explicitly addresses wide-ranging audiences which underlines the importance of their functions to the health of the community as a whole.

This emphasis on the health of the interdependent political body coupled to prudential wisdom is a theme echoed in her *Book of Peace* (1412):

And, thank God, all the estates—along with the people in general, simple though they be—quite rightly recognize, with great loyalty and love, obedience and respect, one single head: the King. O indeed, what power could oppress or trample underfoot such a body, if it is united, with none of its limbs separated? The head that is the king, the shoulders and upper parts that represent the princes and lords, the arms that are the knights, the sides that are the clergy, the loins and belly that are the burghers, the thighs that are the merchants, the legs and feet that are the people. Without doubt, if this body—God protect it!—holds together well, it need fear nothing.[5]

Since consultation is essential to the health of the body, Christine advises that it be exercised even in the most grave of political decisions, such as the decision to go to war, as is exemplified in her *Book of Deeds of Arms and Chivalry* (1410), which is addressed to military leaders, and was dedicated to eighteen-year-old Louis of Guyenne. For Christine, it is not enough for a king to declare war even on the advice of seasoned warriors if that war is based on a passion for revenge, or anger, or even crimes committed against him or his people. Christine emphasizes procedural justice in her discussion: to truly have the conditions of a just war, kingly power and a just *causa* are not sufficient in themselves. A specific process of deliberation and consultation is required as well. A council must be assembled that includes wise advisors and statesmen, including impartial foreign observers along with legal advisors and the king's regular coterie of military men. After frank discussion, if the prince and these advisors decide that his position is righteous, the prince should "summon his adversary" and make his case, as well as ask for restitution for the offenses against him. His adversary should be listened to "without willfulness or spite."[6] If his antagonist refuses to come forward to state his case, or does not agree to restitution, then the ensuing conflict is not vengeance but justice.

As a result, the king's sovereignty over his realm is legitimated and augmented by having followed this procedure, which, in her *Book of Deeds of Arms and Chivalry*, is to be directed to the common good. It resembles an international court of appeal or tribunal in that it includes representatives of numerous affected groups as well as foreign observers, providing both accuser and the accused due process. A war can be considered just only when there is a process of deliberation and the resulting attempts to adjudicate and mediate the dispute have failed. Relying on the principles of consultation directed to the common good, Christine articulates a process by which not only may war be averted but its legitimacy, if it is waged, may be established. Consultation is critical to her practical understanding of sovereignty in the declaration of war as well as being a useful tool for effective solutions to other seemingly intractable international conflicts like the Papal Schism.

The second pillar of legitimate sovereignty is in the exercise of prudence, equally important to a healthy body politic. Across multiple works, which encompass poetry and prose, biography and political works, and her works directed to women, each constituent part of the body is counseled to exercise prudence, understood as foresight, wisdom, discernment, and even mindfulness. "Prudence and wisdom are the mothers and guides of all other virtues,"[7] she notes in her biography of Charles V, *The Book of the Deeds and Good Character of King Charles V the Wise* (1404). In *The Book of the Long Road to Learning* (1402–1403), she writes that "the mother of concord is Wisdom, who gives birth [t]o the virtues, and life to wise men."[8] Likewise, Christine enlists noble women to exercise prudence in the name of the common good in *The Book of Three Virtues* (1405) and in *The Book of the*

City of Ladies (1405), where she employs a definition of prudence that resonated widely in her era:

> ... women are able to judge between good and bad and to learn from the lessons of the past, growing more experienced from the examples they encounter, increasing their ability to conduct today's affairs, and gaining wisdom to deal with the future.[9]

In every aspect of life, prudent conduct on the part of all members of the body politic, regardless of rank or gender, protects the kingdom. *The Lamentation on the Ills of France* (1410)[10] provides an example that is addressed to the leadership of France, both the elderly royal duke, John de Berri, and Queen Isabel of Bavaria. The work implores them to intercede with faction leaders to stop the conflict, and to exercise prudence in the face of Fortune's unpredictability in order to avoid the destruction of the entire kingdom. *The Book of Peace* (1412), *The Book of the Body Politic* (1405–1407), and the *Letter from Othéa* (1400)—Othea is an avatar of Prudence—all emphasize prudence in their advice to Louis of Guyenne (1397–1415), the ill-fated dauphin of France.

The exercise of prudence thus serves both as a means of enhancing the legitimate authority of the king, and also of constraining it, via her insistence on the value of consultation and prudential leadership by all his subjects, regardless of rank. Christine explores prudence explicitly in *The Book of Man's Character*[11] (1405–1406), also known in a later collection as the *Book of Prudence*. This work deserves attention for its direct bearing on the cardinal virtues and their relationship to political authority and good rule.[12] Prudence is the highest form of practical wisdom, she tells us, and is characterized by seven components: understanding, foresight, circumspection, intellectual humility, caution, intelligence, and memory. Manuscript images of prudence during this period are very helpful in conveying the richness of Christine's portrayal: iconographically, Prudence is portrayed as a female figure with three faces, one facing left, the other straight ahead, and the third facing the right.[13] Facing left, Prudence looks towards the past and thus learns from experience and memory. At center, observing the present, she illustrates discernment, intellectual humility, intelligence, and understanding. Facing right, towards the future, she demonstrates foresight and caution. The image of the body reinforces the importance of this understanding of prudence to the body politic: since the eyes are placed in the head, the highest part of the body, the ruler is capable of greater foresight, since he can see both more broadly and farther ahead than any other part of the body politic. Yet prudence is not the goal in and of itself; rather it is the most important and intelligent response to human vulnerability, whether one is a king or a peasant. Just as Fortune's wheel can rise, so too it can fall. The flourishing king today might be a hostage tomorrow, just as a happily married woman can as easily become an impoverished widow overnight. Prudence helps any member of the body politic to learn from the past, to be clear eyed in the present, and to prepare for the future. For rulers, prudence, coupled with respect for interdependence, will buttress a king's authority, moving him from "should be" sovereign to king in fact.

* * *

In summary, during Christine de Pizan's lifetime, every normative claim to sovereignty, whether based on the Church and clergy, custom, patriarchy and social class, or hereditary monarchy, was contested. These traditional sources of a claim to sovereignty were totally inadequate, since they were based on failed institutions and irrelevant customs. The king's mental illness, the schism, the civil war, social violence, and economic pressures had rendered them ineffective. None of these justificatory mechanisms for reclaiming political authority was providing foundational legitimacy for a claim to sovereignty for the rulers of France.

By contrast, Christine strives to ground that foundational political authority on the interdependence of all members of society, projecting an image of a healthy body politic with each member of society both receiving and offering counsel and exercising prudence in their decision making for the good of the whole. The king's personal claim to sovereignty comes then not only from inheritance or by conquest, but also from his willingness to accept counsel and to exercise prudence for the common good.

While Christine's disparate works are discursive and complex, reflecting the wide-ranging audiences for whom she wrote, as well as her own personal insecurity in a chaotic society, her works use every authorial tool that she had at her disposal—mythological themes, philosophical *topoi,* historical *exempla*, epistolary forms, and passionate outbursts—aimed at one overarching insight: royal sovereignty is mediated, incomplete, tangential, and contested. Her model of an idealized interdependent body politic directed to the common good, she believed, could provide guidance for both rulers and ordinary people during chaotic and dysfunctional times. Most important for Christine, sovereignty is defined by its limits rather than its prerogatives. It is curtailed by custom, wise counsel, prudence, other political and social institutions, and especially the concept of the good of the entire people. Across all of her political works, ranging from mirrors for princes and princesses, to her book on chivalry and warfare, and her paean to Joan of Arc, Christine experiments with identifying the practical locus of political authority and legitimacy, and then grounds it in the validation of all parts of the body politic, under the leadership of an ideal king, who values learning and wise counsel and exercises prudence, the quintessential princely virtue.

In effect, Christine has a limited theory of sovereignty. She replaces the inadequate theory of sovereignty she inherited with a functional practice that includes as its cornerstone a vision of interdependence, with an emphasis on broad consultation and prudence in the exercise of political authority, in order to reduce the vulnerability of the whole kingdom.[14]

Notes

1   Christine de Pizan, *The Book of the Body Politic*, trans. Kate Langdon Forhan (Cambridge: Cambridge University Press, 1994), 4. Excerpt modified and italics added by the translator. To facilitate access for the reader, I have used widely available contemporary translations of the works cited whenever possible, although not all of Christine's works have been edited or translated.

2   Ibid., 90. Modified by the translator. Ideas about the functions of the parts of the human body have changed over time. Christine herself ascribed different components of society to different parts of the body, from those of John of Salisbury's *Policraticus* where, for example, the "heart" is the Council or Senate. John of Salisbury, *Policraticus*, ed. and trans. Cary J. Nederman (Cambridge: Cambridge University Press, 1990), 67.

3   Francesco Maiolo, *Medieval Sovereignty: Marsilius of Padua and Bartolus of Saxoferrato* (Delft: Eburon Academic Publishers, 2007), 286. The French equivalent, *souveraineté*, is seen as early as 1283 in Philippe de Beaumanoir, *Coutumes Beauvaisis*, ed. A. Salmon (Paris Picard et fils, 1900), vol. 2, section 1043, 23–4. Electronic text www.koeblergerhard.de/Fontes/BeaumanoirPhilippedeCoutumesdeBeauvaisisBd21900.pdf retrieved March 30, 2020.

4   Charles V (1338–1380) was nicknamed "the Wise" because he was a pragmatic manager who recruited well-educated advisers, built the royal library by commissioning numerous vernacular translations of scientific and political works, replenished the treasury, and reformed the military, among other accomplishments.

5   Christine de Pizan, *The Book of Peace*, ed. Karen Green and Constant Mews (University Park, PA: Pennsylvania State University Press, 2008), 134.

6   Christine de Pizan, *The Book of Deeds of Arms and of Chivalry*, trans. Sumner Willard (University Park, PA: Pennsylvania State University Press, 1999), 18. For a brief account of the later influence of *The Book of Deeds of Arms and of Chivalry* and references to other sources on its reception, see Kate Langdon Forhan, *The Political Theory of Christine de Pizan* (Aldershot: Ashgate 2002), 156–7.

7   Christine de Pizan, *Le Livre des Faits et Bonnes Moeurs du roi Charles V le Sage*, trans. Eric Hicks and Thérèse Moreau (Paris: Stock, 1997), 78. "La prudence jointe à la sagesse est la mère des autres vertus et elle en est le guide, et c'est elle qui l'inspirait en tous ses actes, comme il est apparu au cours de sa noble vie." Translation my own.

8   Christine de Pizan, *The Book of the Path of Long Learning*, trans. Kelly Ramke Lardin (CreateSpace Independent Publishing, 2018), lines 5440–2.

9   Christine de Pizan, *The Book of the City of Ladies and Other Writings*, trans. Ineke Hardy, ed. Sophie Bourgault and Rebecca Kingston (Indianapolis, IN: Hackett Publishing, 2018), 88. Translation modified slightly by the author.

10 Christine de Pizan, "Lamentation on France's Ills," in ibid., 254–5.

11 Christine de Pizan, *Le Livre de Prud'hommie d' l'Homme* (unpublished typescript, courtesy of the late Eric Hicks). Character, integrity, honesty,

rectitude can all be used to translate "prud'hommie." The term changes its meaning quite radically in the seventeenth and eighteenth centuries.

12 In its original iteration, it was presented to Louis of Orleans, younger brother of Charles VI, who was assassinated in 1407 on the orders of his cousin, John the Fearless, Duke of Burgundy. Both men were grandsons of Charles V "the Wise." In its later form, renamed *Book of Prudence*, the dedication to Louis was removed.

13 For an image of prudence, see Claire Richter Sherman, *Imaging Aristotle: Verbal and Visual Representation in Fourteenth-Century France* (Berkeley: University of California Press, 1995), 125.

14 I would like to acknowledge the very helpful feedback from the readers for this volume.

8

Jean Bodin's *République*

Sara Miglietti

*Sovereignty is the absolute and perpetual power of a
commonwealth, which the Latins call* maiestas; *the Greeks* akra
exousia, kurion arche, *and* kurion politeuma; *and the Italians*
segnioria [sic] . . . *while the Hebrews call it* tomech shévet—*that is,
the highest power of command. We must now formulate a definition
of sovereignty because no jurist or political philosopher has defined
it, even though it is the chief point, and the one that needs most to
be explained, in a treatise on the commonwealth . . . If we say that
to have absolute power is not to be subject to any law at all, no
prince of this world will be sovereign, since every earthly prince is
subject to the laws of God and of nature and to various human
laws that are common to all peoples . . . But persons who are
sovereign must not be subject in any way to the commands of
someone else and must be able to give the law to subjects, and to
suppress or repeal disadvantageous laws and replace them by
others—which cannot be done by someone who is subject to the
laws or to persons having power of command over him.*[1]

Jean Bodin's *République* (1576) represents an important milestone in the
history of theories of sovereignty. Of the six books into which the work is
divided, the best known by far is the first, where Bodin defines some key
concepts employed throughout the treatise: first and foremost those of
république, or "commonwealth" ("a just government, with sovereign power,
of several households and of that which they have in common," I.1, vol. 1,

27); and "sovereignty" (*souveraineté*), defined in the excerpt above as the "absolute and perpetual power of a commonwealth" to "give the law to subjects" (I.8, vol. 1, 191). Bodin took great pride in this landmark definition. In his view, the failure of earlier theorists to elucidate this "chief point" of statecraft had not only delayed the advancement of "political science" (Preface, vol. 1, 11), but had also exposed political communities to a twofold danger: on the one hand, the "tyrannical ruses" of "Machiavellian" politicians, who "make impiety and injustice the twin foundations of commonwealths"; on the other, the "licentious anarchy" of those who "push the subjects to rebel against their rightful princes" (Preface, vol. 1, 13–14). To avoid these opposing dangers, a complete reframing of the discourse of statecraft was in order, and defining sovereignty was the necessary first step in this direction.

The urgency of such a task becomes clear when one considers the context in which the *République* was first published. The second half of the sixteenth century was a moment of deep crisis for the kingdom of France, shattered by gruesome civil wars that pitted Catholics against Huguenots for over thirty years (1562–1598). On one level, the *République* can be interpreted as a situated intervention in a specific historical crisis: the response of a learned humanist and experienced civil servant, such as Bodin was, to the "raging storm" that was "tormenting" the "ship of the state" (Preface, vol. 1, 9–10). But the treatise also represented the continuation of theoretical reflections that Bodin had been entertaining for years, certainly as early as 1566, when his first major work—the *Methodus ad facilem historiarum cognitionem* ("Method for the Easy Comprehension of History")—was printed in Paris.[2] In this work, Bodin already tackled many of the issues that he would then develop further in the *République*, including the question of sovereign power. Yet the theory of sovereignty outlined in the *Methodus* differs in many respects from that of the *République*, and a comparison between the two works can illuminate the groundbreaking, if controversial, nature of Bodin's mature positions.

A first difference concerns the question of the prerogatives of sovereign power. In the *République*, as previously mentioned, the most important of these prerogatives is that of making and repealing laws: sovereignty is identified here as a quintessentially legislative power. In the *Methodus*, however, Bodin had expounded a different, and more traditional, view according to which sovereign power consisted in five main functions: first and foremost, "creating magistrates and defining the office of each one"; then, "proclaiming and annulling laws," "declaring war and peace," "receiving final appeal from magistrates," and finally, "the power of life and death" in the last resort (172–3). While law-making does feature in this list, it is secondary to the more important function of appointing officials.

A second important difference relates to the idea of sovereignty as absolute power, which is key to Bodin's definition of sovereignty in the *République*. What Bodin means by "absolute" needs some unpacking, as confusion often arises between "absolute" and "absolutist" in the later, seventeenth-century sense.[3] As Bodin clarifies in the excerpt quoted above, "to have absolute power" does not mean "not to be subject to any law at all," since all earthly rulers are "subject to the laws of God and of nature and to various human laws that are common to all peoples" (I.8, vol. 1, 190). Rather, sovereign power is "unbound from" subjection to what modern jurists call "positive law," as opposed to divine, natural, or common law. Whoever promulgates the law (Bodin reasons) must be above it, for how could one be simultaneously held by the laws and free to "suppress" them and "replace them by others" when necessary?

Now, when one turns to the earlier *Methodus*, one finds a very different view of the relationship between sovereignty and law. In Chapter 6, in the context of a discussion on different types of monarchy, Bodin explains that "of the kings who command lawfully, there are two kinds: those restrained by no law at all; and others who are bound by them" (201). The first type of kings, he notes, was typical of primitive monarchies, when laws had not yet "been made binding" and "the whole state and the rights of citizens depended upon the will of the prince." In modern times, the second type of kings has become more prevalent. Most Christian princes, including the king of France, "bind by law not only officials and private citizens but also themselves," and when being sworn in, they take a solemn oath "to govern the state in accordance with the laws of the country and the public good" (204). Bodin approves of this custom, though he anticipates and acknowledges a possible objection—that it is impossible for a sovereign king to obey his own laws, "for those who decree law ought to be above it, that they may repeal it, take from it, invalidate it, or add to it" (203). This in fact is the position that Bodin himself would come to defend ten years later. Yet in 1566 Bodin quickly dismisses the point: to argue this way, he suggests, is to "use sophistry against the people" and to encourage all sorts of arbitrary behavior on the part of princes (202).

A great hiatus thus separates the *Methodus* from the *République* on the question of sovereign power. In the *Methodus* Bodin still favors a limited sovereignty, tempered not only by the traditional "bridles" of religion, justice, and police, but also by the sovereign's obedience to the law.[4] Respecting the law, Bodin insists, does not detract from the sovereign's power (thus Aristotle "was wrong when he wrote that the kings who were bound by the laws were not kings," 205). Besides, law-making itself is only one of many prerogatives that characterize sovereign power. By the time he wrote the *République*, however, Bodin had not only come to single out law-making as the most distinctive function of sovereign power; he had also shifted away from a limited concept of sovereignty to claim that "either the prince is absolutely sovereign or he is not sovereign at all" (II.5, vol. 2, 73). Thus, although he still stressed in the *République* that sovereigns were bound not only by the laws of God and nature, but also by certain "fundamental" laws aimed at preserving the integrity of the state on matters such as succession and control of the royal domain (I.8, vol. 1, p. 197), he had by then removed many of the constraints which he had previously considered wise to impose on rulers.

To explain such changes, some scholars have drawn attention to the historical context, particularly to the ideological escalation that occurred after thousands of French Huguenots were killed in the St. Bartholomew's Day massacres of August 1572, allegedly under royal orders. From 1573 onwards, a flurry of violently anti-monarchical ("monarchomach") pamphlets appeared in France, proclaiming the people's right to armed resistance against the tyrannical abuses of the royal family. Scholars such as Quentin Skinner have suggested that Bodin's "retreat ... into a far more uncompromising defence of royal absolutism" in the *République* was an alarmed response to this sort of ideological excesses.[5] Textual evidence, however, suggests that Bodin was already revisiting key aspects of his theory of sovereignty (including the prerogatives of sovereign power and whether sovereigns should be bound by the law) as early as 1571—years before the monarchomach wave of the mid-1570s. It seems then that the historical context cannot solely account for Bodin's conceptual shifts (although it may have played an accelerating role in them).[6]

Other commentators have pointed to theoretical reasons for Bodin's change of heart. Already in the *Methodus* Bodin claimed that sovereign power, in order to be truly supreme, cannot be shared among multiple agents. What he did not realize at the time, according to Julian Franklin, was that the notion of "limited supremacy" still accepted in the *Methodus* was inconsistent with this principle of indivisibility, as it implied the existence of "consenting agents" who "must have a share" in sovereign power.[7] When he became aware of this contradiction, Bodin chose to hold on to the principle of indivisibility and concluded that "sovereignty was absolute." Such a solution, Franklin continues, was "seductive but erroneous," as it encouraged "concentration of power in the ruler" as "an essential condition of the state," and thus "helped prepare the way" for dangerous forms of "royal absolutism."[8] Indeed, according to Franklin, Bodin's "celebrated principle that sovereignty is indivisible meant that the high powers of government could not be shared by separate agents or distributed among them, but all had instead to be entirely concentrated in a single individual or group."

This, however, appears to be a misrepresentation of Bodin's principle of indivisibility, interpreted in light of Bodin's rejection of the theory of the mixed constitution—a theory that had its roots in classical authors such as Plato, Aristotle, Polybius,[9] and Cicero, and that found many illustrious supporters in the Renaissance, including Machiavelli and Erasmus. The idea of tempering sovereign power through a system of institutional checks and balances in order to prevent abuse enjoyed great favor in mid-sixteenth-century France, particularly in moderate and (later) monarchomach milieus. Bodin, however, found it "absurd" (*Methodus*, 178), as well as historically unsound: allegedly famous examples of mixed states (such as ancient Rome or the Republic of Venice) were indeed revealed as either pure democracies or pure aristocracies as soon as one considered who held the sovereign prerogatives of appointing magistrates, declaring war, and administering justice in the last resort.

Yet while Bodin unequivocally rejected the idea of a mixed state, he did not reject the idea of power sharing in the daily administration of a country; nor did he ever suggest that all powers must be held by a single person (e.g. the prince) or institution (e.g. the senate) for a country to be stable. For already in the *Methodus*, and then more fully in the *République*, Bodin established an original distinction between the *constitutional form* of a polity (*status* in Latin, *estat* in French) and the way in which that polity is *governed* (*imperandi ratio*, *gouvernement*). On the basis of this distinction, he went on to argue that the best-functioning states are not those in which the sovereign burdens himself with all the duties of public governance (including, for instance, the administration of justice), but those in which such duties are shared with magistrates according to the rules of "harmonic justice" (VI.6, vol. 6, 303–5) and officials enjoy a certain degree of autonomy in the exercise of their functions (IV.6, vol. 4, 170–7; for potential jurisdictional conflict, see VI.6, vol. 6, 261–72).

It is thus incorrect to state that sovereignty's indivisibility meant for Bodin "that the high powers of government could not be shared."[10] Because sovereignty operates on the level of constitutional arrangements, while government has to do with daily administration, Bodin saw no contradiction between the idea of shared government and the principle of indivisible sovereignty. Crucially, his revised definition of sovereignty as a legislative power in the *République* facilitated the task of reconciling the abstract notion of indivisibility with the empirical evidence of power sharing, since it made it easier to justify how functions other than law-making could routinely be discharged by other agents without detracting from the sovereign's majesty. With this in mind, it seems that Bodin's revised theory of sovereignty stemmed in large part from a redefinition of the relationship between sovereignty and law, and particularly from his identification of legislative power as the key prerogative of sovereignty.[11]

Bodin's distinction between *estat* and *gouvernement* also had other important implications. Previous political thinkers had generally accepted that the constitutional form of a state depended partly on *who* exercised the highest power and partly on *how* such power was exercised. For each possible regime (the rule of one, the rule of a few, the rule of many) there existed a "good" and a "bad" form, depending on whether those in power ruled justly or not: thus monarchy could degenerate into tyranny, aristocracy into oligarchy, democracy into anarchy. Bodin departed from this tradition (which had illustrious representatives in Aristotle, Thomas Aquinas, and Erasmus, among others) and argued that there can be only three types of state: "If sovereignty is vested in a single prince, we call the state a monarchy. If all the people share in it, it is a popular state. If only a minority, it is an aristocracy" (II.1, vol. 2, 7–8). The quality of the government does not affect the constitutional form of the regime: a monarchy is always a monarchy whether the king rules virtuously or not.

This is not to say that Bodin is indifferent to how power is exercised. Throughout the *République* he confronts the question of bad rule, decrying the abuses of "tyrants" and reminding all rulers of their responsibility before God. Nevertheless, in another spectacular departure from tradition he denies that unjust rulers can be lawfully resisted (not to mention removed or killed) by their subjects (II.5, vol. 2, 75–8). There is only one case in which resistance is lawful: when the person who is in power is not the legitimate ruler but a usurper (what medieval jurists and theologians called a tyrant *ex defectu tituli*). In this case, Bodin allows and indeed encourages open resistance, on the grounds that the usurper has no legitimate claim to sovereignty and is in fact committing a crime of lèse-majesté against the rightful sovereign (II.5, vol. 2, 69–70). It does not even matter whether the usurper is a good or a bad ruler: he must be removed because he is not entitled to rule. But when one is faced with a legitimate sovereign who abuses his power (i.e. a tyrant *ex parte exercitii*), no amount of atrocities on his part can justify resisting or even disobeying his orders.

Bodin does make allowances for situations in which the sovereign's commands imply an obvious breach of the laws of God and nature. In such cases, Bodin admits that obedience to God must take priority over obedience to the human sovereign (III.4, vol. 3, 96–7). He still does not support open resistance, though: he merely advises that public officials who are ordered to act against God's law had better "leave their position" than obey unjust commands (III.4, vol. 3, 105). But he is also aware that if honest magistrates should quit, the situation would not necessarily improve. It may be that the prince would be so struck by the "constancy and steadfastness" of his officials that he would come to his senses and mend his ways. More likely, though, the prince would find someone less principled to carry out his orders, and would then keep "killing and tyrannizing without opposition" (III.4, vol. 4, 106). If at all possible then, honest magistrates should hold on to their role and work as best as they can to mitigate the injustices carried out under the sovereign's orders.

Is there no hope then for unjustly oppressed subjects? One option that Bodin does not rule out is foreign intervention. While subjects are never justified in taking up arms against their rightful sovereign, foreign princes can choose to use military force to remove a legitimate but abusive sovereign from power and thus "defend the possessions, the honour and the life of those who are unjustly afflicted, when the doors of justice are shut" (II.5, vol. 2, 72). It is also important to note that Bodin concludes the *République* with a long chapter on justice, in which he calls on princes to model themselves after the example of God's majestic rule over the earth (VI.6). Nowhere do Bodin's deep humanism and piety come to the fore more clearly than in this chapter. For him, as for other Christian humanists, God's justice is not just a speculative notion but an experiential truth revealed throughout history, and the certainty that God will intervene to remove and punish abusive rulers strengthens his conviction that subjects should not take it upon themselves to resist injustice by force.[12]

Bodin's rejection of resistance theory does not stem from indifference to the suffering of the downtrodden, nor from a naively optimistic assessment of human nature suggesting that sovereigns entrusted with absolute powers will not abuse them. Precisely because his view of human nature is so pessimistic, in fact, he cannot see how allowing the subjects to rebel would represent a solution to their troubles. To do so would only risk precipitating the country into a state of anarchy, which is "worse than the harshest tyranny in all the world" (Preface, vol. 1, 14). Bodin's anthropological pessimism, however, must not be confused with that of later "absolutist" thinkers such as Thomas Hobbes, for his belief in transcendent standards of justice that will ultimately be enforced by a sovereign God sets him apart from the author of *Leviathan*. For Bodin, it is still possible to explain the existence of evil in the world as the result of a divine plan to "mix good and bad" in perfectly calculated proportions. For Hobbes, good and bad are themselves human-made concepts, non-existent in the pre-moral state of nature and constructed (just like positive law) to enable a modus vivendi between self-interested individuals.[13] The ultimate bridles to sovereign power—justice and religion—were thus removed not with Bodin, but with a later generation of thinkers who made the final move from "absolute" sovereignty to outright "absolutism."[14]

Notes

1   References to the *République* are to Jean Bodin, *Les Six Livres de la République*, six vols (Paris: Fayard, 1986); this excerpt is found in vol. 1, 179 and 190–1 (Book I, Chapter 8). Translations are mine, but whenever possible I have consulted the following two (abridged) editions: *On Sovereignty: Four Chapters from the Six Books of the Commonwealth*, ed. and trans. Julian Franklin (Cambridge: Cambridge University Press, 1992), which I follow in this instance; and *Six Books of the Commonwealth*, ed. and trans. M. J. Tooley (Oxford: Blackwell, 1955).

2   References to the *Methodus* are to: Jean Bodin, *Method for the Easy Comprehension of History*, trans. Beatrice Reynolds (New York, NY: Columbia University Press, 1945).

3   See Mario Turchetti, "Introduction," in Jean Bodin, *Les Six Livres de la République/De republica libri sex. Livre premier/Liber I* (Paris: Garnier, 2013), 63–82.

4   On these "bridles," see Quentin Skinner, *The Foundations of Modern Political Thought*, 2 vols (Cambridge: Cambridge University Press), vol. 2, 293.

5   Skinner, *Foundations*, vol. 2, 297–8.

6 See Sara Miglietti, "Meaning in a Changing Context: Towards an Interdisciplinary Approach to Authorial Revision," *History of European Ideas* 40, no. 4 (2014): 474–94.

7 Julian H. Franklin, "Introduction," in Bodin, *On Sovereignty*, xxiii.

8 Ibid., xiii.

9 For discussions of Aristotle's and Polybius' views on sovereignty, see the relevant chapters in the present volume.

10 Franklin, "Introduction," xiii.

11 For a similar interpretation see Diego Quaglioni, *I limiti della sovranità. Il pensiero di Jean Bodin nella cultura politica e giuridica dell'età moderna* (Padua: CEDAM, 1992), 37.

12 See for instance his discussion of biblical tyrants in *République*, II.5, vol. 2, 76–9.

13 See Hobbes' famous description of the state of nature in *Leviathan*, Part 1, Chapter 13.

14 For a similar conclusion see Skinner, *Foundations*, vol. 2, 293.

9

Hugo Grotius

Absolutism, Contractualism, Resistance

Marco Barducci

When we speak of sovereignty . . . we take it to mean that supreme right to govern the State which recognizes no superior authority among humans, such that no person(s) may, through any right of his (their) own, rescind what had been enacted thereby.[1]

The Civil Power is that which governs the State. The State is a compleat Body of free Persons, associated together to enjoy peaceably their Rights, and for their common Benefit.[2]

The Dutch polymath Hugo Grotius (1583–1645) was an eclectic and cosmopolitan thinker committed to pacifying the political and religious conflicts which had torn apart Christianity in his epoch. With this purpose, Grotius confronted the issues of natural and international law, state–church relations, the fundamentals of Christian theology and ecclesiology, and the origins of civil society and the state. And yet, notwithstanding his "lifelong struggle for peace in Church and State,"[3] Grotius was a controversial author. He was considered either the "heir of Erasmus," a supporter of the Dutch Republic and the Remonstrant-Arminian party within the states of Holland, or a lawyer on the payroll of the United East India Company. Such a combination of scholarship, irenicism and partisanship is reflected in the inherently controversial nature of Grotius' notion of sovereignty. This chapter will provide an overview of how Grotius' analysis of sovereignty evolved over time as a response to the different political and historical circumstances which he confronted in the course of his troubled life. Grotius engaged with Jean Bodin's theory of state sovereignty in the unpublished manuscript *Commentarius in Theses XI (ca.* 1602–8), and developed a form of contractarian absolutism based on a neo-Stoic doctrine of natural law in *De Jure Belli ac Pacis* (1625). However, the underpinning assumption of this chapter is that behind their discrepancies in certain respects, Grotius' views of sovereignty shared both a general aversion to popular government and correlated resistance theories, and a preference for absolutism either in its princely or aristocratic form.

These views are exemplified by the two selected extracts at the beginning of this chapter. In the *Commentarius*, which is an account of sovereignty and a legitimization of the Dutch Revolt against the rule of the Habsburg King Philip II of Spain, Grotius tackled the constitutional problem of *where* sovereignty resided within the state and, consequently, of who within it was entitled to wage a just war and legitimately claim full sovereign rights in consequence of victory. Grotius affirmed that the right to wage war belonged to those who held "marks of sovereignty," which may comprise "the supreme right to introduce legislation and to withdraw it, the right to pass judgment and to grant pardon, the right to appoint magistrates and to relieve them of their office, the right to impose taxes on the people, etc."[4] As also demonstrated by the scrutiny of his notes in the manuscript of *Commentarius*, Grotius' analysis is here mainly developed around Bodin's treatment of the attributes of sovereignty in Book I, Chapter 10 of *Six Livres de la République* (1576), but it differs from the French jurist in some significant respects. As Peter Borschberg has noticed, Grotius firstly omits Bodin's second mark of sovereignty, i.e. the power "to declare war and conclude peace," and secondly, he adds a proviso to the ninth mark entitling the prince to raise taxes without the consent of the people or representative institutions, one which may impede or block such collection.[5] These differences were introduced with the purpose of including among the just causes of war the infringement by King Philip II's plenipotentiary, the Duke of Alba, of an immemorial right of the states of Holland to collect taxes in their territories dating to the *Groote-Privilegie* of 1477.[6]

According to Borschberg, Grotius' engagement with Bodin was preeminently critical: not only did the Dutchman point out the shortcomings of the latter's notion of the indivisibility of sovereignty, but he also used the French jurist's own admission that in certain circumstances the exercise of sovereignty was constitutionally divided between the princes and the estates to justify the Dutch Revolt with arguments borrowed from a leading exponent of royal absolutism.[7] There is certainly some truth in this interpretation, especially as it emphasizes the extent to which Grotius departs from the French jurist in an attempt to demonstrate with both theoretical and historical arguments that sovereignty eventually remains indivisible even though its marks are vested in different institutional bodies (i.e. the prince and the "Senate"). However, Grotius' early manuscript work is neither a celebration of Dutch republican liberties against Spanish tyranny, nor a justification of rebellion inspired by monarchomach resistance theories. What Grotius started to elaborate in *Commentarius*, and further developed in other works such as *De Jure Belli ac Pacis*, was an original though controversial attempt to promote state stability by rejecting private war and reconceptualizing rebellion as a just public war, i.e. a war publicly declared and waged between two (*de facto* or *de jure*) sovereign authorities. With this purpose, Grotius was actually moving *within* a Bodinian framework, specifically by re-adapting his analysis of the marks or attributes of sovereignty to the constitutional organization of the states. In his Thesis 4, Grotius explains that while sovereignty belongs to the whole of the state, and in this respect remains indivisible, constitutional agreements may determine a distribution of sovereign attributes among "a minority" comprising, for instance, the senate and the prince, thus implying an aristocratic government. "The meaning of our thesis—says Grotius— accords well with the views of more reasonable writers. For these themselves will admit that some kingdoms come close to being aristocracies."[8] Bodin, but also Francisco Vitoria in *De potestate civili* (1528)—a work recurrently quoted in *Commentarius*—explained that although there were some states like the Republic of Rome under Augustus, the "Emperor in Germany, the Doge in Venice, and in ancient time the Archon in Athens," in which princes were superior in dignity and authority, the form of state was not monarchical, in that "a principality is nothing but an aristocracy or a democracy which has a single person as president or premier of the republic."[9] Grotius therefore modified Bodin's notion of the marks of sovereignty to align it to the aristocratic government of the states, in which some of the marks of sovereignty pertained to King Philip II while the others were vested in the "people or senate." Consistent with the principle that "whoever undertakes a just war in defence of a mark of sovereignty which lies within his competence also acquires its other marks," Grotius then justifies the acquisition of full sovereignty by the states in consequence of a victorious war waged in defense of their sovereign prerogatives.[10]

Grotius' analysis of the Dutch Revolt as a just public war and the critiques to monarchomach theories devised in *Commentarius* were almost identically reiterated in *De Jure Belli ac Pacis*. Dedicated to the French King Luis XIII, *De Jure Belli ac Pacis* was principally a legal treatise, in which the issue of sovereignty was dealt with in the context of an analysis of the principles regulating the causes (*jus ad bellum*) and conduct (*jus in bello*) of war. In particular, Grotius' analysis of sovereignty was developed in conjunction with a definition of just war as "solemn," "defensive," and waged "by the authority of the sovereign" otherwise called "civil power." To examine in what "supreme" or sovereign power consisted, Grotius utilized the analogy of sight, tracing a significant distinction between the "common" and the "proper" subject of sovereignty: "As the Body is the common subject of Sight, the eye the proper; so the common subject of the Supreme Power is the State." Sovereignty was therefore exercised by "one or more Persons, according to the laws and customs of each nation," but it eventually resided in the state (*DJBP*, I, 259). Grotius defined the state as a "compleat Body of free Persons, associated together to enjoy peaceably their Rights, and for their common Benefit" (*DJBP*, I, 162). The state originated from men's natural "Desire of Society, that is, a certain Inclination to live with those of his own Kind, not in any Manner whatever, but peaceably, and in a Community regulated according to the best of his Understanding; which Disposition the Stoicks termed Οἰκείωσιν" (*DJBP*, "The Preliminary Discourse," 81). "Oikeiosis" or "sociability" was a characteristic of human nature, from which derived a set of natural rights that comprised: self-preservation, "the Abstaining from that which is another's, and the Restitution of what we have of another's, or of the Profit we have made by it, the Obligation of fulfilling Promises, the Reparation of a Damage done through our own Default, and the Merit of Punishment among Men" (*DJBP*, "The Preliminary Discourse," 86).

Grotius firmly rejected the opinion of those "who will have the Supreme Power to be always, and without Exception in the People." By contrast, "[i]t is lawful for any Man to engage himself as a Slave to whom he pleases; as appears both by the *Hebrew* and *Roman* Laws. Why should it not therefore be as lawful for a People that are at their own Disposal, to deliver up themselves to any one or more Persons, and transfer the Right of governing them upon him or them, without reserving any Share of that Right to themselves?" (*DJBP*, I, 261).[11] On the other hand, Grotius' aversion to the theory that people may "restrain or punish their Kings, as often as they abuse their Power" did not prevent him from presenting a list of circumstances in which resistance was allowed (*DJBP*, I, 339; II, 672). In the *Commentarius*, Grotius had already justified armed rebellion against the Habsburgs while defusing the radical implications of popular sovereignty in the case of the newborn Republic. Grotius' attempt to accommodate absolute sovereignty with resistance theory reached its mature elaboration in *De Jure Belli ac Pacis*, in which he pointed out that "if that promiscuous Right of Resistance should be allowed, there would be no longer a State, but a Multitude without Union, such as the Cyclops were." This notwithstanding, he reluctantly admitted that not only inferior magistrates but also private individuals may disobey to "the civil Powers" if they "command any Thing contrary to the Law of Nature," or actively resist them in "cases of extreme necessity" (*DJBP*, I, 337). Since the Middle Ages and throughout the early modern period, writers on resistance usually distinguished between tyrants "by practice," who could be resisted only by inferior magistrates as the people's representatives, and tyrants "by usurpation," who on specific circumstances, such as that of a foreign invader, could be resisted also by private individuals. In these passages Grotius appears in patent contradiction with himself, but as he comes to list seven cases in which resistance was justifiable, he emphatically stresses that these do not transgress the principle previously demonstrated, i.e. "that those who are invested with the sovereign Power, cannot lawfully be resisted" (*DJBP*, II, 372). These cases comprised the circumstances traditionally covered by Catholic and Protestant resistance theories, but they did so without drawing on the natural right of resistance rooted in popular sovereignty. These circumstances included the justification of resistance by the "senate or people" in defense of "a mark of sovereignty," which he had used in his early writings to account for the Dutch Revolt:

> If a King should have but one Part of the sovereign Power, and the Senate or People the other, if such a King shall invade that Part which is not his own, he may justly be resisted, because he is not Sovereign in that Respect. Which I believe may take Place, though in the Division of the Sovereignty, the Power of making War fell to the King, for that is to be understood of a foreign War: Since whoever has a Share of the Sovereignty must have at the same Time a Right to defend it. And when the Case is so, the King may, by the Right of War, lose even his Part of the Sovereignty. (*DJBP*, II, 376)

Furthermore, the seventh case examined by Grotius according to which "if in the conferring of the Crown, it be expressly stipulated, *that in some certain Cases* the King may be resisted; even though that Clause does not imply any Division of the Sovereignty" implicitly referred to the clause of disobedience contained in the Joyous Entry of Brabant of 1356, which provided for a constitutional justification of resistance to Philip II in the early phases of the Dutch Revolt.[12]

So, was Grotius a theorist of absolutism who insisted on political obligation as a means to secure peace in state and church, or was he a supporter of people's sovereignty and, accordingly, of its right to either replace or overthrow tyrannical rulers? And what about the supposed modernity and novelty of Grotius' treatment of sovereignty? Notwithstanding the prevalence of a fundamentally absolutist view of civil (and ecclesiastical) polities, both dimensions actually coexisted in *De Jure Belli ac Pacis*. This is certainly one of the most controversial aspects of Grotius' thought, one that not surprisingly has generated contrasting receptions by modern scholars: Quentin Skinner affirmed that *De Jure Belli ac Pacis* contains both elements of radicalism and of modern-state absolutism, while Richard Tuck similarly observed that the work of 1625 "speak[s] the language of both absolutism and liberty."[13] Knud Haaknonssen rightly argued that this aspect is well exemplified by Grotius' use of the analogy of vision on the basis of which "the ruler is the special agent for the sovereignty of which the state as a whole is the common agent. In other words, sovereignty is not a power that rulers have over subjects, but one that they exercise on behalf of the

corporate body."[14] Furthermore, the inconsistency between a strong claim
for political obligation and the justification of people's right of resistance is
only apparent, in that since his early work on the Dutch Revolt, Grotius had
attempted to reconceptualize the latter within the casuistry either of just war
theory or of constitutionalism as regulated by positive rather than natural
law.

Grotius' alleged oscillation between absolutism and democratic
constitutionalism should be traced to the interplay of absolutist and legalistic
discourses underpinning the paradigm of absolute sovereignty at least from
the twelfth and thirteenth-century Italian and French glossators to neo-
Scholasticism, a legal tradition to which his jurisprudence largely belonged.[15]
According to the Roman legal tradition of sovereignty, which was transmitted
to modern absolutism by the work of medieval commentators like Alessandro
di Hales, Bartolo da Sassoferrato and Baldo degli Ubaldi, princes were
independent from the obligation of positive law, but at the same time they
were bound by a moral duty to abide by a set of principles springing from
nature and God, which eventually restrained their power. So, if obedience
was due *de jure divino, et humano* to the sovereign, the violation of such
principles turned the lawful magistrate into a tyrant, thus justifying resistance
against him.[16]

The dual nature of absolutism inherited from Roman law and medieval
jurisprudence continued to characterize the doctrine of absolutism in the
sixteenth and seventeenth centuries.[17] Early modern absolutist theories can
be generally divided into those that proposed that all rulers received
sovereign power directly from God, so that subjects ought to obey or at least
not to resist their commands unless these breached divine or natural law,
and those for which rulers were transferred their power from the people.
According to Bodin, while princes were not bound by civil law they were
nonetheless subject to divine and natural laws as well as to constitutional
laws (like the "salic law"). Bodin then justified (non armed) resistance
against usurpers (*ex defectu tituli*), but not against tyrants in practice (*ex
parte exercitii*) if "the prince is an absolute sovereign."[18] Johann Sommerville
has explained that the latter, minor tradition of "contractarian" absolutism
postulated either that "the community's transference of power to a ruler had
been unconditional, or that the king's power had arisen by conquest (which
was morally equivalent to an absolute transference)."[19] The idea that the
people had originally been sovereign but that they had transferred their
power to kings by a grant, had already been largely discussed in Spain by
neo-Scholastic authors and in France both by Huguenot authors, who made
a radical use of popular sovereignty in defense of armed resistance to the
king, and successively by Catholics such as Baricave and Cardin Le Bret,
who readapted it to their monarchical and absolutist agendas.[20] It was this
tradition that Grotius sought to accommodate in *De Jure Belli ac Pacis*.

A second reason which may explain the conflict within Grotius' thought
on sovereignty may be ascribed to another unresolved tension which runs

through all his works, such as that between his adoption of a typically humanistic approach to historical *exempla*, and his relying on "the rule and dictate of right reason" to eventually ban armed conflict from intrastate relations. If the first of these actually justifies all atrocities and injustices connected with rebellion and war, the appeal "to a reasonable Nature" is necessary to commend obedience to the state in order to avoid its disaggregation. The emphasis put on state sovereignty did not diminish from the critical engagement with Bodin in *Commentarius* and in *De Jure Belli ac Pacis*, in which he sought to further legitimize sovereign power in an age of religious conflict by rooting it in people's consent rather in God. And although, after 1625, he did not make other attempts to further develop his doctrine of sovereignty, in his late irenic works *Votum pro Pace Ecclesiastica* and *Via ad Pacem Ecclesiasticam*, both published in 1642, Grotius continued to insist on the Christian duty to fully obey the sovereign magistrate for peace's sake.[21]

Notes

I would like to thank Knud Haakonssen for his comments on a draft of this present chapter.

1   Peter Borschberg, *Hugo Grotius "Commentarius in Theses XI"* (Bern: Pieterlen, 1994), 53–6, 215.

2   Hugo Grotius, *The Rights of War and Peace*, ed. Richard Tuck (Indianapolis, IN: Liberty Fund, 2005), I, 162 (from now on *DJBP*). Page references to this edition will be given in parentheses throughout the text of this essay.

3   See H. J. M. Nellen, *Hugo Grotius: A Lifelong Struggle for Peace in Church and State, 1583–1645* (Leiden-Boston: Brill, 2014).

4   Borschberg, *Hugo Grotius "Commentarius in Theses XI,"* 225.

5   Ibid., 54–5, 120.

6   Ibid., Theses 9–11.

7   Cf. Borschberg in ibid., 125–7.

8   Ibid., 291

9   Jean Bodin, *Six Books of the Commonwealth*, trans. M. J. Tooley (Oxford: Blackwell, 1955), 56; *Francisco de Vitoria: Political Writings*, ed. Anthony Pagden and Jeremy Lawrence (Cambridge: Cambridge University Press, 1991), 118.

10 Ibid., 231–2.

11 The material concerning Grotius' analysis of sovereignty and my subsequent analysis of his resistance theory are drawn from my book *Hugo Grotius and the Century of Revolution 1613–1718: Transnational Reception in English Political Thought* (Oxford: Oxford University Press, 2017), 28–9 and 48–50 respectively.

12 Martin van Gelderen, "A Political Theory of the Dutch Revolt and the
    Vindiciae contra tyrannos," *Il Pensiero Politico* 19 (1986): 163–81.

13 Quentin Skinner, *The Foundations of Modern Political Thought*, 2 vols
    (Cambridge: Cambridge University Press, 1978), II, 346–7; Richard Tuck,
    Natural Rights Theories: Their Origin and Development (Cambridge:
    Cambridge University Press, 1979), 79.

14 Knud Haaknossen, "Hugo Grotius and the History of Political Thought,"
    Political Theory 13 (1985), 244.

15 Ennio Cortese, "Sovranità (storia)," in *Enciclopedia del Diritto* (Milano:
    Giuffré, 1990), XLIII, 214.

16 Diego Quaglioni, *La sovranità* (Bari-Roma: Laterza, 2004), 26–32.

17 Pierangelo Schiera, "Assolutismo," in *Dizionario di Politica*, ed. Norberto
    Bobbio, Nicola Matteucci, and Gianfranco Pasquino (Torino: Utet, 1983),
    56–62.

18 Bodin, *Six Books of the Commonwealth*, II, chapters 4–5.

19 Johann P. Sommerville, "Absolutism and Revolution in the Seventeenth
    Century," in *The Cambridge History of Political Thought 1450–1700*, ed.
    J. H. Burns and Mark Goldie (Cambridge: Cambridge University Press, 1991),
    355–6.

20 Sommerville, "Absolutism and Revolution," 361–3.

21 Hugo Grotius, *Opera Omnia Theologica* (Basileæ: 1732), III, 622.

10

Shakespeare on Sovereignty, Indivisibility, and Popular Consent

Stella Achilleos

> REGAN [. . .] How in one house
> Should many people, under two commands,
> Hold amity? 'Tis hard, almost impossible.[1]
>
> SICINIUS What is the city but the people?
> ALL PLEBEIANS True, the people are the city.[2]

Unlike most of the authors covered here—including some of his well-known contemporaries, like Bodin and Hobbes—Shakespeare's prolific career as an author did not include the writing of a comprehensive theory of sovereignty. However, his works have found a prominent place in numerous seminal discussions of sovereignty as they demonstrate a sustained and profound engagement with the concept. Indeed, Shakespeare's works provide reflections on sovereignty at a time of and in response to a complex and often troubled set of historical transitions and transformations: from the Wars of the Roses to Henry VIII's split from the Roman Catholic Church and from Reformation and Counter-Reformation struggles to the political uncertainty over the issue of succession in the final years of Elizabeth I and the troubles that marked James I's first few years on the English throne. Pointing to the intersections between literature and political theory, Shakespeare's plays significantly registered the historical and conceptual crises that marked the development of the concept of sovereignty during this period, thereby focusing his audiences' attention to it as a critical issue, both in historical perspective and in his own time.

Written in the years after the accession of James I in 1603, the two plays from which my opening extracts are drawn, *King Lear* (1605–6) and *Coriolanus* (*ca.* 1608), may be said to provide some of the dramatist's most profound and theoretically engaging reflections on sovereignty. The lines in my first quotation are spoken by Lear's daughter, Regan, after the aged king's abdication from the throne and his decision to divide the kingdom as dowry to his daughters. Ironically, despite Lear's pronouncement that by dividing the kingdom, "[. . .] future strife / May be prevented now" (1.1.43–4), his action has a catastrophic set of consequences that throw the country into chaos. Scholars have commented on Lear's lack of wisdom and his failure to follow some of the principles of good rulership described in early modern advice-to-princes manuals. These are evident in his inability to see how the love contest in Act 1 Scene 1 invites his daughters' flattery, and his failure to take advice from such loyal followers as Kent. As Brian Sheerin also notes, *King Lear* may be read within the context of various discussions in the late Middle Ages and the early modern period, such as John Fortescue's *Governance of England* (1407), which referred to the extravagant distribution of royal property in the form of gifts as a sign of bad governance. In Sheerin's words, this led to "a peculiar kind of kingly self-cancellation."[3]

Perhaps more importantly, Lear's distribution of his kingdom as dowry to his daughters involves an important question concerning the legality of land distribution by kings. As R. A. Foakes observes, this question had been raised during the Elizabethan period when the Queen inquired about the possibility of disposing property. Her counselors' advice on this was that "any property [. . .] had to be regarded as part of the royal estate and not as owned by the monarch as an individual."[4] Indeed, for a number of Shakespeare's contemporaries, the distribution of royal property constituted an illegal violation of the "body politic," that always remained superior to the king's "body natural," despite the inseparable fusion of the two in the schema analyzed by Ernst Kantorowicz as "the king's two bodies."[5] In this respect, *King Lear* takes part in a much larger debate on the limits of sovereign power and the extent to which it should be limited by law; a debate that would give shape to much of the proto-republican discourse of the early modern period.

Yet, the havoc that ensues from Lear's action is not so much an outcome of the fact that he gives his lands away, but of the fact that he *divides* the kingdom.[6] This involves a multiple fracturing of sovereignty that pertains not only to the division of power between Lear's daughters and of a previously unified country into distinct territorial jurisdictions, but also to Lear's idea that while "divest[ing]" himself "of rule, / Interest of territory, cares of state" (1.1.49–50), he should preserve some of the most important prerogatives of sovereignty. This includes not only the name and the ceremonies—"th'addition" (1.1.137)—of kingship, but also one of the most important marks of sovereignty: namely, the right to retain an armed force in the form of his one hundred knights. Goneril and Regan both find this most destabilizing for their own, newly established power and authority, and the issue comes at the centre of their heated discussion with their father in Act 2 Scene 2, where they ask him to reduce and ultimately disband his group of knights. It is within the context of this discussion that Regan, who now "sp[ies] a danger" (2.2.439), raises the question in my opening extract, about the impossibility of divided sovereignty being effective or possible. The broader political implications of her reference to "one house [. . .] under two commands" are hard to miss given the family's royal status but also the conventional analogy between the household and the state.

The untenability of divided sovereignty is further suggested in the play by Goneril and Regan's failure to keep peace with each other. The ensuing chaos involves a complete collapse of power and authority that is reminiscent of the condition Hobbes would later call the "state of nature." *King Lear* may therefore be said to highlight the significance of what Bodin had referred to as the indivisibility of sovereign power a couple of decades earlier, in *Les Six Livres de la République* (1576). Bodin's book appears to have been one of the works of political theory that enjoyed popularity among educated readers in England,[7] and in 1606 it appeared in an English translation by Richard Knolles that enabled its further dissemination to English audiences. It may be impossible to know if Shakespeare had any direct familiarity with the *République*, but he certainly appears to have been conversant with the ideas found therein.

While Bodin's theory of sovereignty's indivisibility was shaped within the context of the ravaging wars of religion between Catholics and Huguenots in France, Shakespeare's treatment of this question in *King Lear* came in the aftermath of his long preoccupation with the medieval civil wars he had previously dramatized in his English history plays. But *King Lear* also touches on a more immediate set of issues that marked the early rule of James I, in front of whom the play was probably staged in December 1606. Earlier in that year, following the Gunpowder Plot of 1605, English Catholics were required to take the controversial Oath of Allegiance that stipulated their obedience to James and their allegiance to him over the Pope.[8] The oath, that clearly aimed to assert James' undivided sovereignty, also denounced the idea that the Pope had any authority to depose the king. With this, it addressed a broader issue that was central in the monarchomach theory of the period (i.e. the issue of violent resistance to the temporal sovereign). James' own take on this question in *The Trew Law of Free Monarchies* (1598) may be said to have been written in response to such well-known tracts as the *Vindiciae, contra tyrannos* (of uncertain authorship, 1579) and George Buchanan's (James' former tutor) *De jure regni apud Scotos* (1579), both of which advocated the right to resist rulers. On the contrary, James, who championed the divine right of kingship, upheld what Shakespeare's Richard proclaims in *Richard II*, that "The breath of worldly men cannot depose / The deputy elected by the Lord" (3.2.56–7). For James, resistance to kingly authority was unacceptable even in the case of a wicked king.[9]

At the same time, *King Lear* may be read within the context of James' ultimately unsuccessful attempt to officially unify the kingdoms of England and Scotland, both of which he came to rule (along with Ireland) following his ascendance to the English throne in 1603.[10] By staging the division of the kingdom, the play, as Andrew Hadfield points out, "both reflects and inverts the contemporary political situation of James."[11] James thought it fit he should warn his eldest son Henry about the dangers of dividing a unified kingdom. So, his advice to Henry in *Basilicon Doron* (first published in 1599 and reprinted in 1603) is that, if he gets a unified Britain, he should hand it over in its entirety to his eldest son and endow the rest of his children with private property only: "Otherwayes by deuiding your kingdomes, yee shall leaue the seed of diuision and discord among your posteritie."[12] Evidently, James ardently supported the Bodinian notion of sovereignty both as an absolute and an indivisible power.

In this respect, *King Lear* seems to provide a nod of approval to James' ideas on sovereignty's indivisibility. However, the play does not otherwise offer an endorsement of his absolutist politics. Indeed, while the play dramatizes the horrors that may ensue upon the division of sovereignty, it also calls into question the absolute type of sovereignty that transcends law: it is precisely Lear's attachment to this position, his blindness or indifference to the possible illegality of his division of the kingdom, and his refusal or inability to pay heed to honest advice, that produce the subsequent chaos. Lear's obstinate rejection of Kent's advice has duly been read alongside James' definition of the role of the king as the father of his people, an analogy that reduced subjects to an infantilized position and precluded their political participation or intervention.[13]

Likewise, attention has been drawn to James' conception of the role of Parliament as a body that should only be summoned at the king's will, function at his sufferance, and could only provide advice that the king had the freedom to take or discard. In *The Trew Law*, James also highlighted that the prerogative to make laws belonged to the king, who was God's "lieutenant" (65), and not to his subjects. Further, as he claimed, being "aboue the law," the king himself "is not bound thereto but of his good will" (75). Unsurprisingly, James came to have a troubled relationship with the House of Commons: his very first English Parliament in 1604 was marked by the so-called Buckinghamshire election dispute that urgently raised the issue of who should be the judge in cases of disputed elections and the more portentous question of whether authority ultimately rested with parliament or the king. In Andrew Hadfield's words, "the resulting conflict became the first of many serious constitutional conflicts between parliament and crown in the next half-century."[14]

King Lear's emphasis on the significance of political counsel thus implies an indirect critique of James' absolutist politics. This is in line with various other Shakespearean plays that offer critical portrayals of monarchs, but also draw attention to the instability of sovereignty when it is not based on the consent of the people. Shakespeare often has kings themselves acknowledge the significance of this element. An example may be found in *Richard II*, where Bolingbroke's popularity—"[. . .] his courtship to the common people, / How he did seem to dive into their hearts / With humble and familiar courtesy" (1.4.24–6)—is revealed as one of the motives behind his banishment by Richard. When he deposes Richard, Bolingbroke himself reveals his anxiety to secure the consent of the people by claiming the legitimacy of this action. Thus, in the famous deposition scene, Bolingbroke makes sure to note that Richard "had been willing to resign" (4.1.190), while Richard is required to read *in public* (a Shakespearean contrivance) a list of the "grievous crimes" (4.1.223) he committed "Against the state and profit of this land," so "That, by confessing them, the souls of men / May deem that you are worthily deposed" (4.1.225–7). This attempt by Bolingbroke and his supporters to have "The commons [. . .] satisfi'd" (4.1.272) is all the more urgent given the awareness that many would see the rebellion as illegitimate and the new king as a tyrant *sine titulo* (i.e. a ruler without title, who has illegitimately seized power).[15]

Similar concerns are found in various other Shakespearean plays that explore the question of legitimate sovereignty. Even the most ruthless of usurpers, Richard III, shows awareness of the need for popular support, as he asks his follower Buckingham to deliver a public speech with which to cast doubts about the legitimacy of King Edward's rule and present Richard himself as the solution to the political crisis faced by this "ungovern'd isle" (*RIII* 3.7.109). The citizens, as Richard is informed, respond to this speech with deafening silence. Later, Richard puts up a show of piety, religiosity, and virtuous reservation that evokes the rationalized political advice offered to rulers in Machiavelli's *The Prince* (published in 1532). During this, "[his] citizens" (a suggestively ambiguous term here) "entreat" (3.7.200) Richard to assume sovereign power in order to serve what Buckingham refers to as "our general good" (3.7.67). One also recalls the example of Macbeth, who avoids using "bare-fac'd power" (3.2.118) to kill Banquo and instead secretly hires murderers to do it, thus "Masking the business from the common eye" (3.2.124). Even though his subsequent escalation of violence exposes Macbeth openly as a tyrant *exercitu* (i.e. by practice) as well as one *sine titulo*, at this stage at least he seems to be concerned with preserving the support both of influential friends "Whose loves I may not drop" (3.2.121) and, one would say, of his subjects more broadly.

These examples demonstrate Shakespeare's engagement with a range of sources and ideas that interrogated kingly authority, but also, more broadly, drew attention to the limits of sovereign power and its dependence on the consent of the governed. His preoccupation with these ideas is also revealed in his treatment of mixed government and republicanism in such plays as *Othello* and *The Merchant of Venice*, where he explores the political institutions of Venice, but especially in his engagement with Rome's republican past in the Roman plays. *Coriolanus* arguably provides

Shakespeare's most sustained treatment of the political institutions of the Roman republic. Like *King Lear*, *Coriolanus* also invites a theoretically engaging reflection on the concept of sovereignty that would have found special currency within the context of early- to mid-seventeenth-century constitutional debates.

The play starts with a group of starving plebeians protesting over the inadequate distribution of food by the patricians—a possible allusion to the Midlands Uprising of 1607. A senator called Menenius tries to pacify the rioters with a version of the famous fable of the belly (also found in Shakespeare's source, Plutarch's *Life of Coriolanus*). In this story, the belly is accused by "all the body's members" (1.1.95) for its inactivity. The belly's response to this is to indicate how its accusers in fact owe it gratitude as it undertakes the life-preserving task of digesting food and distributing it to the rest of the body. As Menenius explains to the plebeians, "The senators of Rome are this good belly, / And you the mutinous members" (1.1.147–8). This authoritarian version of the body politic is not very far from the political views expressed by Coriolanus, whose relationship with the plebeians is marked by mutual enmity. In a furious outburst against the two tribunes, Sicinius and Brutus, who later come to inform him that "The people are incense'd against him" (3.1.32), Coriolanus expresses his complete aversion to the concept of popular rule. Reflecting, like Regan in *King Lear*, on sovereignty's indivisibility and on the "confusion" that "May enter 'twixt the gap of both, and take / The one by th'other" (3.1.110–2) when "two authorities are up, / Neither supreme" (3.1.109–10), Coriolanus castigates the idea that the plebeians should be allowed to take any part in government. Repeatedly expressing his disapproval of Greek democracy, where "the people had more absolute rule" (3.1.116), he countenances the possibility of the plebeians challenging the rule of the patrician senate with utter dismay.

The relevance of these ideas within the context of Jacobean politics is hard to miss, especially given the affinity between Coriolanus' and Menenius' authoritarian views and those expressed by James I in his writings.[16] James had notably advanced his own version of the body politic in *The Trew Law*, where he argued that "the proper office of a King towards his Subiects, agrees very wel with the office of the head towards the body" (76). Menenius' authoritarian model of a body politic in which the stomach/senate controls bodily functions is here turned into a royal-absolutist model in which the king, as the head rather than the stomach, does not only control such important processes as decision-making but enjoys absolute power over the body. For James, this is a power that involves the right, in caring for the body, to "cut off some rotten member [. . .] to keepe the rest of the body in integritie" (78). This may, of course, be read as an allusion to the king's right to punish rebellion, but its implications are far broader: the figurative act of amputation pertains to the sovereign's power of life and death over the subjects.

In exclaiming that "the people are the city" (as in the second of my opening quotes), the plebeians in *Coriolanus* clearly express an altogether different conception of the state, on the basis of which the people cannot be excluded from political participation. Theirs is a republican understanding of the body politic as a body whose health relies on the mutual dependence and co-activity of all members. Sicinius and Brutus assert this notion when, in response to Coriolanus' expression of his authoritarian views in Act 3 Scene 1, they claim their right to charge him with treason and have him apprehended as "A foe to th' public weal" (3.1.176). Drawing attention to the issue of popular consent, the two also defend the structures of political representation that enabled the plebeians to have their voice heard in the republic through the election of tribunes: "By the consent of all we were establish'd / The people's magistrates" (3.1.201–2). As Brutus further exclaims "Or let us stand to our authority / Or let us lose it [. . .]," it becomes clear that the central question here is that of sovereignty.

As the development of the conflict in *Coriolanus* puts the republic itself in serious danger, the play seems to carry another reminder of the significance of the indivisibility of sovereignty. Yet, the question of *who* sovereignty should fall to ultimately remains equivocal. As with many other Shakespearean plays, this renders it practically impossible to provide a definitive answer to the question of "Shakespeare's politics" or his views on sovereignty. But, the attempt on our part to determine whether Shakespeare adhered to the idea of absolute monarchy or championed the values of civic republicanism rather misses the point. For the value of Shakespeare's engagement with these ideas may be found more in his opening up of questions rather than foreclosing answers, and in how he invited his audiences to reflect on a broad set of theoretical dilemmas regarding sovereignty that would dominate political discussion and constitutional debates in England for many decades to come.

Notes

1 William Shakespeare, *King Lear* 2.2.432–4. Cited from *The Arden Shakespeare Complete Works*, rev. ed., ed. Richard Proudfoot, Ann Thompson and David Scott Kastan (London and New York: Bloomsbury, 2011).

2 William Shakespeare, *Coriolanus* 3.1.199–200, cited from ibid. Shakespeare's works will hereafter be cited parenthetically in the text from this edition.

3 Brian Sheerin, "Making Use of Nothing: The Sovereignties of *King Lear*," *Studies in Philology* 110, no. 4 (Fall 2013): 789–811 (793).

4 R. A. Foakes, "Introduction," in *King Lear*, ed. R. A. Foakes, The Arden Shakespeare: Third Series (London: Thomson Learning, 1977; reprint. 2005), 17.

5 Ernst Kantorowicz, *The King's Two Bodies: A Study in Medieval Political Theology* (Princeton: Princeton University Press, 1957).

6   For a more extensive discussion than the one offered here, see Stella Achilleos,
    "Sovereignty, Social Contract, and the State of Nature in *King Lear*," in *The
    Routledge Companion to Shakespeare and Philosophy*, ed. Craig Bourne and
    Emily Caddick Bourne (London and New York: Routledge, 2019), 267–78.

7   See Andrew Hadfield, *Shakespeare and Renaissance Politics* (London and New
    York: Bloomsbury, 2004), 17.

8   For a concise discussion of the Oath of Allegiance controversy, see Philip
    Lorenz, *The Tears of Sovereignty: Perspectives of Power in Renaissance Drama*
    (New York: Fordham University Press, 2013), 1–5.

9   Cited from *King James VI and I: Political Writings*, ed. Johann Sommerville
    (Cambridge: Cambridge University Press, 1994), 62–84 (72). The text is
    hereafter cited parenthetically from this edition.

10 James' position as King of England and Scotland inevitably involved a certain
    fracturing of sovereignty, as the two kingdoms were discrete states with
    different laws, constitutions, and churches.

11 Hadfield, *Shakespeare and Renaissance Politics*, 99.

12 "Basilicon Doron," in *King James VI and I: Political Writings*, 1–61 (42).

13 Hadfield, *Shakespeare and Renaissance Politics*, 100–2.

14 Ibid., 103–9 (103). For a discussion of some of the constitutional conflicts that
    later marked the eruption of a civil war, see Michael Mendle's essay on Henry
    Parker and Charles I in this volume.

15 For a discussion of the figure of the tyrant in Shakespeare's plays, see Stephen
    Greenblatt, *Tyrant: Shakespeare on Politics* (New York and London: W. W.
    Norton, 2018).

16 See, for instance, W. Gordon Zeeveld, "*Coriolanus* and Jacobean Politics," *The
    Modern Language Review* 57, no. 3 (1962): 321–34.

11

Sovereignty and the Separation of Powers on the Eve of the English Civil War

Henry Parker's *Observations* and Charles' *Answer to the XIX Propositions*

Michael Mendle

The fountain and efficient cause [of political power] is the people . . . the king, though he be singulis major *[greater than anyone], yet he is* universis minor *[less than the whole], for if the people be the true efficient cause of power, it is a rule in nature* quicquid efficit tale, est magis tale *[the cause is greater than the effect].*

*   *   *

I come now to those seven doctrines, and positions, which the king by way of recapitulation lays open as so offensive—And they run thus:
1. That the parliament has an absolute indisputable power of declaring law, so that all the right of the King and people, depends upon their pleasure. *It has been answered, that this power must rest in them, or in the king, or in some inferiour court, or else*

all suits must be endless, and it can nowhere rest more safely then in parliament.

2. That parliaments are bound to no precedents. *Statutes are not binding to them. Why then should precedents? Yet there is no obligation stronger then the justice and honour of a parliament.*

3. That they are parliaments, and may judge of public necessity without the king, and dispose of anything. *They may not desert the king, but being deserted by the king, when the kingdom is in distress, they may judge of that distress, and relieve it, and are to be accounted by the virtue of representation, as the whole body of the State.*

[. . .]

5. That the sovereign power resides in both houses of parliament, the king having no negative voice. *This power is not claimed as ordinary, nor to any purpose, but to save the kingdom from ruin, and in case where the king is so seduced, as that he prefers dangerous men, and prosecutes his loyal subjects.*[1]

There being three kinds of government amongst men, absolute monarchy, aristocracy and democracy . . . [t]he experience and wisdom of your ancestors hath so moulded this out of a mixture of these, as to give to this kingdom (as far as human prudence can provide) the conveniencies of all three, without the inconveniencies of any one, as long as the balance hangs even between the three estates, and they run jointly on in their proper channel . . . .
In this kingdom the laws are jointly made by a king, by a House of Peers, and by a House of Commons chosen by the people . . . . The government *according to these laws is trusted to the king, power of treaties of war and peace, of making Peers, of choosing officers and councilors for State, judges for law, commanders for forts and castles . . . are placed in the king . . . the House of Commons (an excellent conserver of liberty, but never intended for any share in* government, *or the choosing of them that should* govern) *is solely entrusted with the first propositions concerning the levies of moneys*

(which is the sinews as well of peace, as war) and the impeaching of
those, who for their own ends, though countenanced by any
surreptitiously gotten command of the king, have violated that law,
which he is bound (when he knows it) to protect. . . . And the Lords
being trusted with a judicatory power, are an excellent screen and
bank between the prince and people.
[Agreeing to the Nineteen Propositions] would be a total subversion
of the fundamental laws, and that excellent constitution of this
kingdom [and would bring on a cascade of disasters, ultimately
leading the "common people" to] set up for themselves, call parity and
independence, liberty; devour that estate [viz., the House of
Commons] which had devoured the rest; destroy all rights and
proprieties, all distinctions of families and merit; and . . . end in a dark
equal chaos of confusion . . . Our answer is, Nolumus leges Angliae
mutari *[We do not wish the law of England changed] . . .*[2]

In England, the "War of the Three Kingdoms" (1642–51) was a civil war. While religious differences supplied much of the energy, the core issues leading to armed conflict were political and constitutional. These were hashed out in early and mid-1642 in the so-called war of words—exchanges between the writers for the Houses of Parliament (and, indeed, largely the writers in and for the House of Commons) and those writing in the name of King Charles. Ostensibly negotiating positions, these very public pronouncements simultaneously exacerbated the conflict and clarified the issues. Along with official pronouncements, both sides had their less official scribblers, whose efforts grew more numerous as the actual conflict superseded the war of words.

The official exchanges were later collected in a good-sized volume, while pamphlet wars filled many others.[3] Two pieces, though, had a disproportionate influence. Henry Parker's *Observations upon some of his Majesties late Answers and Expresses* stated the parliamentary case with perhaps too-exceptional candor. A little later Charles' spokesmen, in *His Majesty's Answer to the XIX Propositions,* stated the king's case in a way that would define a constitutional crux for centuries forward.

*   *   *

The most common understanding of England's constitutional arrangement came from the fifteenth-century lawyer and courtier, Sir John Fortescue. Famously, he defined England's arrangement in (unfair) comparison to that of France. France was, he said, a *dominium tantum regale*—a simple monarchy. England, however, was a *dominium politicum et regale*, usually glossed as a "mixed" or "limited" monarchy. But what did that mean? Fortescue and others meant that in England royal power flowed through two channels. The "political" channel expressed the royal will through Parliament and the law. The subject's life and property could only be taken or restrained through the legal process and the courts. Taxation was granted only through Parliament, and the Commons had the (theoretical) initiative about grants of money. The framing of laws through the agreement of king, Lords, and Commons, was often taken as the highest expression of the king and the kingdom's will. The Houses of Parliament and the courts remained the king's (viz., they did not possess an independent existence and right of action.). However, the king could not act independently of them within their spheres of competence. The "regal" or "royal" channel encompassed a substantial range of powers that were (again, in theory) exercised by the king alone. They were usually taken to include the packet of rights called the royal prerogative, and were more or less taken to mean everything we mean by foreign policy, war and peace, general executive authority, as well as the governance of the royal household and appointments to office. In those areas he could act alone, absolutely.[4]

For those adopting a Bodinian or Hobbesian reductionist standard of sovereignty (Who's in charge here? Only one answer allowed!) Fortescue's formulation was maddening. To others, it was merely confusing. Naturally, there had been skirmishes over the boundaries of the political and the regal channels. These were, in effect, potential disputes over sovereignty. Repeatedly, the Stuarts raised revenue through devices that avoided the label of "tax" by using the *dominium regale* (prerogative authority): import duties via the prerogative right of regulation of commerce with foreign powers; forced loans, money-saving quartering, and ship money via the royal power and duty to defend the realm. Charles used the logic of national security ("reason of state") to override common-law restraints upon incarceration without cause. Equally, the impeachment process, albeit indirectly, reached into the royal power of appointment; the Commons chafed at restrictions upon their involvement with foreign policy. In 1628, an attempt was made— the famous Petition of Right—to find a common ground. Though the Petition was accepted, the king and his opponents held radically different understandings of what the Petition meant. The "patriots" insisted upon language that unreservedly declared the supremacy of law without any prospect of royal emergency override, while the king and his allies just as insistently attempted to insert "savings" (i.e. exceptions) for the royal prerogative. The bitterness and intractability of that dispute led to the eleven years of rule without Parliament (1629–1640).

The convening of the Long Parliament in November 1640 heralded a progressive weakening and dismantling of the apparatus of Charles' *dominium regale*. Arrests, impeachment proceedings and the so-called "bridge appointments" (in which leading opposition figures were given ministerial appointments) led to a near-collapse of prerogative government. The Privy Council became more or less irrelevant, the government control of the press dissolved (with the two houses fitfully stepping into the breach). Charles progressively ceded his right to control the calling and dissolving of Parliament, allowed that ship money had been illegal, and agreed to the elimination of the Star Chamber and High Commission courts. Meanwhile, both houses took it upon themselves to intervene as they chose in church governance, in matters grand and small, in direct contravention of the royal supremacy as conventionally understood. When Charles went to Scotland in summer 1641 (with rumors flying that he had a deal on offer to the Covenanters to occupy London on his behalf), the Commons pushed its nose into the executive tent with "ordinances" not involving the king's assent in areas hitherto understood as the domain of royal proclamations under the *dominium regale*.[5]

This was the context of Henry Parker's two ripostes to the king's position papers on the war of words with the Houses of Parliament.[6] In fits and lurches, seldom fully appreciated at the time, the houses had been claiming as their own territory what had been earlier the realm of the *dominium regale*. The unmissable final straw came with the militia ordinance of March 1642, in which the two houses (after what was in practice a purge of the House of Lords, through the elimination of bishops' seats and the intimidation of the royalist peers)[7] declared that an emergency (the king's refusal to agree with them by way of bill) required them to take control of the military might of the kingdom, a total break with the king's control over the means of warfare.

Charles' spokesmen had brutally pointed this out, ending their answer to a remonstrance of the two houses of May 26, 1642, with seven positions they charged the houses with holding. Parker either quoted or closely paraphrased them in the lines italicized above. He then countered them in a triumphalist assertion of the two houses' supremacy over the king, which followed from his three conjoined propositions that the people were supreme, that the Houses of Parliament fully represented the people, and that they, without the king if need be, constituted the whole Parliament. All departures from settled practice were undertaken through the logic of the emergency, an approach that had been used by Charles in the 1620s and 1630s to govern in his own way, and that linked up closely to a wider European discourse about "reason of state." At that time, many legal minds denied that the law was so easily dismissed. In 1642, the tables having been turned, it was Parker's mission to declare that in an emergency of their own defining, the Houses of Parliament could do whatever they thought necessary to "save" the kingdom. Following the Bodinian line that sovereign power resided in either in one locus or another, or it did not exist, Parker agreed that "parliament" (as Parker always called the Houses of Parliament) had the ultimate power of court and legislature (viz., to "declare" law); that, moreover, law set no boundaries upon what a parliament could do or the property it could take "in public necessity." Finally, the king's voice in legislation could be dispensed with, as necessity dictated.

The boldness of Parker's exposition did not bear the house's official imprimatur. But Parker was the insider grandee Lord Saye's nephew, and soon to be secretary to Parliament's war-managing Committee of Safety, and he made clear the implications of the houses' less explicit, less general formulations. When the houses offered Charles the Nineteen Propositions, amounting to a demand for Charles' surrender of the *dominium regale*, Charles' spokesmen riposted with their *Answer to the XIX Propositions*. Part of their response addressed the larger concerns raised by Parker, though only indirectly. The two pieces "crossed in the mail," as it were.

The *Answer* was done well, but not without missteps born of haste and weariness.[8] One was to prove a long-term royalist embarrassment. Probably to respond to the houses' rejection of the king's absolute veto of legislation, the *Answer* described the king, Lords, and Commons as equally necessary "estates." But this formulation abandoned the traditional scheme (clergy, nobility, and commons) that put the "three estates" under the king, and also seemingly threw the cause of episcopacy to the wolves. Some parliamentary propagandists used this verbal slip to misread the *Answer* and find within it a hard doctrine of a general "co-ordination" of power in king, Lords, and Commons.

The *Answer* further muddied its meaning by using a key term, "government," in two distinct ways. In the excerpt, the first usage of "government" is largely consonant with our own. "Government" here referred to the entire constitutional/ruling framework. In the subsequent usages, "government" meant something quite different, and was the core of the *Answer's* message. This second sense was based on a strong medieval distinction of *jurisdictio* from *gubernaculum*. The former literally meant "law-saying," and covered activities ranging from dispute adjudication, crime punishing, and legislation (which this same legal tradition comprehended within law-saying). The latter term comes out as "government," meaning specifically administration and regulation (in fine, the *dominium regale*), but not law making, or taking of life, liberty or property, matters for the king within the *dominium politicum*.

Accordingly, the *Answer* stressed that while king, Lords, and Commons had a joint responsibility for legislation and taxation, in other respects, the power of each "estate" was restrained to its "proper channel." In particular, the Commons had no "share in government, or the choosing of them that should govern" or control of the forts of the kingdom. In this way, the *Answer* responded to the Nineteen Propositions with that bugbear of Bodinian sovereignty, the separation of powers. In doing so, it condensed claims of popular sovereignty into parliamentary absolutism (which Parker did not deny), the equal and opposite of the nightmare of royal absolutism. Parliamentary absolutism equaled the collapse of the restraints and checks of the ancient constitution,[9] and a likely prelude to further dissolution of all order into a "dark equal chaos of confusion."

Along with a stubborn attachment to the established church, this doctrine formed the grounds of Charles' resistance to the two houses. Charles had claimed the two houses had committed the same absolutist misdeeds of which he had been accused, and while he had been rehabilitated through reform legislation and personnel changes, his reckless opponents had done far worse. His opponents rejected the argument as a false moral equivalence; his supporters embraced it as welcome polemical high ground.

The immediate context aside, however, the issues lingered on, as new contingencies redefined them. Parker, pamphleteer of the moment and scribbler on behalf of political insiders, restated and expanded key ideas in his most theoretical tract, *Jus Populi* (1644). He showed considerable familiarity with Jean Bodin and some with Hugo Grotius, while trying to ground popular sovereignty in a historical and conceptual separation of the political from the familial. But Parker did little to firm up his heady, facile identification of popular and parliamentary sovereignty. The identification could not survive the self-interest and self-dealing of the "new class" of perpetual politicians of the Long Parliament.[10] Accordingly, the "reserves" of the famous first *Agreement of the People* of the army radicals of 1647 cordoned off those things that even an otherwise omnicompetent Parliament could not do: force religion, impress men, and modify the foundational commitment to a soldiers' indemnity. Leveller writers joined Royalists in tracing the Long Parliament's transgressions to its seizure of executive and judicial power. Later, in 1654, the most powerful justification for the Instrument of Government echoed the *Answer*'s claims of ancestral wisdom for the separation of legislative and executive power.[11]

Another enduring constitutional conundrum for the English has been the relationship of two profoundly central constructs of national political identity—the sovereignty of Parliament and the primacy of the common law. Were they ultimately at odds or could an accommodation be found? Could *jurisdictio* be separated into legislation and jurisprudence? One answer was to use the separation of powers to preserve, though also to tame, the populist beast within republican thought. In this way, the separation of powers became the widest bridge linking the republican-populist and constitutionalist-liberal traditions. That it should be so closely tied to an otherwise obscure royalist salvo in an interminable but mostly forgotten war of words, is an irony both to ponder and savor.

Notes

1   Henry Parker, *Observations upon some of his Majesties late Answers and Expresses* (London, 1642), 2, 45.

2   Charles I, "Answer to the XIX Propositions," in *An Exact Collection of All Remonstrances*, comp. Edward Husbands (London, 1643), 320–2. Emphasis of "government" and "governed" added.

3   The single volume is Husbands, as cited above; the many pamphlets were most fulsomely collected in George Thomason's collection, now incorporated into EEBO.

4   Sir John Fortescue, *On the Laws and Governance of England*, ed. Shelley Lockwood (Cambridge: Cambridge University Press, 1997).

5   On the first ordinances, see Michael Mendle, "The Great Council of Parliament and the First Ordinances: The Constitutional Theory of the Civil War," *Journal of British Studies* 31, no. 2 (1992): 133–62.

6   Parker's celebrated *Observations* was preceded by the less noticed *Some Few Observations*. For the details, see Michael Mendle, *Henry Parker and the English Civil War: The Political Thought of the Public's "Privado"* (Cambridge: Cambridge University Press, 1995), 82–8, 192.

7   The most recent treatment is David Como, *Radical Parliamentarians and the English Civil War* (Oxford: Oxford University Press, 2018), 107–22. See also Michael Mendle, *Dangerous Positions: Mixed Government, the Estates of the Realm, and the Answer to the XIX Propositions* (University, AL: University of Alabama Press, 1985), 165–70.

8   Mendle, *Dangerous Positions*, ch. 1, 8.

9   The *locus classicus* of this notion remains J. G. A. Pocock, *The Ancient Constitution and the Feudal Law: A Study of English Historical Thought in the Seventeenth Century*, 2nd ed. (Cambridge: Cambridge University Press, 1987 [1957]).

10 I am using the term in the spirit of Milovan Djilas, *The New Class: An Analysis of the Communist System* (New York: Praeger, 1957).

11 On these writings, see Michael Mendle, "The Royalist Origins of the Separation of Powers" in *Royalists and Royalism in the English Civil Wars*, ed. Jason McElligott and David L. Smith (Cambridge: Cambridge University Press, 2007), 182–5.

12

Thomas Hobbes, Sovereign Representation, and the English Revolution

Glenn Burgess

And in him [the Leviathan] consisteth the essence of the commonwealth, which (to define it) is one person, of whose acts a great multitude, by mutual covenants one with another, have made themselves every one the author, to the end he may use the strength and means of them all, as he shall think expedient, for their peace and common defence.
And he that carrieth this person is called SOVEREIGN, *and said to have* Sovereign Power; *and every one besides, his* SUBJECT.[1]

Thomas Hobbes' *Leviathan* was published in 1651 in the wake of a tumultuous decade in England. Civil wars, Scottish armies, and ideas of popular sovereignty conspired to bring Charles I, king since 1625, to a temporary scaffold erected outside the banqueting hall in Westminster. There, he was beheaded on January 30, 1649. England became for the first and only time a republic. Though he makes relatively few direct references to contemporary events, Thomas Hobbes was a deeply engaged writer. He wanted his work to be understood as a solution to the political problems that plagued England in the 1640s, and so he could say of *Leviathan*, "I completed the work, and in my native language, so that it might be read, beneficially, by very many of my English countrymen."[2] He produced a rhetorical masterpiece in which he sought to undermine those ideas that, in his view, fed the revolutionary zeal that brought low the Stuart monarchy.[3]

Leviathan is, among other things, a tissue of word definitions: there was nothing innocent in those definitions. They served a purpose. There is no better illustration of his loaded approach to word definition than Hobbes' discussion of sovereignty.

How did sovereignty come into existence? Hobbes imagined the human condition in its natural state before the existence of political communities. This was a condition of freedom: everyone had a right to all things, and to do what was needed to preserve themselves. But this freedom was useless, worse than having no freedom whatsoever. It was a state of war, in which fear and mutual suspicion drove people into conflict. There was no power from which to seek protection or to maintain any peace for long. Certainly, people could understand rational principles, called the laws of nature, which revealed how one could live in a better way. The first law was to seek peace when it was safe to do so. But these laws of nature were of no effect at all in the natural state: it never would be safe to follow them.[4]

Escape from such a miserable condition was possible only "if each man subjects his *will* to the *will* of a single other, to the *will*, that is, of one *Man* or of one *Assembly*, in such a way that whatever one wills on matters essential to the common peace may be taken as the will of all and each."[5] This outcome may be imagined to come about when a person "by an Agreement with each of the rest" obliges himself "not to resist the *will* of the *Man* or *Assembly* to which he has submitted himself." The agreement creates a "union" or "commonwealth" ("one person whose will . . . is to be taken as the will of them all") and the person or assembly to which they have submitted is the sovereign, to which "each of the citizens has transferred all his own force and power."[6]

The account given so far follows *De Cive* (published in 1642). The passage from *Leviathan* that opens this chapter was Hobbes' later summary of the nature of this sovereign authority. In *Leviathan* new concepts were introduced into the description of the process by which sovereignty was created, and they functioned to tighten the argument and provide fewer footholds for disagreement. In *Leviathan* the sovereign was the authorized representative of the commonwealth and of every subject in it.[7] Subjects did not alienate or transfer rights and powers to the sovereign; instead they "*give up*" their right to govern themselves, provided that everyone else does the same, and create a sovereign "*and Authorise all his Actions*" (17; 2, 260). By this process a "Multitude of men, are made *One* Person, when they are by one man, or one Person, Represented" (16; 2, 248). There could be no other representative of the people (19; 2, 286).

Hobbes' account of the process by which subjects abandoned their rights and authorized their sovereign can sound like a piece of history, something that had happened at some point in the past. But there is no reason to suppose that Hobbes believed this to be so. He was well aware that in many cases sovereigns won authority by force or fraud. Such sovereigns "by acquisition," however, were no different from sovereigns "by institution."

Their authority, too, rested on consent and hence on the free choice of those who became their subjects. The subjects of a conquering king or usurping oligarchy always had an option: they could submit, and thus recognize and authorize the authority of the sovereign, or they could refuse, possibly at the cost of their lives (20; 2, 306).

A sovereign was a sovereign, regardless of how power was obtained or exercised. Furthermore, a sovereign was a necessary feature of civil society. No sovereign, no society. Subjects either accepted their sovereign or they cast themselves back into the state of nature. There, they were again entirely free to do whatever they thought necessary for their own protection. But in nature everyone else was similarly free. And as a consequence, this was a state of war, real or threatened, and life "solitary, poore, nasty, brutish and short."[8] A taste of what this might be like was given by civil war, and for Hobbes even the greatest "incommodity" that can be suffered under a monarch was preferable to "the miseries and horrible calamities, that accompany a Civil Warre." In short: "Soveraigne Power not so hurtfull as the want of it" (18; 2, 282). Subjects could never be *justified* in refusing to obey their sovereign, still less in engaging in overt acts of resistance or rebellion, though subjects did retain a right *in extremis* to preserve themselves from death. But even if they used that right in an attempt to protect themselves against their sovereign, that sovereign was nonetheless entirely justified both in placing their subject's life in jeopardy and in quashing by whatever means necessary subjects' attempts to protect themselves.[9]

Hobbes made no effort to soften the implications of this theory. The sovereign's immunity from any subject's claims was entirely without limit. Hobbes traced in detail the implications of this, and listed the powers sovereigns possessed. The sovereign could not be deprived of authority or forfeit it in any way. Subjects could not change the form of government, nor stand against the sovereign (except in those extreme cases where the subject's right of self-protection might be involved); the sovereign could never be guilty of injustice to their subject. The sovereign's actions were always just by definition, for "nothing the Soveraign Representative can doe to a Subject, on what pretence soever, can properly be called Injustice, or Injury; because every Subject is Author of every act the Soveraign doth" (21; 2, 326–30). The subject had authorized whatever the sovereign did, and thus consented even to her or his own punishment, which therefore could not be unjust. The sovereign, though, was unpunishable, and had the sole authority to determine public doctrine and action (political and religious). All judicial authority lay with the sovereign, as did the power to make war, to punish, to bestow honors, and to choose ministers and advisers (18; 2, 264–83). Certainly there was a sort of ethical framework constituted by the laws of nature.[10] Hobbes said that "although those who hold sovereign power among men cannot be subject to laws properly so called . . . it is nevertheless their *duty* to obey right reason in all things so far as they can." This meant ruling for the safety of the people.[11] But no one could without injustice enforce these limitations or take away the sovereign's right to ignore them.

Many of Charles I's opponents were driven by their religious convictions, and resisted their king on religious grounds. Hobbes denuded churches of any independent authority. Religious doctrine (i.e. public teaching or orthodoxy) was defined by the sovereign. Religious observance was whatever the sovereign determined it to be. And in so far as obedience to any scriptural precepts was required of subjects, only the sovereign had the power to make a precept into a law. No one could claim that conscience justified their disobedience to the sovereign or its laws. The church could have no authority or power independent of the sovereign. Hobbes redefined the requirements that their faith imposed upon Christians so that they could never be in conflict with the public authority of the sovereign.[12]

None of this means that Hobbes could not distinguish between good and bad rulers. *Leviathan* was full of advice on how to use sovereign power well and how to use it ethically. He advised the sovereign to administer justice equally to rich and poor, to ensure that the offences of the rich against the poor did not go unchecked, to impose taxes equally, and to provide public charity for those unable to work (30; 2, 536–40). Hobbes showed no sign of relishing lawless or violent rule. But the choice between living in peaceful subjection or in violent chaos was a stark one. The one thing all human beings could agree on was that peace was better than war, and this alone required absolute subjection to an absolute sovereign.

This understanding of sovereignty entirely cut away the ground from beneath the opponents of Charles I in the English Revolution. They just did not understand what sovereignty meant. Were there any weak spots in the armor that Hobbes had cast for Charles I? Many of those who argued against the king in the 1640s claimed that England was not a pure monarchy. In other words, they said, in England sovereignty took the form of mixed monarchy, shared between King, Lords and Commons in Parliament (the institution known as King-in-Parliament). Hobbes repelled this argument partly by reading English constitutional law in such a way that sovereignty in this particular polity was assigned to the king alone, even though he might (on sufferance) govern through parliament or even entrust law-making powers to it (19; 2, 286). Like all such delegation, though, this was purely "at will" and did not in any way bind the sovereign. But this interpretation of the English constitution was underpinned by the further argument that mixed sovereignty was, in any case, an incoherent idea (29; 2,512). The opponents of Charles I "were averse to absolute Monarchy, as also to absolute Democracy, or Aristocracy; all which Governments they esteemed Tyranny, and were in love with Monarchy, which they us'd to praise by the name of mixt Monarchy, though it were indeed nothing else but pure Anarchy."[13] Sovereignty could not be shared. There had to be a single locus for sovereign authority, and in England there was no other contender for this role than the king.

Hobbes' political thought was an oddly incongruous mixture of the liberal and the illiberal.[14] For example, his account of what sovereigns were entitled to do is utterly illiberal and highly authoritarian, with subjects having almost no rights against their sovereign, but his account of how sovereignty was created by consent is echoed in liberal (even democratic) thought.[15] It is worth wondering why a political theory that seems in our eyes a bizarre mash-up of ideas that do not belong together made sense to Hobbes himself. The answer to this must lie in the relationship between Hobbes and his immediate context. What was he trying to do?

The work of scholars who have sought to understand Hobbes as anti-"republican" has been immensely illuminating.[16] But the term republican is itself a little problematic. We tend to understand a republican as someone who wants to abolish monarchy. But when the term is used in relation to Hobbes it refers primarily to an ideal of what constitutes a "free state," an ideal which was derived from ancient (especially Roman) republican writers. It did not necessarily take forms that are republican in the sense of requiring government that was not monarchical. At the heart of this idea was that to live in a free society—to be a free citizen and not a subject or a slave—it was not enough to be free from immediate restraint or coercion. One had to live in a condition of non-domination. "[T]he conception of freedom as non-domination . . . requires that no one is able to interfere on an arbitrary basis—at their pleasure—in the choices of the free person."[17]

Hobbes was quite clearly repudiating such a view. It is tempting, indeed, to think that he was, for polemical reasons, actually *inventing* something like republicanism (in our sense) and attributing it to all of the enemies of Charles I, whatever they may actually have said or thought. Inspired by the Dutch example, as well as by Greek and Roman authors, these enemies of their king thought "there needed no more to grow rich, than to change . . . the forme of their Government" (29; 2, 506). But any challenge to the person (or persons) who rule as sovereign threatened the destruction of sovereignty itself (and of political order with it). In England that meant the destruction of monarchy. Charles' opponents were republicans set on destroying the monarchy, whether they knew it or not, whether they declared it or not. They could not be anything else.

Hobbes' most emphatic means of making such positions untenable—indeed, unthinkable on his own definitions—was to understand the status of being a *subject* in such a way that it was indistinguishable from the status of being a *citizen*. Sovereign power was identical in every form of government, whether a hereditary monarchy or an aristocratic republic (in practice, these were the two main options, though not the only ones, in early modern Europe). It was one of the false beliefs that could be learned from the ancient authors "that the Subjects in a Popular Common-wealth enjoy liberty; but that in a Monarchy they are all Slaves" (29; 2, 508). Though the citizens of a republic might think of themselves as more free than the subject of a monarch, or even as living in a free state, they were deluded. In any society, to be free was to be able to do the things that the laws allowed you to do. All sovereigns imposed laws on their subjects in similar ways and those laws covered similar ground. Consequently, the citizen of Venice or the Dutch Republic was no freer to disobey laws than the subjects of the kings of England or France or those of the Ottoman sultan. Though in a democracy (which was a possible form for sovereign authority to take) a citizen might have some voice in making the laws, sovereign power was really no different than in a monarchy. The sovereign was authorized by all and spoke with the voice of all. And as Hobbes understood freedom, participation in rule did not add one jot to the degree of freedom you possessed. As we have seen, one of the versions of Hobbes' political thought was entitled *Of the Citizen* (*De Cive*) and in it Hobbes usually referred to citizens (*cives*); the passage from *Leviathan* that opens this chapter talks of the same person as a "subject"; the Latin *Leviathan*, Hobbes' final systematic political statement, makes the equivalence clear, referring in the equivalent passage to "*Subditi & Cives*" (subjects and citizens) (17; 2, 263).

The dividing line between a free man (or citizen) and a slave was shockingly fine.[18] Within a civil society, freedom in the proper sense was not infringed by the imposition of law. A person "restrained by threats of punishment from doing all he wants to do is not oppressed by servitude, he is governed and maintained."[19] It was always possible for such a person to disobey, even at the risk of being punished, unless physically chained up or otherwise prevented by external force from doing so. In *Leviathan* Hobbes also maintained "that all actions which men doe in Commonwealths, for *feare* of the law, are actions which the doer had freedom to omit" (21; 2, 326). In considering liberty within a political society, he argued that "[t]he Liberty of a Subject, lyeth therefore only in those things, which in regulating their actions, the Sovereign hath praetermitted [i.e. omitted to regulate]" (21; 2, 328). The liberty of subjects or citizens in this sense existed purely on sufferance. Every freedom possessed by the citizen could be taken away in the future, lawfully and justly but also arbitrarily. This was the opposite of non-domination. To be free on sufferance was not to be free at all.

The combination of the "liberal" and the "illiberal" in Hobbes enabled him to say that subjects were, in effect, self-ruling citizens. They authorized their own rule and exercised it through their sovereign representative. Any subject could feel as proud as the citizens of Rome to have as much freedom as was compatible with maintaining peace and avoiding war. The subjects of Charles I seem to have forgotten, not just that they had never had it so good, but that it would never be possible to have things any other way. No other form of rule could give citizens more freedom or a less authoritarian sovereign, for all sovereigns were absolute. Sovereigns, in the proper understanding of matters, should have nothing to fear from free citizens, for they ruled them—absolutely and without check—as their subjects. Conversely the subjects of a king, like those of Charles I, could not gain more freedom by changing their ruler or their government. They could become free by returning themselves to the anarchy of nature. But who could want that?

Hobbes' powerful analytical clarity had considerable appeal to some later thinkers. His idea of the state as a fictional person ("Leviathan") represented by the sovereign, had a long life ahead if it, and was arguably influential on Bentham.[20] His thought also shadows the thinking of modern legal positivists, from J. L. Austin onwards,[21] including that of Carl Schmitt, philosopher and legal theorist in sympathy with Nazism.[22] But this was a long way from Hobbes' "moment" in the English Revolution and his defense of Charles I.

Notes

1   Thomas Hobbes, *Leviathan*, ed. Noel Malcolm, 3 vols (Oxford: Clarendon Press, 2012), vol. 2, ch. xvii, 260–2. References to *Leviathan* are to this edition, and are generally given parenthetically in the text (chapter number; volume in this edition, page).

2   Hobbes' Latin autobiography, qtd. in Hobbes, *Leviathan*, vol. 1, 10.

3   David Johnston, *The Rhetoric of Leviathan: Thomas Hobbes and the Politics of Cultural Transformation* (Princeton, NJ: Princeton University Press, 1986); Quentin Skinner, *Reason and Rhetoric in the Philosophy of Hobbes* (Cambridge: Cambridge University Press, 1996).

4   Hobbes, *On the Citizen [De Cive]*, ed. and transl. Richard Tuck and Michael Silverthorne (Cambridge: Cambridge University Press, 1998), i–ii, 21–42; *Leviathan*, 13–4; 2, 188–219.

5   Hobbes, *On the Citizen*, v.6, 72.

6   Ibid., v.7–11, 72–4.

7   See Quentin Skinner, "Hobbes on Political Representation," in Skinner, *From Humanism to Hobbes: Studies in Rhetoric and Politics* (Cambridge: Cambridge University Press, 2018), ch. 9, 190–221; A. P. Martinich, "Authorization and Representation in Hobbes's *Leviathan*," in *The Oxford Handbook of Hobbes*, ed. A. P. Martinich and Kinch Hoekstra (New York: Oxford University Press, 2016), ch. 14, 315–38.

8   This is, of course, Hobbes' famous description of the state of nature, *Leviathan*, 13; 2, 192.

9   On the implications of some of this see Glenn Burgess, "On Hobbesian Resistance Theory," *Political Studies* 42 (1994): 62–83; and Susanne Sreedhar, *Hobbes on Resistance: Defying the Leviathan* (Cambridge: Cambridge University Press, 2010).

10 See especially the chapter on "The Office of the Sovereign Representative," in Hobbes, *Leviathan*, 30; 2, 520–3.

11 Hobbes, *On the Citizen*, xiii.2, 143.

12 For more on Hobbes' ecclesiology see Jeffrey R. Collins, *The Allegiance of Thomas Hobbes* (Oxford: Oxford University Press, 2005), and the variety of perspectives in *Oxford Handbook of Hobbes*, Part IV.

13 Thomas Hobbes, *Behemoth, or An Epitome of the Civil Wars of England, from 1640 to 1660* (London, 1679), 120–1.

14 Noel Malcolm, "Thomas Hobbes: Liberal Illiberal," *Journal of the British Academy* 4 (2016): 113–36.

15 On Hobbes and democracy see the essays by Kinch Hoekstra and Richard Tuck, in *Rethinking the Foundations of Modern Political Thought*, ed. Annabel Brett, James Tully, and Holly Hamilton-Bleakley (Cambridge: Cambridge University Press, 2006), chs. 10 and 11.

16 Especially Quentin Skinner, *Hobbes and Republican Liberty* (Cambridge: Cambridge University Press, 2008).

17 Philip Pettit, *Republicanism: A Theory of Freedom and Government* (Oxford: Clarendon Press, 1999), 271.

18 Hobbes, *On the Citizen*, ix.9, 111–2.

19 Ibid., ix.9, 111.

20 See Quentin Skinner, "Hobbes and the Concept of the State," in Skinner, *From Humanism to Hobbes*, ch. 12, 341–83. However, as Skinner shows, the relationship between Hobbes and Bentham is problematic: see James E. Crimmins, "Bentham and Hobbes: An Issue of Influence," *Journal of the History of Ideas* 63 (2002): 677–96.

21 Cf. Mark C. Murphy, "Hobbes (and Austin, and Aquinas) on Law as Command of the Sovereign," in *Oxford Handbook of Hobbes*, ch. 15, 339–58, pointing out some of the differences between Hobbes and Austin.

22 John P. McCormick, "Teaching in Vain: Carl Schmitt, Thomas Hobbes, and the Theory of the Sovereign State," in *The Oxford Handbook of Carl Schmitt*, ed. Jens Meierhenrich and Oliver Simons (Oxford: Oxford University Press, 2017), ch. 9.

13

John Locke and the Language of Sovereignty

Geoff Kemp

Though in a Constituted Commonwealth, standing upon its own Basis, and acting according to its own Nature, that is, acting for the preservation of the Community, there can be but one Supream Power, which is the Legislative, to which all the rest are and must be subordinate, yet the Legislative being only a Fiduciary Power to act for certain ends, there remains still in the People a Supream Power to remove or alter the Legislative, when they find the Legislative act contrary to the trust reposed in them . . . and carry on designs against the Liberties and Properties of the Subject. . . . And thus the Community may be said in this respect to be always the Supream Power, but not as considered under any Form of Government, because this Power of the People can never take place till the Government be dissolved.[1]

The words above from paragraph 149 of the second of the *Two Treatises of Government* (1690) are among those most likely to feature, in whole or part, when any discussion of sovereignty turns to the views of John Locke (1632–1704). There is good reason for this in terms of illuminating Locke's perspective on supreme power, considered politically. The words of 2:§149 convey his conviction that governments govern by popular concession, acting at two levels: a governing executive is subordinate to a law-making body entrusted by the people to act for them; and "the People" reserve a power to constitute government anew when it has failed their trust by gross betrayal of the public good. The latter provision arises from the terms of agreement by which individuals would contract to unite their powers in government and underpins the right of resistance and revolution with which Locke concludes the *Second Treatise*. It also highlights the potential theoretical and practical tension between legislative and popular authority considered as twin supreme powers co-existing in relation to a single political community. The tension was present in Locke's day and continues to be apparent today.

In one important regard, however, the present chapter's "head quote" differs from most of those that adorn other chapters in this book: the quotation does not include the term "sovereignty" or cognates like "sovereign." Locke did not leave any clear alternative in the works he published, because they all demonstrate an aversion to using the term "sovereignty" in expressing his thinking to describe what others might class as political sovereignty. In the *Two Treatises*, the terminology of sovereignty occurs eighty-nine times but there is a striking discrepancy. Eighty-two instances appear in the *First Treatise*, but these arise in quotations and paraphrases of Sir Robert Filmer's *Patriarcha* (1680) as part of Locke's rebuttal of this work. In the *Second Treatise*, where Locke sets out his own theory of government, six of the seven remaining examples occur in further references to Filmer and his theme of familial authority (2:§4, §61, §69, §83) or to pre-political society (2:§108). The other instance (2:§6), considered below, uses the terminology in a way marginal to most discussions of political sovereignty.

Locke's reticence in saying "sovereignty" when he may seem to mean political sovereignty has attracted only occasional notice. One effect is that Locke is a frequent but not inevitable presence in books or discussions about sovereignty as a historical concept, unlike Jean Bodin and Thomas Hobbes. When he does appear, commentators who register the terminological issue must decide whether to declare the absence, whether to proffer an explanation and whether to specify how it may affect interpretation. It is more common for interpreters to "correct" or gloss Locke's vocabulary, believing that the language of sovereignty captures what he meant by "supreme power."

There need be little doubt, in fact, that Locke took the word "sovereignty" to mean "Absolute Unlimited Sovereignty," a single source of unaccountable and "unlimitable Power," as he paraphrased Filmer (1:§9, §67). The question is why he resisted its political application. He had known the work of Bodin as well as Filmer since at least the early Restoration, when he committed to manuscript (in Latin) the Bodinian view that in a commonwealth a power with "no superior on earth to which it is bound to give an account of its actions" can be considered "supreme" (using *suprema* not *maiestatem*, Bodin's term for "souveraineté").[2] In his writings, Locke quite often used "sovereign" as an adjective connoting all-powerful ("sovereign remedy" is a favorite), but never as a noun naming the supreme political power in his conception of government. His letters avoid the formality of calling the monarch the sovereign. If silences can cry out for attention, Locke's reticence regarding political "sovereignty" does so. The following account, after reviewing earlier interpretations, argues that an explanation lies in Locke's conviction that sovereign power is unavoidably theomorphic, not anthropomorphic—to Locke, sovereignty was for God alone.

The adaptation of Locke's arguments to the language of political sovereignty is itself of interest when studying the concept historically. Anyone paraphrasing the ideas in the quotation above will find themselves drawn inexorably towards using the word "sovereign." This was already the case in Locke's time. When the *Second Treatise* appeared in French in 1691—in which form it would be read by Montesquieu and Rousseau— Locke's original was translated into the language of popular sovereignty: the legislative was "un Pouvoir Suprême" but the people retained "le pouvoir souverain."[3] Pierre Bayle declared "the gospel of the day" to be Locke's argument that "la Souveraineté" rested with the people, who could retrieve it from the hands of so-called sovereigns.[4] In the eighteenth century, with the *Two Treatises* more often harnessed to the sovereignty of crown-in-parliament, Sir William Blackstone presumably believed he was merely rendering Locke into English when he inserted "sovereign" into a quotation where Locke had written "he" (referring to the "chief magistrate").[5] Against the revolutionary background later in the century, John Cartwright deployed the wording of 2:§149 to insist that the people represented the only "absolute sovereignty," while Charles James Fox told Parliament he was "ready to say with Locke" that "the people were the legitimate sovereign in every community."[6] In the following century, T. H. Green took the same text (§149) to be a rhetorical move in declaring the ultimacy of popular "sovereignty" (while noting that "Locke does not use the term"), it being evident that a unified "act of the sovereign people" might be broached as a caution to government but was a practical impossibility.[7] In the first half of the twentieth century, commentators converged on a view that Locke had failed to provide an adequate account of sovereignty, although without discussing his avoidance of the word: he simply had "no clear view," no "clear-cut theory of sovereignty," "no theory of Sovereignty at all."[8] Ernest Barker decided Locke was best considered an "exponent of the sovereignty of Natural Law" in furnishing an oppositional discourse of natural rights, principally for "Whig grandees."[9] C. E. Vaughan concluded that the discourse of rights meant that, for Locke, "the real sovereignty resides in the individual," which Vaughan thought an assault on "the very idea of sovereignty."[10]

In more recent decades, a disinclination to refer directly to Locke's linguistic lacuna has continued and his conversion into the language of political sovereignty remains common. The standing of some scholars who have done either or both suggests this can claim justification. Peter Laslett's introduction to his standard edition of the *Two Treatises* affirms Locke as a theorist of "the sovereignty of the people."[11] John Dunn's *The Political Thought of John Locke* discusses Locke's "legislative sovereign" and is the authority on "Locke on popular sovereignty" to which Quentin Skinner directs readers.[12] Richard Tuck's *The Sleeping Sovereign*, quoting 2:§149, aligns Locke's twin supremacies with the "common" and "proper" "sites of sovereignty" he finds in Grotius and Pufendorf. To John Simmons, Locke "takes the people (society) to be sovereign," while James Tully finds him presenting a "classic theory of individual popular sovereignty" combining collective power and individual rights.[13] The underlying absence is so readily glossed over that Julian Franklin's *John Locke and the Theory of Sovereignty* describes 2:§149 as an "explicit" statement of a "new idea of sovereignty" dividing "ownership and use of sovereignty."[14]

Of these authors, Tuck notes the terminological issue in passing, while Laslett's account insists against Green that Locke "used the term sovereignty in the way his contemporaries did," though of the scattered passages cited in support, four out of five from the *Second Treatise* do not even use the word.[15] Locke's omission has received notice from other commentators, however, if not necessarily concluded to be of theoretical significance. An early and continuing surmise, initially by J. W. Gough in 1950, is that Locke thought the word too tainted by recent associations with absolute monarchy to be retrieved from the supporters of Filmer or Hobbes.[16] This may be part of an explanation but Locke was not averse to using the word "sovereign" as such, and antipathy to the word's monarchical associations does not go far in explaining his position. He could, after all, have called the people "supreme" and the legislative something else; or vice versa. The issue for Locke lay not only with the word but with the idea of sovereignty.

A number of writers have contended in consequence that whether or not Locke was disdaining tainted terminology, his purpose was forging a revised concept. Richard Cox claimed that Locke's silences accorded with displacing sovereignty to the commonwealth as a "sovereign body" among other sovereign states, empowering the executive.[17] More often it has been suggested that by avoiding the term sovereignty, Locke invited acceptance of politics as a negotiation between sources of authority. Views differ on whether this implies shared sovereignty or none. To John T. Scott, Locke envisaged a "sovereignless state" with "several coexisting claimants to supreme authority."[18] In Ross. J. Corbett's account, Locke's theory requires "sovereignless government" because the rule of law binding the people by their own agreement also requires that law's limitations (silences, slowness, lack of discretion) are supplemented by prerogative actions accepted on the people's part not on the basis of obligation but their judgement as to public good.[19] "The People shall be Judge," declares Locke (2:§240), but in the case of irresolvable dispute not answered by law, there is no sovereign to decide: "there can be no Judge on Earth" (2:§168).

According to his various interpreters, Locke did or did not avoid the language of sovereignty; he does or does not have a theory of sovereignty; the theory when identified locates sovereignty as the attribute of a single ultimate power, of multiple powers, or of none; and the locus of sovereignty, singly or in combination, is the crown in parliament, the legislature alone, the people, the individual, the commonwealth through its executive, the law, or natural law. More could be said about these interpretations, but the final part of the present account offers another answer to the puzzle. As already suggested, Locke avoided the language of political sovereignty but had no aversion to taking the word and concept of sovereignty to mean a single ultimate power. If we return to the section of the *Two Treatises* which remains after discounting the other eighty-eight paragraphs containing the language of sovereignty—2:§6 rather than §149—Locke is found declaring humankind to be "all the Workmanship of one Omnipotent, and infinitely wise Maker; All the Servants of one Sovereign Master," whose will is that they preserve themselves and each other (cf. 1:§17). From this premise unfolds the *Second Treatise*'s account of the rise, structure, function, and limits of government. As Michael Davis has observed, Locke "rejects all forms of sovereignty except the sovereignty of God."[20] Locke repeats the identification in his other writings, most directly in the *Essay Concerning Human Understanding*, where he refers to "that Sovereign Being, which we call God, being all boundless and infinite." In the late *Paraphrase and Notes on the Epistles of St Paul* (effectively his final thoughts on the matter) he writes of the "prerogative of gods soverainty" and the divine will being "Soverain over all mankind."[21]

Locke's affirmation of divine sovereignty is not itself distinctive, of course, being a claim that early-modern writers were unlikely to deny: Bodin and Hobbes no less than Filmer declared God to be sovereign. The significance for Locke's political theory lies in his evident rejection of the possibility that "unlimited and unlimitable Power" could have the limitation of being divided or shared, even between heaven and earth, and consequently his avoidance of the language of sovereignty in characterizing political authority. For Locke, sovereignty was theomorphic, not anthropomorphic. In adhering strictly to the logical-semantic exclusivity of the notion, Locke was in some ways a more thoroughgoing theorist of sovereignty than either Bodin or Hobbes. His conception of sovereignty was arguably as political in effect as theirs, however, because it precluded their insistence on the exclusivity of political supremacy. Locke instead invoked the possibility or necessity of coexisting powers in a polity, notably those identified in §149. Interpretations registering this implication of his terminology are therefore on the right track, if potentially misleading in suggesting that he intended the sharing of "sovereignty," or "abandoning the concept of sovereignty."[22]

The further corollary of Locke's reservation of "unlimited and unlimitable Power" to the divine law maker is that no earthly power can be considered without limits. Most obviously, this applied to government in being liable to judgment by the people, as well as duty-bound to serve them: responding to Romans 13:1 in the *Paraphrase*, Locke identified the "higher powers" as being that "supreme civil power" having the (God-given) end of "the good of the people sincerely pursued."[23] Limitations also applied to the people, however, each person's end being to preserve themselves and others, obeying the law (natural and civil) that restrains contrary inclinations (2:§6). In the *Paraphrase*, again, Locke contended that God could not countenance such inclinations "without foregoeing his soverainty."[24] The "Body of the People" was a "proper Umpire" in disputes over whether government acted for the good of the people; but the people's right to revolution when rebuffed implied an "appeal to Heaven" which carried a duty to ensure this recourse served the public good in divine as well as democratic terms, in accord with "God and Nature" (2:§168. 242).

An all-powerful sovereign on Locke's definition did not require that the people be "all his slaves," as Davis suggests.[25] Locke made an explicit distinction between slaves subject to arbitrary power and the servant who remains a free man in undertaking service for "the Wages he is to receive" (1: preface; 2:§85). For individuals as "Servants of one Sovereign Master" the wages are those of sin or righteousness—death or eternal happiness— according to God's covenant through Christ, a view Locke elaborates elsewhere. In the *Two Treatises*, his observation that for any master and servant there is a "Contract between 'em" (2:§85) nevertheless cannot mean that God's sovereignty is contractual in the manner of the civil supremacy of the legislature—forfeitable on failed performance. To Locke, sovereign power *is* control over all final outcomes; by definition, the sovereign cannot fail.

In an era distant from the *Two Treatises*, the interest of Locke's conception of sovereignty may lie mainly in its informative divergence from his contemporaries and ours on the role requisite to God. One dimension might be Locke's case for toleration, wherein his insistence that in religion individuals owed an obligation to their maker ahead of their magistrate could be seen to reflect God's sovereignty rather than human self-sovereignty. On the other hand, an orientation to political sovereignty akin to Locke's may not need his faith and theology so much as a sense that a notion of unitary, ultimate and unlimited power over others belongs in a metaphysical more than political realm. The displacement of the false god of civil sovereignty arguably serves political realism, pluralism and due limitation, whatever it accords a spiritual sovereign. Locke believed that a rule of rectitude governing ethical and just conduct emanated from a source outside politics, supplying a law of nature giving individuals reasons for action (2:§6). Natural law was not itself sovereign since it supposed a higher power: a law maker supplying reasons and sanctions to motivate adherence to the moral law. But in politics, Locke held that the sovereign left the question of political supremacy to his subjects to resolve in pursuit of the end set for them, the good of the people. Indeed, in theological mode he contended that the move from politically prescriptive Mosaic law to a new dispensation was another instance of "the prerogative of gods sovereignty." In the *Paraphrase*, having argued that the sovereign could not forego concern with humanity's fate, and therefore with political power as such, Locke added that "how men come by a rightfull title to this power; or who has that title" was a matter of "civil rights" on which the divine sovereign's word was "silent."[26] Only in the extreme case of the revolutionary appeal to heaven would the sovereign be seen to have the final say. The *Second Treatise* from §6 to §243, not least §149, represented Locke's response to the challenge of a politically silent sovereign, which he met in part by his own silence on political "sovereignty."

Notes

1   John Locke, *Two Treatises of Government*, 2:§149 (original italics suppressed). References to the *Two Treatises* are given in parentheses in the text, indicating treatise and paragraph number. Peter Laslett's edition (Cambridge: Cambridge University Press, 1960/1988) has been used.

2   John Locke, *Two Tracts on Government*, ed. and trans. Philip Abrams (Cambridge: Cambridge University Press, 1967), 201, 231; Jean Bodin, *On Sovereignty*, ed. Julian H. Franklin (Cambridge: Cambridge University Press, 1992), 1.

3   John Locke, *Du Gouvernement Civil* (Amsterdam, 1691), 190. The translation is attributed to the Huguenot exile David Mazel.

4   Pierre Bayle to Vincent Minutoli, 14 September 1693, in Bayle, *Oeuvres Diverses*, vol. IV (Hague, 1737), 700.

5   William Blackstone, *Commentaries on the Laws of England*, 4 vols (Oxford, 1765–9), i, 52, 236.

6   John Cartwright, *An Appeal, Civil and Military, on the Subject of the English Constitution* (London, 1799), 290; *Authentic report of the debate in the House of Commons, on the 6th and 7th of May, 1793, on Mr. Grey's motion for a reform in Parliament* (London, 1793), 132.

7   Thomas Hill Green, *Lectures on the Principles of Political Obligation*, ed. Paul Harris and John Morrow (Cambridge: Cambridge University Press, 1986), §59–63.

8   Ernest Barker, *Essays on Government* (Oxford: Oxford University Press, 1951), 102; Richard I. Aaron, *John Locke* (2nd ed., Oxford, 1955; first published 1937), 281; C. E. Vaughan, *Studies in the History of Political Philosophy Before and After Rousseau*, ed. A. G. Little (2 vols, Manchester: Manchester University Press, 1925), i, 185.

9   Barker, *Essays*, 94, 103. Barker's essay drew on an article he wrote for the *Times* in 1932 (August 29), 11.

10 Vaughan, *Studies*, i, 134, 193.

11 Locke, *Two Treatises*, ed. Laslett (1988), 115, 121; cf. Laslett's initial "Critical Edition" (1960), 114, 119.

12 John Dunn, *The Political Thought of John Locke: An Historical Account of the Argument of the "Two Treatises of Government"* (Cambridge: Cambridge University Press, 1969), 17, 148; Quentin Skinner, *From Humanism to Hobbes:*

Studies in Rhetoric and Politics (Cambridge: Cambridge University Press, 2018), 361.

13 Richard Tuck, *The Sleeping Sovereign: The Invention of Modern Democracy* (Cambridge University Press: Cambridge, 2015), 119; A. John Simmons, *On the Edge of Anarchy* (Princeton: Princeton University Press, 1993), 159; James Tully, *An Approach to Political Philosophy: Locke in Contexts* (Cambridge: Cambridge University Press, 1993), 14, 101.

14 Julian Franklin, *John Locke and the Theory of Sovereignty* (Cambridge: Cambridge University Press, 1978), 64, 94, 123.

15 Locke, *Two Treatises*, 235.

16 J. W. Gough, *John Locke's Political Philosophy* (Oxford: Clarendon Press, 1950), 114–5.

17 Richard Cox, *Locke on War and Peace* (Oxford: Oxford University Press, 1960), 108–11, 122–5.

18 John T. Scott, "The Sovereignless State and Locke's Language of Obligation," *American Political Science Review* 94, no. 3 (2000): 547–61. Cf. Martin Seliger, *The Liberal Politics of John Locke* (London: Allen & Unwin, 1968), 326–7; Ruth W. Grant, *John Locke's Liberalism* (Chicago: University of Chicago Press, 1987), 108–9.

19 Ross J. Corbett, *The Lockean Commonwealth* (Albany: State University of New York Press, 2009), 48–53.

20 Michael Davis, "Locke's Political Society," *Journal of Moral Philosophy* 11, no. 2 (2014): 209–31 (227).

21 John Locke, *An Essay Concerning Human Understanding*, ed. Peter H. Nidditch (Oxford: Clarendon Press, 1975), II, xxiii, 34; John Locke, *A Paraphrase and Notes on the Epistles of St Paul*, ed. W. A. Wainwright (2 vols, Oxford: Clarendon Press, 1987), ii, 485, 582.

22 See above, and Corbett, *Lockean Commonwealth*, 48.

23 Locke, *Paraphrase*, ii, 587.

24 Ibid., 553. Space precludes discussion of Locke on divine voluntarism.

25 Davis, "Locke's Political Society," 226–7.

26 Locke, *Paraphrase*, ii, 484, 587.

14

Rousseau's Sovereignty as the General Will

David Lay Williams

[O]nly the general will can direct the forces of the state according to the end for which it was set up, that is, for the common good. For if the opposition of particular interests made the institution of societies necessary, the agreement among these same interests made it possible. What these different interests have in common creates the social bond, and if there were not some point on which all the interests were in agreement, no society could exist. Now, this common interest is the only basis on which society must be governed.

Therefore, I maintain that, since sovereignty is nothing but the exercise of the general will, it can never be alienated, and that the sovereign, which is only a collective being, cannot be represented except by itself. The power can be readily transferred, but not the will.

In fact, if it is not impossible for a particular will to agree on some point with the general will, it is at least impossible for this agreement to be durable and constant, for the particular will tends by its nature towards things it prefers, and the general will towards equality. It is even more impossible to have a guarantee of this agreement, even if it should always exist. That would be a result, not of art, but of chance. The sovereign could well say, "I now will what such and such a man wills or at least what he says he wills,"

*but it cannot say, "What this man is going to will tomorrow, I shall
will as well," because it is absurd that the will gives itself fetters for
the future and because no will is required to consent to anything
contrary to the good of the one doing the willing. Thus if a people
promises simply to obey, by that act it dissolves itself and loses its
quality as a people. The instant there is a master, there is no longer a
sovereign, and from that point on the body politic is destroyed.*[1]

While there have historically been many conceptions of and approaches to
understanding sovereignty, there is a good argument to be made that Jean-
Jacques Rousseau's (1712–78) conception of sovereignty remains one of the
most original, important, and influential in the history of political thought.
Not only would his conception of sovereignty inspire the upheavals of the
French Revolution,[2] but it would also go on to inspire countless influential
political theorists in his considerable wake, from Kant to Fichte to Hegel,
extending all the way to John Rawls in the twentieth century. And in an age
in which democratic regimes are flirting dangerously with variants of
right-wing populism and authoritarianism, there is a good case to be made
that Rousseau's conception of sovereignty is more important now than it
ever has been.

Rousseau conceives of his idea of sovereignty as a response to Thomas
Hobbes (1588–1679), who had characterized the sovereign as "that *mortal
god* to which we owe, under the *immortal God,* our peace and defense."[3]
For Hobbes, it is the essential nature of sovereignty that the power be
embodied in some person or persons—whom he calls the "sovereign" or
"Leviathan." While Hobbes urges that sovereigns follow what he called the
"laws of nature" in exercising their authority, there is no legal necessity that
they do so. Further, for Hobbes, sovereign authority must encompass all the
so-called branches of government—legislative, executive, and judicial. To
separate them, on his logic, would be to divide sovereign authority itself and
ultimately condemn the commonwealth to dissolution and destruction.

Rousseau would seek to reverse the course of the modern notion of
sovereignty in all these respects. First, he would not use the sovereign to
generate the Hobbesian terror to bring about the conformity of wills.
Second, he would unite the very notion of sovereignty with objective moral
and political truth. Third, he would separate the idea of sovereignty from
any particular individual. And finally, he would unite the sovereign with the
people united by their common interests, and then separate it from the
government or executive branch.

The excerpted passage above from Rousseau's *Social Contract* represents
the core argument that makes this unique conception of sovereignty possible.
Key to this passage is the central political concept in his political philosophy:

the general will—without which it is impossible to grasp his understanding of sovereignty, "since," as he insists, "sovereignty is nothing but the exercise of the general will." Although the general will had previously existed as a theological concept prior to Rousseau,[4] he would make it his own and convert it into a political one.

As he stresses in the above passage, and as he does repeatedly throughout his *Social Contract*, Rousseau describes the general will in contrast to a particular or private will. Every citizen has both a particular and a general will. The particular will tends toward what is personally beneficial; the general will tends toward what individual citizens have in common with their fellow citizens, or as he emphasizes above, toward equality. In much of our personal lives, according to Rousseau, we tend to be animated by our particular will. We do not, for example, consult the general will before deciding what to have for breakfast or what to wear on a given day. And this is perfectly fine, so far as it goes, since these decisions only affect ourselves. But where our decisions affect matters bearing on the common interest, we are morally obligated to make decisions according to the general will.

The most fundamental way in which citizens affect others is in their legislative capacity, which Rousseau assigns exclusively to the people.[5] The people must author their own laws, and they must do so according to their general will, rather than an aggregation of their particular wills (*SC*, 2.3).[6] That is to say, for Rousseau, the people are sovereign—but only insofar as their expressed wills correspond to the general will. Should the people—or, rather, a majority thereof—issue laws that seek to oppress or dominate any subset of the population, or legislate unjustly, there is no general will, and hence no sovereign.

This has three important implications for Rousseau's theory of sovereignty. First, sovereign power does not reside in the government, as it does for Hobbes. Rather, it resides with the people themselves. This position underwrites claims to *popular sovereignty*—an historically important doctrine in the development of sovereignty. Secondly, Rousseau goes a step further than the assertion of popular sovereignty to suggest that it cannot involve "the people" simply conceived. It must involve the people insofar as the will of its members conforms to the idea of the general will. This condition signals a clear departure from Hobbes' understanding that sovereignty resides in a particular concrete political office, because it connects it to an abstract political idea. Thirdly, whereas for Hobbes and Hobbesians the political authority of the government, qua sovereign, is absolute, for Rousseau governmental authority, being a mere servant of the sovereign people, is never absolute in itself.

It is worth exploring these elements of Rousseauian sovereignty and their implications further. First, it bears emphasizing that Hobbes' theory of sovereignty actually involves a *transfer* of authority in the social contract.[7] In the state of nature, individuals have what he calls the "right of nature"— the right to do whatever they want—but because they cannot exercise it effectively to maintain peace and stability, they are compelled by their precariousness and their reasoning faculties to transfer their rights to the Leviathan. This argument, as Helena Rosenblatt has noted, was developed by eighteenth-century Genevan natural law theorists, such as Jean Barbeyrac and Jean-Jacques Burlamaqui, who understood the "right of nature" to amount to individual sovereignty. For them, "sovereignty resided in the people originally, and once it had been transferred to the magistrates, the people were no longer sovereign."[8] Rousseau attributes this theory, somewhat cynically, to Grotius. Arguing that Grotius was attempting to ingratiate himself with King Louis XIII, he comments, "He spares no effort to rob the people of all their rights and to invest kings with them by every possible artifice" (SC, 2.2).

Rousseau's dramatic innovation in social contract theory was, rather than *transferring sovereignty* to a government, to facilitate the people in *retaining their own sovereignty*. This is what he means when he insists that sovereignty "can never be alienated" (SC, 2.1). For the people to transfer sovereignty to someone else, such as found in the political theory of Hobbes, Grotius, Burlamaqui, and Barbeyrac, is to institute a master–servant relationship between the government and the people: "if a people promises simply to obey, by that act it dissolves itself and loses its quality as a people. The instant there is a master, there is no longer a sovereign, and from that point on the body politic is destroyed" (SC, 2.2).[9] This is precisely the despotic relationship between masters and slaves Rousseau had described in his earlier work, The Discourse on the Origin and the Foundations of Inequality among Men (1754), in which "the despot is master only as long as he is the strongest."[10] For Rousseau, the choice is stark: a state may either have democratic sovereignty or despotism. There is nothing in between.

Rousseau's conception of democratic or popular sovereignty, however, needs further elaboration by considering the second important implication above: that popular sovereignty cannot be "the people" simply conceived. As suggested above, *sovereignty belongs to the people to the degree that they express the general will*, "since the sovereignty is nothing but the exercise of the general will" (SC, 2.1). While I have already explained that the general will is to be understood in contrast to particular wills, there remains a great deal more to be said. Most fundamentally, Rousseau's general will is grounded in his idea of justice. As he elaborates in his Discourse on Political Economy, "the most general will is also the most just."[11] Justice itself, for Rousseau, has metaphysical dimensions, insofar as it is "universal" (SC, 2.6) and "eternal."[12] As such, its content is "independent of human conventions" (SC, 2.6).[13] This means that in order for the people to legislate legitimately (viz., as sovereign, rather than as a collection of people), their laws must express the general will, or the idea of justice.[14] Rousseau's notion of sovereignty, thus, has a constraint absent in the Hobbesian system, since Hobbes' sovereigns are technically free to legislate in whatever way they choose, and as such, represent a threat to act arbitrarily.[15]

This being said, a metaphysical idea of justice can seem abstract and devoid of content. Yet Rousseau is careful to supply that content in his *Social Contract*. For him, "the goal of every system of legislation . . . comes down to these two principal objects: *liberty* and *equality*" (*SC*, 2.11). By "liberty" here Rousseau has in mind *civil liberty*, which he defines as the right to do what one wants, so long as it does not violate the general will— namely, the legitimate laws enacted by the sovereign people (*SC*, 1.8). But his conception of equality here is much more carefully sketched because, as he argues, there can be no meaningful liberty without equality. By "equality" he means a relative equality between citizens in both power and material circumstances. And since, for him, power is largely reducible to wealth,[16] his real focus is on economic equality. Thus it is a fundamental responsibility of the sovereign to ensure that "no citizen is rich enough to be able to purchase another, and none so poor that he is forced to sell himself" (*SC*, 2.11). The problem with economic inequality is that in facilitating the disproportionate and unjust influence of the rich, it undermines the civil liberty of the poor. The poor work in order to serve the rich and lack liberty for their own pursuits, depending as they must on the will of the rich.[17] Thus, he insists, it is imperative to "[b]ring the extremes together as much as possible. Tolerate neither rich people nor beggars. These two conditions, by nature inseparable, are equally fatal to the common good" (*SC*, 2.11n).[18]

For the people to arrive at the general will requires a rational effort on the part of individual citizens to transcend their own selfishness or particular wills. This distinguishes Rousseau, once more, from Hobbes, who rarely assumes the people are capable of this effort of moral psychology without external coercion. Once Rousseau's government has been established, its responsibility is to create an environment where citizens more instinctually gravitate toward willing the common good than their private interests.

The third implication of Rousseau's theory of sovereignty, distinguishing it again from its Hobbesian counterpart, is that while the sovereign general will of the people is absolute, its government is not. Namely, citizens can and should be free to challenge their government when that government deviates from the principles of the general will. Because the government is not sovereign, it has merely what Rousseau characterizes as a "borrowed and subordinate life" (*SC*, 3.1). Where a government acts beyond its mandate to carry out the general will, especially in pursuit of its own private will, as executives are sometimes tempted to do, they have effectively dissolved themselves, theoretically inviting revolution. While Rousseau himself is cautious about revolution,[19] others, including the French revolutionaries, found him inspirational.

To be sure, while Rousseau's conception of sovereignty as the general will has great appeal in theory, there remain unanswered questions about how it might play out in practice. For instance, what happens if people stubbornly pursue selfish and unjust practices? Rousseau argues that it is the role of the government to "force" these subjects "to be free" (*SC*, 1.7). At such moments, is the government sovereign and the people mere subjects? The answer is that the people are only sovereign when they are legislating, and legislating the general will at that. When they are doing so, they are to be called "citizens." When the government enforces the law enacted by citizens, the people are to be called "subjects" (*SC*, 1.6). But at no time, for Rousseau, is the government to be considered sovereign as it consists in nothing more than civil servants empowered merely to uphold the law passed by citizens. As he clearly insists, "the dominant will of the prince is not or should not be anything other than the general will or the law ... As soon as he wishes to derive from himself some absolute and independent act, the links of the whole begin to loosen ... and at that instant the social union would vanish and the body politic would dissolve" (*SC*, 3.1).

Such passages were an inspiration to figures involved in the French Revolution, who evoked Rousseau's conception of sovereignty to argue that the *Ancien Regime* had exceeded its mandate. But beyond this, Rousseau's legacy would also substantially influence Kant, who expressly embraces the general will in his *Metaphysics of Morals*.[20] Rousseau's legacy continues to this very day as perhaps the most compelling of all arguments for popular sovereignty, insofar as he challenges the people to be the very best version of themselves. Yet its associations with the more violent dimensions of the Revolution have likewise fostered less enthusiastic interpretations that also persist to the present.[21] All this serves as a reminder that Rousseau's conception of sovereignty remains as influential and contested a theory of sovereignty as any in the history of political thought.

Notes

1   Jean-Jacques Rousseau, *The Social Contract*, 2.1. All references to the text are by book and chapter numbers of the version found in *Jean-Jacques Rousseau: Fundamental Political Writings*, ed. Matthew W. Maguire and David Lay Williams (Peterborough, Ontario: Broadview Press, [1762] 2018).

2   Although Rousseau surely would have objected to the Revolution's excesses, especially the Terror.

3   *Leviathan*, 17.13. Cited from Thomas Hobbes, *Leviathan*, ed. A. P. Martinich and Brian Battiste, 2nd ed. (Peterborough, Ontario: Broadview Press, [1651] 2011). All Hobbes references are to chapter and paragraph number.

4   See Patrick Riley, *The General Will before Rousseau: The Transformation of the Divine into the Civic* (Princeton, NJ: Princeton University Press, 1986); and James Farr and David Lay Williams, *The General Will: The Evolution of a Concept* (Cambridge: Cambridge University Press, 2015).

5   I speak here of ordinary legislation, or the passing of statutes. He assigns extraordinary legislation, or the authoring of constitutions, to the character of the "lawgiver" (*SC*, 2.7).

6   Some have asked if Rousseau's introduction of the character of the Lawgiver (*SC*, 2.7) complicates or even undermines the people's sovereignty. See Patrick Riley, *Will and Political Legitimacy: A Critical Exposition of Social Contract Theory in Hobbes, Locke, Rousseau, Kant, and Hegel* (Cambridge, MA: Harvard University Press, 1981), ch. 4.

7   *Leviathan*, 14.8–10.

8   Helena Rosenblatt, *Rousseau and Geneva: From the "First Discourse" to the "Social Contract," 1749–1762* (Cambridge: Cambridge University Press, 1997), 99.

9   One important implication of this argument is Rousseau's rejection of representative government (*SC*, 3.15).

10 Jean-Jacques, Rousseau, "The Discourse on the Origin and the Foundations of Inequality among Men," in *Jean-Jacques Rousseau: Fundamental Political Writings*, 160.

11 Jean-Jacques Rousseau, "Discourse on Political Economy," in *The Social Contract and Other Later Political Writings*, ed. Victor Gourevitch (Cambridge: Cambridge University Press, [1755] 1997), 8.

12 See also Jean-Jacques Rousseau, *Letter to M. d'Alembert on the Theater*, trans. Allan Bloom (Ithaca, NY: Cornell University Press, [1758] 1960), 66; Jean-Jacques Rousseau, *Emile, or On Education*, trans. Allan Bloom (New York: Basic Books, [1762] 1979), 259, 292, 473.

13 I note here that my interpretation of the general will in this respect is at sharp odds with much of the scholarship (e.g. Leo Strauss, *Natural Right and History* (Chicago: University of Chicago Press [1953] 1965); Roger D. Masters, *The Political Philosophy of Rousseau* (Princeton: Princeton University Press, 1968); Arthur M. Melzer, "Rousseau's Moral Realism: Replacing Natural Law with the General Will," *American Political Science Review* 77, no. 3 (1983): 633–51; and John T. Scott, "Politics as an Imitation of the Divine in Rousseau's *Social Contract*," *Polity* 26, no. 3 (1994): 473–501). I address their interpretations in some depth in David Lay Williams, *Rousseau's Platonic Enlightenment* (University Park, PA: Pennsylvania State University Press, 2007) 98–114; and *Rousseau's "Social Contract": An Introduction* (Cambridge: Cambridge University Press, 2014), 255–9.

14 See Jean-Jacques Rousseau, "Letters Written from the Mountain," in *Letter to Beaumont, Letters Written from the Mountain, and Related Writings*, ed. Christopher Kelly and Eve Grace, vol. 9 of *The Collected Writings of Rousseau* (Hanover, NH: University Press of New England [1764] 2001), 232.

15 This being said, Hobbes strongly believes it is prudent for sovereigns to legislate in accordance with the laws of nature.

16 See Part II of his "Discourse on Inequality," 158.

17 Rousseau expressly elaborates on the dangers of dependence in Book II of his *Emile* (85). For discussions of Rousseau's treatment of dependence see Timothy O'Hagan, *Rousseau* (London: Routledge, 1999), 92–100; and Frederick

Neuhouser, *Rousseau's Critique of Inequality: Reconstructing the Second Discourse* (Cambridge: Cambridge University Press, 2015), 168–75.

18 I note here that in specifically this respect, Rousseau is not radically different from Hobbes, who compares the concentration of "too much abundance in one or a few private men" with the disease of pleurisy (*Leviathan*, 29.19). I address this in my forthcoming book, *"The Greatest of All Plagues": Economic Inequality in Western Political Thought* (Princeton, NJ: Princeton University Press).

19 *Emile*, 310; see Blaise Bachofen, "Why Rousseau Mistrusts Revolutions: Rousseau's Paradoxical Conservatism," in *Rousseau and Revolution*, ed. Holger Ross Lauritsen and Mikkel Thorup (London: Continuum, 2011).

20 "[S]overeignty . . . is itself the united will of the citizens," Immanuel Kant, *The Metaphysics of Morals*, trans. Mary Gregor (Cambridge: Cambridge University Press, [1797] 2017), 121.

21 E.g. Isaiah Berlin, *Freedom and its Betrayal: Six Enemies of Human Liberty*, ed. Henry Hardy (Princeton: Princeton University Press, 2002), 49; Bertrand Russell, *A History of Western Philosophy* (New York: Simon and Schuster, 1945] 1972), 700; Karl Popper, *The Open Society and its Enemies, Volume I: The Spell of Plato* (Princeton: Princeton University Press, [1945] 1971), 257, n. 20. Against this reading of Rousseau's conception of sovereignty as hostile to individuals, see Michael Locke McLendon, *The Psychology of Inequality: Rousseau's "Amour-Propre"* (Philadelphia, PA: University of Pennsylvania Press), 116–7.

15

Sovereignty in the American Founding

Michael Zuckert

*There is and must be in all forms of government a supreme,
irresistible, absolute, and uncontrolled Authority, in which Jura
summi imperii, or rights of sovereignty reside.*[1]

*Be it declared that the colonies in America have been, are,
and of right ought to be, subordinate unto and dependent
upon the Imperial Crown and Parliament of Great Britain in
all cases whatsoever.*[2]

*Each state retains its sovereignty, freedom and Independence,
and every Power, jurisdiction and right which is not by
this confederation expressly delegated to the United States,
in Congress assembled.*[3]

*But is not the Constitution itself necessarily the offspring of a
sovereign authority? What but the highest political Authority, a
sovereign Authority, could make such a constitution? And where
does the sovereignty which makes such a constitution reside? It
resides not in a single state but in the people of each of the several
states, uniting with those of the others in the express and solemn
compact which forms the Constitution. To the extent of that
compact or Constitution therefore, the people of the several states
must be sovereign as they are a united people.*[4]

The United States was born in one debate about sovereignty and nearly died in another. The American Revolution was prompted largely by a conflict over where sovereignty lay in the extended British Empire and nearly collapsed in a Civil War prompted largely by debate over where sovereignty lay within the American Union.

The ten years of constitutional conflict with Britain leading up to the Revolution featured sovereignty as one of its leading elements. As William Blackstone said in his Commentaries on the Laws of England, quoted in the first excerpt above, "there must be a supreme, irresistible, absolute, and uncontrolled Authority," possessing the rights of supreme dominion in every political community, no matter its particular form of government. As "supreme," the sovereign authority must, among other things, be undivided and indivisible, for if truly divided there would be no supreme authority.

The idea of sovereignty emerged in its mature form in the writings of Jean Bodin during the sixteenth century, but it was a product of a long gestation period during the Middle Ages. The impetus to the development of the idea was the long contest between sacred and secular authorities, which prompted thinking about the problem of supremacy as such.[5] The force of the idea derived from a combination of logical and practical considerations, which entranced thinkers of the seventeenth and eighteenth centuries. The very logic of the idea of sovereignty was irresistible, elevating it for many to the status of a "first principle, upon which all subsequent reasoning must depend." Such first principles contained, as Alexander Hamilton put it, "an internal evidence, which, antecedent to all reflection or combination, commands the assent of the mind."[6] What proved so compelling was the simple logic of "supremacy": Supremacy is supremacy is supremacy.[7] Here was a truth that no reasoning and no evidence could shake. As Samuel Johnson said during the British–American conflict: "in sovereignty, there are no gradations."[8]

The power or right to give law, the characteristic of the state, implies or derives from "supremacy"; that power or right cannot be controlled or controllable, for then the controller would be "supreme" over the one supposed to be sovereign. There can then be no enforcement of limits on sovereign power; such limits as may exist are moral or theological, that is, without enforcement in this world; such responsibility as there is to those limits is to God or to the sovereign's conscience alone. For all practical purposes, then, sovereign power is absolute and arbitrary. As Martin Howard, a parliamentary sympathizer, said during the Stamp Act crisis in 1765: "it is of the essence of government, that there should be a supreme head, and it would be a solecism in politics to talk of members independent of it."[9] The logic of supremacy was reinforced by an appreciation of the dangers of anarchy and disorder, which were the heritage of the Reformation-inspired political disorders often based on reservations on behalf of individual conscience against the claims of political authority. No group and no individual could be granted a right to withhold obedience or even to judge of the rightfulness of obedience. The demands of political life are in principle illimitable; however prudent it may be not to exercise some power or other, one could never say in advance that the public good may not require its exercise. *Salus populi suprema lex*, the welfare of the people is the supreme law, as even John Locke said in his constitutionalist *Two Treatises of Government*.[10] The American Thomas Hutchinson gave a fine statement of the way the logical and the practical arguments coalesced when he asserted that "it is essential to the being of government that a power should always exist which no other power can have a right to withstand or control."[11]

The medieval struggle between sacred and secular authorities had led to the initial emergence of the doctrine of sovereignty, and the struggle between crown and Parliament in seventeenth-century England ultimately committed Britain to a doctrine of parliamentary sovereignty.[12] Not the older constitution of the common lawyers, more or less oblivious to the very notion of sovereignty, but the sovereignty-affirming constitution of Blackstone emerged from these struggles: Parliament possessed the sovereignty, that is, unbridled legal power.[13] It was as though the very idea of sovereignty had a Midas-like power to transform whatever it touched, for the parliamentary party, at first only attempting to redress or restore the constitutional order unbalanced by the Stuarts and to resist the claim to sovereignty raised by Stuart spokesmen, ended up claiming for itself the powers it denied the king. Once launched, "the doctrine of sovereignty was the single most important abstraction of politics of the entire revolutionary era", as historian Gordon Wood averred.[14] The second opening excerpt, the main test of the Declaratory Act of 1766, reveals that the parliamentary claim of sovereignty was extended over the colonies as well as the homeland, in its assertion of a right to legislate for the colonies "in all cases whatsoever."

In the earlier phases of the conflict, American spokesmen felt able either to evade the issue of sovereignty altogether while attempting to resist parliamentary authority, or to endorse it at the same time that they sought to resist parliamentary authority by staking out positions that coexisted most uneasily with their affirmations of sovereignty. In the latter category, for example, belonged the great hero of the 1760s, James Otis. According to Otis, government is founded on laws as unchangeable and necessary as the law of gravity. It cannot, therefore, rest on "mere compact"; men are not free to make governments according to their arbitrary will. But following Locke, he insisted they cannot rightfully make an absolute arbitrary government, for the ends of government, the security of rights, the *salus populi*, the satisfaction of "the great law of self-preservation" are incompatible with that kind of government.[15]

On the other hand, men are not free to create government arbitrarily lacking in power either: there must be supreme legislative and supreme executive power somewhere. In the British Empire, that supreme power is lodged in Parliament, which "has an undoubted right to make acts equally binding [on the colonists] as upon the subjects of Great Britain." Thus Otis put no weight on the colonial charters, for he conceded Parliament's right to rescind these.[16]

Even without the charters, however, Americans possess rights as "men, citizens, and British subjects." Those rights stand as limits to what government may rightfully do, and in the final analysis would justify revolution if government failed to respect or secure them. Actions taken against those rights by Parliament are "void." Thus Otis takes away with one hand the sovereign authority he gives with the other. Spokesmen for the British position both in England and in America, as well as many contemporary historians, found Otis' position obscure, or even contradictory. Otis recognized Parliament as sovereign, but he denied it the power to, for example, tax the Americans. The contradiction was visible to the British and to many Americans as well. Once one admits sovereignty, it is difficult to draw limits around it, as Otis tried to do. In response to this problem the Americans eventually modified their stance on sovereignty.

The most common American position, however, until around 1774, was to dodge the issue of sovereignty.[17] At first, then, American opinion was not dominated by the logical juggernaut of sovereignty. But as the conflict wore on and as the colonists themselves were driven deeper into the issues by the shifting character of the challenges they faced, they too fell under the sway of sovereignty.[18] But they refused to concede the British position. If sovereignty there must be, agreed the Americans, Parliament cannot be the possessor of it. In the course of their controversy with the British, they insisted that political power as such must be understood as subordinate to and for the sake of security of rights. Recognition of parliamentary sovereignty did not promise to conduce to the ends of government, since, under conditions of life in the British Empire, the Americans were not and could not effectively be represented in Parliament. The logic of their thinking meant sovereignty must lie elsewhere, not in Parliament, but in agencies more responsible to the governed. That is to say, the legislative power must lie in the colonial legislatures. The king, not Parliament, was the head and unifying force of the Empire. This "mature" constitutional position was premised on an acceptance of the logic of sovereignty, and a rejection of the idea that Parliament possessed it.[19] The Americans saw the Empire as a unit composed of separate and independent political entities, sharing a common king, but possessing separate legislative authorities. Since the Americans, under the aegis of the idea of sovereignty, had reinterpreted the Empire as a certain sort of confederacy, it is no wonder that when they had a freer hand, under the aegis of the same idea, they constructed a particularly pure or principled sort of Constitution in the Articles of Confederation. As my third opening excerpt illustrates, they bannered the principle of sovereignty very early in its text when they pronounced each state to retain its sovereignty within the confederacy.

The concern with sovereignty went much deeper than mere declarations. The Articles created a system especially scrupulous in treating its member states as its citizens, treating them as sovereign entities in their own right. Each state was therefore equal in political rights in the Confederacy. Changes in the terms of the agreement, that is, amendments of the Articles, required unanimity. Article III stated the purpose of the Confederacy: The States created a "firm League of friendship", for their "common defense, the security of their [that is the states'] liberties, and their [again, the states'] mutual and general welfare." The general government had responsibility for matters of peace and war, but had no control of the instrumentalities of peace and war, depending entirely on requisitions or requests to the states for men and money.

Indeed, so sovereignty-obsessed was the Article of Confederation's system that the very name of government could be denied to it. In order to vindicate the labeling of the member states as sovereign, there was no coercive authority whatever granted to the federation government to compel state compliance with confederation policy. But, according to Madison,

> government implies the idea of making laws. It is essential to the idea of a law, that it be attended with a sanction or, in other words a penalty or punishment for disobedience. If there be no penalty annexed to disobedience, the resolutions or commands which pretend to be law will, in fact, amount to nothing more than advice or recommendation.[20]

Unfortunately, that "government" failed, as Madison diagnosed, to provide effective governance. The Articles' "government" was made a creature of the states in the deepest way: it had no higher legal status than any ordinary piece of legislation passed by a state legislature. As an intellectual fabric, the Articles of Confederation possessed an austere beauty, deriving from the consistency and purity of the logic of its construction. They reveal the power of that transformative idea of sovereignty, which gave to the world a beautiful model of pure, that is, sovereignty-obsessed federalism. The result, however, was that not only the Federalists, but even those who became Anti-Federalists conceded that the system required remodeling. Successful remodeling of Union would require, at the minimum, the taming of sovereignty.

As is well known, the first foundation for the new constitution was laid in the so-called Virginia Plan, a sketch of government introduced early in the Constitutional Convention by the delegates from Virginia. That plan in effect addressed the issue of sovereignty in its final resolution, which provided that the product of the convention should be considered for adoption by "an assembly of Representatives expressly chosen by the people to consider and decide thereon." Unlike the Articles of Confederation, adopted by the state legislatures, the new constitution was to be adopted by the people or rather their representatives chosen expressly for that purpose.

This was understood by the founding generation to establish the authority of the new constitution directly on the sovereign people and thus to place it in a position of (at least) equality with the state governments. It was to rest as much on the people as the state governments did and thus not to be conceived as in any way a creature of and thereby subordinate to the states. This practical development was based on an adaptation of the theoretical insight that underlay the Articles and was nestled within the American political philosophical orientation all along: the notion of popular sovereignty affirmed within the Lockean political theory most of the Americans adhered to. This doctrine allowed a distinction between the sovereign and the government, and thereby the maintenance of the qualities of sovereignty in the people—supreme, indivisible, and all that—while allowing with no logical contradiction the division of governmental powers. The Americans could then institute both federalism and separation of powers, two sets of institutions that the theretofore reigning doctrine of sovereignty had rendered extremely problematical.

The application of the popular sovereignty idea to the American order was complex, for what the people were consenting to in their exercise of their sovereignty was the total constitutional order, according to which the pooled people of the entire consenting states were adopting and legitimating the Constitution for the government of the United States and at the same time putting the constitutional order of their own states on the solid footing of popular sovereignty. The people were legitimizing not only the two different constitutional orders but the relations between them as specified in the Constitution of the United States.

This solution proved to be both a brilliant and a problematic resolution to the problem the rights-oriented Americans faced in their effort to set up governments limited by divided and checked powers. Although in theory the American solution should have been clear enough, there were sufficient ambiguities that there arose the claim that sovereignty remained as much with the states as it had before the new Constitution. The ambiguity arose chiefly from the fact that ratification occurred state by state and was interpreted by some to be a mere exercise of the continuing sovereign power of the people of each state.

On this notion arose the idea of the legitimacy of state nullification of federal laws that individual states considered unconstitutional, and finally of the constitutional right to secede from the Union. As Madison makes clear in my fourth opening excerpt, neither of these claims is theoretically valid. The sovereign authority authorizing the Constitution is not the individual state but the pooled populace of the states that ratified the Constitution—all of them as it happened. The individual state constitutions and the US Constitution in effect have two different but overlapping authorizing bodies—the whole people of the United States, what Madison called "the people of the several states," in the case of the Constitution of the United States, and the people of each separate state in the cases of the state constitutions. Vis-à-vis the US Constitution the people of the individual states are not the sovereign body. They have pooled their sovereignty to create a new sovereign body of which they are only a part. The individual states have as little right to withdraw from the union as an individual county or town would have to withdraw from its state.

The theory may be clear if complex but it took a Civil War to supply a more definitive resolution to the problem of sovereignty in practice. After the war, amendments were added to the Constitution that led the Supreme Court to put forth a formula for the nature of the union that no longer could be held to support the idea of state sovereignty: an indestructible union of indestructible states.[21]

The Court thus embraced a conception of the nation that the doctrine of sovereignty had declared to be an impossibility. Although the American resolution had its difficulties, it has nonetheless served as a vehicle for the taming of sovereignty. It has shown that the inexorable logic of "supremacy is supremacy is supremacy" need not stand in the way of efforts to divide and limit political authority and thus to institute free and non-authoritarian regimes.

Notes

1   William Blackstone, *Commentaries on the Laws of England* (1765; Chicago: University of Chicago Press, 1979), vol. 1, 49.

2   "The Declaratory Act" (1766), in *Documents of American History*, ed. Henry Steele Commager, 7th ed. (New York: Appleton Century Crofts, 1963), 60.

3   "Articles of Confederation" (1781), Article II, in Commager, *Documents*, 111.

4   James Madison, "Notes on Nullification" (1836), in *The Mind of the Founder: Sources of the Political Thought of James Madison*, ed. Marvin Meyers (Waltham, MA: Brandeis University Press, 1973), 436–7.

5   For a useful survey of the history of political thinking on sovereignty, see Ferdinand E. M. Bullowa, The *History of the Theory of Sovereignty* (1895; Mishawaka, IN: Palala Press, 2015).

6   "The Federalist No. 31," in Alexander Hamilton, John Jay, and James Madison, *The Federalist Papers*, ed. George W. Carey and James McClellan (1788; Indianapolis: The Liberty Fund, 2001), 150.

7   The word "sovereign" derives from the Latin "superannus", which means "supreme." Bullowa, 5–6.

8   Samuel Johnson, *Taxation no Tyranny*, quoted in Randolph G. Adams, *The Political Ideas of the American Revolution: Brittanic-American Contributions to the Problem of Imperial Organization, 1765–1775* (New York: Barnes and Noble, 1939), 9.

9   Martin Howard, "A Letter from a Gentleman at Halifax," reprinted in *Tracts of the American Revolution, 1763–1776*, ed. Merrill Jensen (Indianapolis, IN: Bobbs-Merrill, 1967), 67.

10 John Locke, *Two Treatises of Government* (Cambridge: Cambridge University Press, 1992), II, 158; and see the chapter on Locke in this volume.

11 Quoted in Bernard Bailyn, *The Ideological Origins of the American Revolution* (Cambridge, MA: Harvard University Press, 1967), 222.

12 See Chapter 11 on the debate between Henry Parker and King Charles in this volume.

13 Cf. George L. Mosse, *The Struggle for Sovereignty in England: From the Reign of Queen Elizabeth to the Petition of Right* (East Lansing, MI: Michigan State College Press, 1950); Adams, *Political Ideas*, 123–4.

14 Gordon Wood, *The Creation of the American Republic, 1776–1787* (Chapel Hill, NC: University of North Carolina Press, 1969), 345.

15 James Otis, "The Rights of the British Colonies Asserted and Proved," in *Pamphlets of the American Revolution*, ed. Bernard Bailyn (Cambridge, MA: Harvard University Press, 1965), I, 423–6.

16 Ibid., 426.

17 Bailyn, *Ideological Origins*, 208.

18 Wood, *Creation*, Ch. IX.

19 See Thomas Jefferson in his "A Summary View of the Rights of British America," John Adams in his "Novanglus" essays, and James Wilson in his "Considerations on the Nature and Extent of Legislative Authority of the British Parliament." The former two are reprinted in Jensen, *Tracts*. For a discussion of other sources of this theory, see Adams, *Political Ideas*, Ch. III.

20 James Madison, "Vices of the Political System of the United States," in *The Mind of the Founder*, 59–60.

21 *Texas v White* 74 US 700 (1869).

16

Thomas Paine

Reinventing Popular Sovereignty in an Age of Revolutions

Carine Lounissi

Every government, let its form be what it may, contains within itself a principle common to all, which is, that of a sovereign power, or a power over which there is no control, and which controls all others: and as it is impossible to construct a form of government in which this power does not exist, so there must of necessity be a place, if it may be so called, for it to exist in.

In despotic monarchies this power is lodged in a single person, or sovereign. His will is law; which he declares, alters or revokes as he pleases, without being accountable to any power for so doing. Therefore, the only modes of redress, in countries so governed, are by petition or insurrection. And this is the reason we so frequently hear of insurrections in despotic governments; for as there are but two modes of redress, this is one of them.

Perhaps it may be said that as the united resistance of the people is able, by force, to control the will of the sovereign, that therefore, the controlling power lodges in them; but it must be understood that I am speaking of such powers only as are constituent parts of the government, not of those powers which are externally applied to resist and overturn it.

In republics, such as those established in America, the sovereign power, or the power over which there is no control, and which controls all others, remains where nature placed it—in the people; for the people in America are the fountain of power. It remains there as a matter of right, recognized in the constitutions of the country, and the exercise of it is constitutional and legal. This sovereignty is exercised in electing and deputing a certain number of persons to represent and act for the whole, and who, if they do not act right, may be displaced by the same power that placed them there, and others elected and deputed in their stead, and the wrong measures of former representatives corrected and brought right by this means. Therefore the republican form and principle leaves no room for insurrection, because it provides and establishes a rightful means in its stead.[1]

As early as January 1776 Paine reshaped the modern concept of revolution, i.e. a radical change through which the people would replace an illegitimate despotic government by a legitimate democratic one. In contrast to John Locke's idea that the consent of the people might be legitimately invoked to found any type of government, including monarchy,[2] Paine was convinced from the very start of his career as a successful pamphleteer that this consent could only lead to the setup of a democratic or representative government. This meant that monarchy, whether hereditary or not, could not have been the result of the deliberative process taking place in the primary assembly that naturally gathered the first people in the state of nature or in a settlement by immigrants in the case of North America. Paine would henceforth never stop endeavoring to convince his readers that all forms of monarchy were illegitimate and could have only been imposed on the people through the invention of fictional and fictitious origins whose veracity it was forbidden to investigate. So, popular sovereignty was the only possible source of legitimacy for a regime and the only legitimate government was that which enabled the people to exercise their sovereignty continuously.

Therefore, sovereignty was a key concept in Paine's political thought, for Paine was a thinker as well as a brilliant polemicist. Yet, he did not use the word itself very often, especially because he had to retrieve it from the monarchical language that had, in his opinion, usurped the word as well as the power it designated. One of the few writings in which he dwelt on this notion longer is a text he published at the end of his first stay in America. He published *Dissertations on Government* in 1786 in the context of the debates triggered by the democratic experiment in Pennsylvania. This writing has been quite neglected by Paine scholars who have instead focused on the works that circulated most extensively in America and in Europe.

Dissertations on Government, which appeared after *Common Sense* (1776) and before *Rights of Man* (1791–2), is a major step in Paine's reflection on representative governments and may be considered as connecting his two most famous writings. It is indeed the only text of the known Paine corpus in which he provided a definition of sovereignty. Paine's understanding of the term as "the power over which there is no control, and which controls all others" is reminiscent of Bodin's view of it as "absolute and perpetual."[3] Yet, in contrast to Bodin, Paine posited that this "sovereign power" belonged to all men equally and that this right could rationally be exercised only in order to consent to a government defending the fundamental rights of the people, including the right to have a say in the affairs of the polity or the right to vote and to petition. Nevertheless, Paine kept from Bodin's definition (whatever the medium through which he saw it) the notion that sovereignty perpetually belonged to those who had delegated it and that once the term for holding an executive or a legislative power was over, it had to revert to the original source of sovereignty. In addition, Bodin's sovereign power was limited only by "the law of God or of nature."[4] In Paine's view this limitation meant the natural rights of the people. As a result, Paine reinterpreted Bodin's concept in order to fit it in his theory of the representative regime.

Paine showed that the only regime in which sovereignty could be effectively exercised was a republic, whereas Bodin's flexible idea of the republic as referring to any form of regime encompassed monarchy. This was a point that Paine could never endorse, even in 1792 in the second part of *Rights of Man*, in which he commented on the "res publica."[5] In Paine's system the only way to the commonwealth or the common good is in a republican regime that necessarily coincides with the exercise of true, popular sovereignty. Paine did not distinguish monarchy from "despotism" or tyranny. All three originated in a usurpation of sovereignty that was both political and linguistic. As "monarch" and "sovereign" had become synonymous, Paine deconstructed the traditional language of sovereignty used by monarchs and courtiers. In *Common Sense*, he famously proposed a ritual which would symbolically place sovereignty back where it belonged through the physical destruction of a crown whose parts should be "scattered among the people" (CS, 34). In the second part of *Rights of Man*, he explained that "representation is of itself the delegated monarchy of a nation" (RM2, 233). So, what he expounded in *Dissertations on Government* is the more theoretical side of his argument, which he simplified in the other two writings.

As Paine clearly stated in the extract selected here, sovereignty is a power but not one based on mere "physical" force. Even if resisting a despotic regime is an act of sovereignty, the meaning and legitimacy of a revolution lies in the natural right of all to take part in the government. Coercion and

force do not make a more legitimate ground for revolution than they do for
a despotic regime, which is itself founded on this forceful seizure of power.
Violence alone cannot therefore be the basis for any stable and free political
regime. This would be one of the bones of contention between Paine and
Burke in 1791–2. Burke contended that the French Revolution was an
illegitimate form of upheaval since the people and the National Assembly
had resorted to sheer and gratuitous violence to overthrow the French
monarchy. Paine then had to explain to what extent violence was sometimes
necessary in revolutions and to reinforce his theory that what made the
revolution legitimate was both the right on which it relied and its confirmation
through the constructive phase of the revolution.

Sovereignty seems to have been in Paine's view a power, a right and a will.
It belongs to each individual, but it makes up a collective power, a collective
right and a collective will. The "will" of the usurper of sovereignty, the
monarch or despot, is not sufficient to guarantee the government's focus on
the public good. The common will of the people only can aim at the
common weal. The executive power cannot be a sovereign power in a
republic. As Paine demonstrated in *Dissertations on First Principles of
Government*, published in the context of the debate of the new republican
constitution in France, "it is impossible to conceive the idea of two
sovereignties, a sovereignty to *will* and a sovereignty to *act*" (DFP, 406,
Paine's emphasis). The will of the monarch is a fake sovereignty since it is
most of the time only fancy and impulsion. Reason is thus not compatible
with the exclusive rule of one individual. As Paine asserted in 1786 in
Dissertations on Government a few paragraphs below the excerpt above,
"sovereign power without sovereign knowledge" is despotism.[6] The
deliberative process alone can lead to potentially rational decisions or at
least to compromises based on debates in which reason may have a chance
to prevail. Later, in the context of the French Revolution, Paine would adopt
the phrase "general will," but without ascribing the precise meaning
Rousseau had given to it.

As a result, the republican government is a representative one. Founding
a political regime is an act of sovereignty on the part of the people and
voting is essential to guarantee and preserve this sovereignty. The continuous
exercise of sovereignty through elections maintains the vitality of the system
that is kept in "constant maturity," as Paine pointed out in *Rights of Man II*.
It prevents the separation of the political and physical bodies of the sovereign,
as was the case in monarchies. In the same passage of *Rights of Man II*,
Paine even called for a Copernician decentering in politics as he rejected the
Hobbesian view of the body of Leviathan as made up of the nation. He
offered to replace it by the quite Vitruvian (or Da Vincian) image of the
body politic "within a circle, having a common center, in which every radius
meets; and that center is formed by representation" (RM2, 233). This image
visually conveyed what Paine said about the need for a combination of
"knowledge" and "power" which is "concentrated" or literally at the center

of the circle of sovereignty, whereas monarchy is outside this circle and is "eccentric" (RM2, 233).

Replacing what Paine sees as an absurd political construction of sovereignty by a more "natural" one is both a political and an intellectual revolution. The republican scheme will then guarantee the freedom of all, governed and governors alike. As the rights of all are secured through the system of representation, it means that "sovereignty" and "freedom" coincide. As Paine concluded a few lines below the extract selected here, "wherever the sovereignty is, there must the freedom be." When the people exercise their sovereignty, they substitute autonomy for heteronomy and can see to it that neither constitutional clause nor ordinary law will damage their interests. They will indeed have the "rightful means" to question the actions of their representatives and obtain redress through debate and deliberation.

Paine wrote this passage on sovereignty in a context of agitation in Pennsylvania in the mid-1780s, which would ultimately lead to the writing of a new Constitution for the State in 1790. The argument relies on at least two assumptions: the people always deliberate in the right way in the end and never willingly agree to measures against their own rights and interests; deliberation is conducted in a rational way or in such a manner that reason or common sense may prevail. In Pennsylvania in the mid-1780s Paine avowedly faced situations that did not meet the second requirement. He deplored the partisanship that had corrupted the deliberative process and meant that representatives acted as members of factions or parties, not as representatives of the people. As a consequence, representation itself did not secure either the rational character of the debates or the public good. Paine felt the need to remind the citizens of Pennsylvania that the republican regime was based on a moral agreement among them. Since a republic is the opposite of despotism in terms of governmental organization, it means that it should reflect this principle at an individual level as well. In other words, sovereignty as a right implies the duty of being fair to one another. In *Dissertations on Government*, Paine epitomized this idea by underlining that "a republic, properly understood, is a sovereignty of justice, in contradistinction to a sovereignty of will."[7]

Partisanship may have been the most serious threat on the exercise of sovereignty as conducive to the public good and to the fairest decision. In the second part of *Rights of Man*, Paine endorsed Madison's conclusion in *The Federalist* according to which representation was better "even in small territories" (RM2, 233). Yet, it is not clear whether he agreed with Madison's theory of factions. He suggested the temporary division of the legislative during the deliberative phase before the several committees be reunited in one assembly for the final vote (RM2, 254). He was soon faced even more directly with the limits of the first postulate of his republican theory. He indeed experienced the divergence between the people and their representation in France after 1792 as a member of the French Convention. During Louis XVI's trial, Paine argued in favor of the sentence that the Convention was authorized to pass, i.e. banishment. A death sentence would have required a resort to the electorate or primary assemblies. Paine rejected such a referendum in January 1793 both in his speech dated January 7 and during the vote on this question ten days later. He perceived this moment as one of conflict between sovereignty and representation. It would intensify in the coming months. In the spring, Paine witnessed what may have been the most serious crisis in the representative system with which he was ever confronted. In the letter he sent to Danton on May 6, 1793, he denounced the open conflict between sovereignty and representation, this time opposing the Parisian sections, the "representatives of the departments" and "the representation itself."

Paine was imprisoned in December 1793, both because he was a foreigner and an alleged "Girondin." After he was released and rehabilitated in the winter 1794, he defended the right to continuous sovereignty through universal male suffrage, in contrast to conservatives who blamed the Terror on this very form of suffrage. It was in the context of the debate in the spring and summer 1795 on both the new French constitution and the origins of the Terror that he had to defend the right to vote as the soil in which the republican regime is rooted. In *Dissertation on First Principles of Government*, he explained that "the right of voting is the primary right by which other rights are protected" (DFP, 398). He also confirmed and specified what he had written in 1786 about the fact that "the republican form and principle leaves no room for insurrection." In this context, he addressed the question of minority and majority in a republic. In the case that the minority was "right" whereas the majority was "wrong," he posited that the minority would soon manage to convince the majority provided two essential conditions were met: "freedom of opinion and equality of rights" (DFP, 405). Paine thus admitted that democracy did not always lead to the best decision making as reason was not always on the side of the majority. In other words, democracy could work only if combined to republican principles, i.e. equal rights and a free public sphere where debate could take place, which would both put things back in order again as if by a natural mechanism. The association of sovereignty, democracy and republic would guarantee the public good and prevent the tyranny of the majority.

Even if during the summer 1795 Paine opposed the restriction of the right to vote in the new French Constitution, he eventually supported the Directorial republic against the threats of monarchists, as did many French and American republicans after 1795. In *Agrarian Justice*, published in 1797, Paine still saw the lack of universal suffrage as the source of both the conservative and communist uprisings against the *Directoire*. Yet, a few months later, in September, he defended the resort to force to invalidate the results of the elections in which representatives in favor of the restoration of monarchy obtained the majority. The potential return to monarchy justified exceptional measures, even if it implied violating the rule of the majority. In this *Letter to the People of France and the French Armies on the Event of the 18th Fructidor*, Paine did not repeat his attacks against the restricted franchise. He instead extolled the Constitution of 1795.[8] He failed to probe the implications of what he had stated in 1795 and the potential contradiction with his support of the 18th Fructidor coup, thus missing an opportunity to further explore the complex question of the balance between majority and minority in a representative regime.

Despite the moments of violence and injustice he lived through in France, Paine did not renounce his commitment to republicanism and popular sovereignty. When he came back to the United States in the early 1800s, he attempted to revive the flame of 1776, but he found a country quite different from the one he had left more than a decade earlier. Paine elaborated his concept of sovereignty in specific contexts that he perceived as critical. *Common Sense* and *Rights of Man* were and still are Paine's bestsellers, but it was maybe in less pressing moments, in 1786 in Pennsylvania and in 1795 in France, once the republican principle was secured, that he managed to probe the notion of sovereignty. Paine's view on popular sovereignty as the uniquely sound basis on which to build a legitimate and just government did not change. He made this principle explicit in *Dissertations on Government* and also began to recommend an extended suffrage for men. However, Paine did not actively defend the right to vote for other categories of the American or European populations, women and blacks. He barely touched on the subject, so it is hard to know what he really thought about it. Yet, even if the sovereignty he defended was not fully "universal" by our own standards, this does not undermine the value and validity of his theory. Popular sovereignty was the keystone of his conception of the republic and his reflections on these topics may be a valuable legacy to think about these issues in the present day.

Notes

1   Thomas Paine, "Dissertations on Government," in Thomas Paine, *The Writings of Thomas Paine*, coll. and ed. Moncure Daniel Conway, 4 vols (New York: G.P. Putnam's Sons, 1894), vol. 2, 133. https://oll.libertyfund.org/titles/paine-the-writings-of-thomas-paine-vol-ii-1779-1792, accessed 31/01/2020

2   See, for example, the final chapter of *The Second Treatise of Government* in which Locke explained that a legitimate revolution might consist in changing either the regime or the ruler as the people think fit. See John Locke, *Two Treatises of Government*, ed. Mark Goldie (London: Everyman, 1993), ch. 19, § 220 and 243, 226 and 240.

3   Jean Bodin, *Les six livres de la République* (A Paris: chez Jacques du Puys, 1576), livre I, ch. 9, 152. For a discussion of Bodin's theory of sovereignty, see Sara Miglietti, Chapter 8 in the present volume.

4   Ibid., 129.

5   Thomas Paine, *Rights of Man, Common Sense and Other Political Writings*, ed. Mark Philp (Oxford: Oxford University Press, 1995), 230. All subsequent references to Paine's writings, other than *Dissertations on Government* and *Letter to the People of France and the French Armies on the Event of the 18th Fructidor*, will be to this edition and citations will be made parenthetically in the text.

6   *The Writings of Thomas Paine*, vol. 2, 133.

7   Ibid., 141.

8   Thomas Paine, *The Complete Writings of Thomas Paine*, ed. Philip S. Foner, 2 vols (New York: The Citadel Press, 1945), vol. 2, 595 and 598.

17

Sovereignty and Political Obligation

T. H. Green's Critique of John Austin

John Morrow

In those states of society, in which obedience is habitually rendered by the bulk of society to some determinate superior . . . who in turn is independent of any other superior, the obedience is so rendered because this determinate superior is regarded as expressing or embodying what may properly be called the general will, and is virtually conditional upon the superior being so regarded. It is by no means an unlimited power of compulsion that the superior exercises, but one dependent in the long run, or dependent for the purpose of insuring an habitual obedience, upon conformity to certain convictions on the part of the subjects as to what is for their general interest. . . . Thus, quite apart from any belief in the rights of revolution, from the view that the people in any state are entitled to an ultimate sovereignty, or are sovereign de jure, and may withdraw either legislative or executive power from the hands in which it has been placed in the event of it being misused, it may be fairly held that the ostensible sovereign—the determinate person or persons to whom we can point and say with him or them lies the ultimate

power of exacting habitual obedience from the people—is only able
to exercise this power in virtue of an assent on the part of the
people, nor is this assent reducible to the fear of the sovereign felt
by each individual. It is rather a common desire for certain ends—
specially the . . . [peace and security of life]—to which observance of
law or established usage contributes, and in most cases implies no
conscious reference on the part of those whom it influences to any
supreme coercive power at all.[1]

This passage appears in a section of Green's *Lectures on the Principles of Political Obligation* that focuses critical attention on the account of sovereignty presented by the utilitarian political philosopher and jurisprudential writer John Austin. Austin, a disciple of Jeremy Bentham and close friend of John Stuart Mill, was an obvious subject for Green's attention. Green's political philosophy was advanced as an alternative to prominent contemporary utilitarian theories of ethics and politics. By the time he was delivering his lectures at Oxford in the late 1870s, Austin's major work on "the positive philosophy of law" was already in its fourth edition and established as a standard textbook on the subject. Thanks largely to the editorial labors of his wife Sarah, Austin had become a major figure in English jurisprudence, one who was regarded, as Green put it, as a "master of precise definition"' (Austin xi–xii; Green 66). Austin's association with Bentham placed him at the center of a powerful current in contemporary political philosophy (one to which Green was adamantly opposed), and his conception of sovereignty relied upon ideas that Bentham and his followers derived from Thomas Hobbes' political philosophy.[2] In this respect, it is significant that Green's preliminary survey of early modern sovereignty theory included a trenchant critique of what he took to be Hobbes' position (Green 39–45).

These connections are signaled in references to "supreme coercive power" in the quotation at the head of this essay. In Green's passage, the Hobbesian and Austinian characterizations of sovereignty are juxtaposed with Rousseau's ideas about the relationship between sovereignty and the "general will." Green thought that Rousseau's theory was a partial pre-figuration of a truer (because more complete) account of political authority by reference to the moral interests and expectations of members of political communities in pursuit of their "common good." That is, a good "common to the person conceiving it with others, and good for him and them, whether at any moment it answers their liking or no" (264).

The idea of the common good lay at the heart of Green's foundational contribution to what was later termed "new liberalism."[3] He emphasized the social context of free action and argued for a view of freedom that took account of the positive requirements of self-directed action which enhanced the common good, rather than focusing exclusively on removing legally and socially prescribed restraints on individual liberty. In the hands of earlier liberals this approach had been important in freeing western European societies from some of the worst constraints and inequities of the aristocratic political culture of the early modern period. Green thought, however, that the time had now come to reconsider the role the state could play in fostering "positive liberty," that is,

> a positive power or capacity of doing and enjoying something worth doing or enjoying, and that, too, something that we do or enjoy in common with others . . . [T]hough . . . there can be no freedom amongst men who act not willingly but under compulsion . . . the mere removal of compulsion, the mere enabling of a man to do as he likes, is in itself no contribution to true freedom. (199)

Depending on the circumstances, positive freedom may justify an active role for the state in removing a range of cultural, economic, legal and political hindrances to free action. Green's idea of positive liberty underwrote a theory of the state conceived as a network of authoritative and voluntary institutions that embodied the shared moral aspirations of members of the community and maintained conditions which fostered the pursuit of them. As we shall see, Green argued that sovereignty needed to be understood by reference to the state as an agent of moral change, rather than the state being seen as a product of sovereign power.

In the early sections of the *Lectures* Green canvassed a range of theoretical statements on "the obligation of the subject to the sovereign, of the citizen towards the state, and the obligations of individuals to each other as enforced by a political superior" (13). This approach exemplified the long-established connection between discussions of sovereignty, the rationale of political authority and obligation within political communities.[4] Green argued that Spinoza's, Hobbes', Locke's and Rousseau's theories were vitiated by their adherence to a conception of natural rights as moral attributes of pre-social individuals that could only be aligned with social and political demands through consensual processes. His historical survey concluded with an examination of Austin's analysis of sovereignty and a consideration of what it implied for the grounds of political obligation and the character of the state.

As a follower of Bentham, Austin avoided the mistaken assumptions of natural rights theorists. He regarded "Divine law" as the only basis for a coherent conception of natural law but insisted that it played no role in jurisprudence. This field of enquiry dealt with "positive law," "law . . . established by a political superior" and upheld by sanctions at their exclusive disposal. Positive and divine law were to be distinguished from "positive morality" that derived from "*mere opinion*" and was only regarded as a species of law by an improper analogy (Austin 18–20).

Austin traced positive law to "society political and independent" and the relationship between subjects and sovereigns that were distinctive to it. Sovereignty existed where the "*bulk* of [a] given society" were "in a *habit* of obedience to a *determinate* and *common* superior" whilst that superior "is *not* in a habit of obedience to a determinate human superior" (166). Positive law derived from the commands of sovereigns was the source of legal rights and the duties arising from them. Other rights and duties were either products of divine law specified and upheld by the power of god or derived from systems of positive morality that rested on the uncertain and contested ground of opinion. In these cases, "law," "rights," and "duties" were analogues of the true forms derived from the commands of human and divine sovereigns.

Although Austin held that the purpose of government was to maximize the happiness of the members of the community, he thought that this objective would only serve as the ground of political obligation if subjects were perfectly rational and government wholly fulfilled its utility-maximizing role (Austin 246–8). In other circumstances obedience sprang from habit, from fear of the sanctions which sovereigns imposed on those who disobeyed them, and from a Hobbesian recoil from actions that would undermine sovereignty and reduce human life to a condition of anarchy. In Austin's account, fear of sanctions and fear of the state of nature thus played a major role in subjects' conscious obedience to their sovereign: "[T]he habitual obedience of the people in most or many communities" arises "wholly or partly from their fear of the probable evils which they might suffer by resistance" (249). Austin regarded this fear as the basis of obligations between subjects and their sovereign: "Being liable to evil from you, I am *bound* or *obliged* by your command, or I lie under a *duty* to obey it" (22).

The quotation reproduced at the head of this essay summarizes Green's response to Austin's views on law and sovereignty and particularly the role he attributed to subjects' fear of coercion in explaining sovereign power and the basis of law and rights. Green accepted Austin's definition of sovereign power and recognized the need for it, but he rejected his explanation of its basis and reversed the relationship between sovereignty on the one hand and law and rights on the other. Thus, while Austin regarded law and rights as creatures of sovereign power, Green argued that rights were products of social life that provided a moral basis for law and sovereignty. Sovereign power was a *necessary* condition for political society, but not a *sufficient* one.

The Austinians, having found their sovereign, are apt to regard it as a much more important institution than, if it is to be identified with a determinate person or persons, it really is; they are apt to suppose that the sovereign, with the coercive power (i.e. the power of operating on the fears of the subjects) which it exercises, is the real determinant of the habitual obedience of the people—at any rate of their habitual obedience in respect of those acts and forbearances which are prescribed by law by law. (69)

Green traced both the fact of "habitual obedience," and the moral obligation of subjects towards their sovereign, to what modern "communitarians" have termed an "embedded" conception of individuality.[5] He thus rejected early-modern natural rights theory, arguing that rights are products of social interaction that is sustained by the mutual recognition of claims by members of the community because they are conducive to their shared commitment to a "common good,"

> The capacity . . . on the part of the individual conceiving a good as the same for himself and others, and of being determined to action by that conception, is the foundation of rights; and rights are the condition of that capacity being realised. (28)

This conception of rights sprang from Green's understanding of moral personality as a potentiality and from his insistence that the development or "realization" of moral capacities necessarily involved the freely willed pursuit of a good that was recognized and endorsed by other members of the community. Rights were the products of the shared values embedded in social interaction, and the means through which individuals made freely determined contributions to the moral quality of their shared existence. Green emphatically rejected the idea of rights as "arbitrary creatures of law," insisting that they rested on a "consciousness of common interest on the part of members of society" (29).

Green thought that his conception of the common good as the object of moral endeavor and basis of legitimate political authority had been pre-figured in Rousseau's theory of the general will. Regrettably, however, Rousseau's adherence to conventional ideas about natural rights led him to argue that this will was only expressed comprehensively in the vote of a popular assembly. Green regarded this position as flawed in principle since it rested on the assumption that the claims of the holders of natural rights could only be set aside with their consent and thus ignored the social basis of rights. "A right against society, in distinction from a right to be treated as a member of society, is a contradiction in terms. No one therefore has a right to resist a law . . . on the grounds that it requires him to do what he does not like, and that he has not agreed to submit to the authority from which it proceeds . . ." (79–80). Moreover, Rousseau's position was inoperable in practice because it meant that only those who voted with the majority were bound to obey particular legislative enactments. In light of Rousseau's assumptions about the general will, sovereignty and democratic decision making, Green thought it was misleading to treat the general will as the source of sovereignty. He saw his own formulation, which linked the obedience constitutive of sovereign power to the idea of the common good, as avoiding these difficulties and making sovereignty possible in monarchical and aristocratic governments as well as in representative and direct democracies (Green 69, 80).

Although natural rights theorists and John Austin and his utilitarian associates started from markedly different positions, Green thought their conceptions of sovereignty were vitiated by a common error.

> They make no inquiry into the development of society and of man through society. They take no account of other forms of community than that regulated by a supreme coercive power, either in the way of investigating their historical origin and connection, or of considering the ideas and states of mind which they imply or which render them possible. (89)

In response to theories which relied on Austinian images of abstract power or abstract conceptions of moral personality found in natural right theories, Green argued that the recognition of a shared sense of moral purpose that underpinned rights was the foundation of all forms of human regulation, including those arising from sovereign power.

> The sovereign should be regarded, not in abstraction as the wielder of coercive force, but in connection with the whole complex of institutions in political society. It is as their sustainer, and thus as the agent of the general will, that sovereign power must be presented to the minds of the people if it is to command habitual loyal obedience; and obedience will scarcely be habitual unless it is loyal not forced. (74)

This argument was the focus of a lecture in which Green rejected Austin's idea that laws can be adequately characterized as commands enforced by penalties. Command and enforcement are essential elements of law but are not its defining characteristics. The purpose of law is to define and specify rights and these, Green argued, rest on the recognition that the claims in question are conducive to the pursuit of the common good by members of the community. Laws are derivative of pre-political (but not pre-social) rights and are not, as Austin argued, products of them: the commands of sovereigns give "fuller reality to rights already existing" (Green 103).

This account of the relationship between sovereignty, law and rights underwrote Green's attempt to reconcile positions which his liberal predecessors treated as mutually exclusive. On the one hand, he regarded free action directed by a commitment to advancing the common good as a necessary feature of moral conduct. At the same time, however, Green rejected laissez-faire liberals' suspicions of an active state and argued that state action could support free agency by removing a range of legal and social impediments to it. He thus supported legislation that promoted the well-being of the bulk of the population through regulating housing and public sanitation. Such measures were necessary if contemporary society was to secure to all of its members the conditions necessary to develop and exercise their capacities to contribute to the common good. Green regarded this requirement as the "object of civil society" and thought that in mid-Victorian Britain it also justified state regulation of the liquor trade and factory labor, and government provision of public education and legally enforced participation in it (201).

Green treated the state as a focal point of the shared moral aspirations of members of the community and a key agency in securing their realization. These aspirations were often inchoate but their hold on the minds of ordinary citizens could be seen in the widespread endorsement of claims to free life and to other rights as being necessary to it. They were also apparent in a range of social agencies including the family and the countless popular self-help institutions which supported moral striving in contemporary society. These institutions constituted the "state" in the broader sense of the term. Through them individuals received invaluable assistance in exercising their rights. They were also supported by the state construed far more narrowly in common parlance as "government." Governments created systems of law that defined and upheld rights. Insofar as laws acted through coercive sanctions they played no direct role in realizing the moral objective of the free pursuit of the common good. They were, however, morally necessary in the sense that they made moral action possible by protecting right-holders from illegitimate interference in the free exercise of their rights. They were also morally useful in that they provided guidance for those who were inclined to do what was right and coordinated their attempts to pursue this goal. For example, Green observed that the existence of a law obliging parents to send their children to school did not trench on the liberty of those who were already committed to educating their dependents. When such a law was accompanied by government-organized provision of education it was a means of coordinating social efforts to prepare children to take their place within the community.

Green's stress on the positive ethical implications of law and his insistence that it rested on the moral aspiration of the population, explains why he thought it necessary to develop a theory of political obligation through a series of related critiques of earlier sovereignty theory, including, as we have seen, the revival of a Hobbesian approach in the work of John Austin. Austin's view of law as the product of sovereign power that operated on individuals through their fear of sanctions and fear of anarchy, seemed to Green to empty political obligation of any fundamental moral content, and the state of any distinctly moral dimensions. From this perspective, political authority was at best seen as providing practical assistance to the requirements of negative freedom. It provided the basis of legal systems that prevented interference with subjects' exercise of their rights, but were not conducive to advancing the conception of freedom which Green espoused. Austinian sovereignty left no space for free action within and alongside frameworks of coercive constraints that Green regarded as a necessary but not a defining characteristic of the state. "[W]hen we come to think of the state as distinguished by sovereignty" we "suppose that supreme coercive power is essential to a state, forgetting that it is rather the state that makes the sovereign than the sovereign that makes the state" (Green 102).

Because Green saw sovereign power as being grounded in the shared moral aspirations of members of communities, he treated subjects' obligations to political superiors as conditional upon their commitment to the common good. He insisted that individuals had the right the judge whether governors satisfied this requirement and might rightfully resist those who did not. Resistance was both a right and a duty: "there can be no *right* unless on the ground that it is for the common good, and if so there is a duty" (185). Green cautioned, however, that subjects' reaction to the unjust actions of sovereigns must be constrained by their own responsibilities for advancing the common good and their recognition of the range of benefits produced even by far-from-perfect states. Thus Green argued that in constitutional regimes, subjects' moral responsibilities would be fulfilled most effectively by utilizing mechanisms for addressing injustices that were embedded in the political system, and that even in despotisms like Czarist Russia resistance was only justified where it posed less of a threat to the common good than the injustices which provoked it.[6] He thought that was unlikely to be the case if the bulk of the population did not appreciate the issues at stake. Where it did, an informed commitment to the common good would minimize disruptions to it and provide the basis for refocusing the general will into a new form of sovereignty.

Notes

1   T. H. Green, *Lectures on the Principles of Political Obligation and Other Writings*, ed. Paul Harris and John Morrow (Cambridge: Cambridge University Press, 1986), 68. All parenthetical in-text references to Green are to this edition. In-text references to Austin's works are to John Austin, *The Province of Jurisprudence Determined*, ed. Wilfrid E. Rumble (Cambridge: Cambridge University Press, 1995).

2   See Mark Francis, "The Nineteenth-Century Theory of Sovereignty and Thomas Hobbes," *History of Political Thought* 1, no. 3 (1980): 517–40.

3   *The New Liberalism: Reconciling Liberty and Community*, ed. Avital Simhony and David Weinstein (Cambridge: Cambridge University Press, 2001), passim.

4   See F. H. Hinsley, *Sovereignty* (London: Watts, 1966), 17–18.

5   See Michael Freeden, "Liberal Community," in *The New Liberalism*, 26–31.

6   Green's views on how democratic subjects should react to perceived injustice
    thus differs from Thoreau's "civil disobedience" since that removes the citizen
    from political obligation; see Henry Thoreau, *Political Writings*, ed. Nancy L.
    Rosenblum (Cambridge: Cambridge University Press), 233–5.

18

Divided Sovereignties

Lenin and Dual Power

Antonis Balasopoulos

The highly remarkable feature of our revolution is that it has brought about a dual power. *[. . .]* Nobody *previously thought, or could have thought, of a dual power.*
What is this dual power? Alongside the Provisional Government, the government of the bourgeoisie, another government has arisen [. . .] the Soviets of Workers' and Soldiers' Deputies.
[. . .]
What is the political nature of this government? It is a revolutionary dictatorship, i.e., a power directly based on revolutionary seizure, on the direct initiative of the people from below, and not on a law enacted by a centralised state power. It is an entirely different kind of power from the one that generally exists in the parliamentary bourgeois-democratic republics [. . .] of Europe and America. [. . .] The fundamental characteristics of this type are: (1) the source of power is not a law previously discussed and enacted by parliament, but the direct initiative of the people from below [. . .] (2) the replacement of the police and the army, which are institutions divorced from the people and set against the people, by the direct arming of the whole people [. . .] (3) officialdom, the bureaucracy, are [. . .] similarly replaced by the direct rule of the people themselves [. . .]

*The bourgeoisie stands for the undivided power of the bourgeoisie.
The class-conscious workers stand for the undivided power of the
Soviets [. . .]*[1]
Two powers cannot exist *in a state. One of them is bound to pass
away. [. . .] The dual power merely expresses a* transitional *phase in
the revolution's development, when it has gone farther than the
ordinary bourgeois-democratic revolution,* but has not yet *reached a
"pure" dictatorship of the proletariat and the peasantry.*[2]

The two texts from which I have drawn were written in the space of a few
days of feverish activity after V. I. Lenin's return to Russia from exile, on
April 3, 1917. "The Dual Power" was published in *Pravda* on April 9; "The
Tasks of the Proletariat in Our Revolution" was first published in September
of that year but dates back to April 10. Lenin's schedule as organizer and
agitator was particularly hectic because of the situation that had unfolded
as a result of the so-called "February Revolution": after Czar Nicholas II
abdicated, monarchy in Russia was de facto abolished. A "Provisional
Government" was appointed, under Georgy Lvov, with the mission of
organizing national elections for the convention of the Russian Constituent
Assembly. The Soviets (workers' and soldiers' councils) gave the Provisional
Government their support, contenting themselves, as Lenin notes, with the
role of "an observer, a supervisor of the convocation of the Constituent
Assembly" ("Tasks" 60). At the same time, however, they—particularly the
Petrograd Soviet—maintained control of several vital aspects of government,
including the railway, local factories, and, vitally, the army. The military
units that participated in the February Revolution were not disarmed or
disbanded (and indeed, could not be so); conversely, the Czarist police was
replaced with units subordinated to the local authorities and severely
weakened.[3]

Writing in 1922, conservative German jurist Carl Schmitt famously
remarked that "it is precisely the exception that makes relevant the subject
of sovereignty."[4] Likewise, the exceptional circumstances of April 1917, the
appearance of what Lenin correctly saw as a revolutionary situation that
could well outstrip the control of the bourgeoisie, may be said to have led
him (a first-generation Bolshevik generally averse to bourgeois legalism)[5] to
an exceptional engagement with the nature of sovereign power.[6] Sovereignty
thus divulged itself as a theoretical question to him at the very moment of
its crisis, under the light of the historical exception. It could be argued that
shortly thereafter, when Lenin composed *The State and Revolution* (in
August and September 1917), the question of sovereignty had become
almost entirely subordinated to that of the past and future nature of state
power more broadly.[7] But this shift does not diminish the significance of the

brief excursions into the question of dual power undertaken in April. Rather, they can be deployed to shed light on a theoretical and practical context marked by Lenin's privileging of force and of civil war as the respective content and form of state revolution.

In his "Letters on Tactics," written in the same fateful month of April, Lenin characterized the situation in Russia as "extremely original, novel and unprecedented," since it featured "side by side [. . .] simultaneously, both the rule of the bourgeoisie [. . .] and a revolutionary-democratic dictatorship of the proletariat and the peasantry."[8] He thus seized on the significance of a feature of the contemporary Russian situation that went against one of the basic orthodoxies of much modern theory of sovereignty, namely, the emphasis on its *indivisibility*. This insight did not mean that Lenin rejected sovereignty theorists' stress on indivisibility. On the contrary, he considered the situation in Russia to be as unsustainable as thinkers as diverse politically as Bodin, Hobbes and Rousseau would have found it:[9] "There is not the slightest doubt that such an 'interlocking' [of powers] cannot last long. Two powers *cannot exist* in a state. One of them is bound to pass away" ("Tasks" 61).

Lenin's tacit subscription to one of the cornerstones of pre-Marxist (and indeed absolutist) political theory is evident in his conviction that dual power must lead into either revolution or counter-revolution, and in both eventualities decision by force. The de facto, and exceptional, division of sovereign power thus does not alter its function as direct and forceful *expression* (rather than mediated representation) of a monolithically conceived and absolute (i.e. unrestrained by "rule of law") class *will*: it is telling in this regard that though Lenin's April writings conceded that sovereign power was at the time dual, he also envisioned each of its two branches as "undivided" ("Dual" 41).[10]

Thus, at the same time that they take stock of the extraordinary and explosive concatenation of two forms of sovereignty in a single state, Lenin's April writings are revealing of his broader assumptions, particularly those that would come to the fore in *The State and Revolution* and in a number of his post-revolutionary writings. In this regard, the reference to the emergence, alongside "centralized state power," of "revolutionary dictatorship" (or "dictatorship of the proletariat") as power consisting in "the *direct* rule of the people themselves," power, too, that is based "on the *direct* initiative of the people" (emphases added) and not on "a law," is both significant and portentous. Both "Dual Power" and "Letters on Tactics" noted that the second, parallel power that asserted itself in April "is of *the same type* as the Paris Commune" ("Dual" 38). In part, this meant that it was based neither "on the law" nor "on the previously expressed will of the people" ("Tasks" 61); rather, it was both *extra-legal* and *immediate* (or direct) in nature. In both of these regards, Soviet power is at the antipodes not merely of liberal dualisms resting on the distinction between state and civil society and therefore of the complex institutions which mediate them, but also of Hobbesian sovereignty, which presupposes the alienation of individual wills to sovereign will and the function of this presumed pact of delegation (the *pactum subjectionis*) as foundation of sovereign legitimacy.[11] Lenin's conception of Soviet power *qua* sovereign power is far closer to the Rousseauian understanding of the general will, with the vital provision that in Lenin, as in Marx and Engels, this will is always already *divided* by class, so that what is to rise to sovereign power, at least when the conceptual horizon is determined by the incipience of revolution, is the (representationally unmediated) will of the "toiling" *majority*.[12]

The rejection of representational mediations aiming at a prevention of too high a concentration of power in the hands of a single actor brings us to a second aspect attending to the identification of Soviet power with the type of power emerging in the Paris Commune, equally anti-dualistic in character, namely, the conflation of executive and legislative powers. In *The Spirit of the Laws* (1748), Montesquieu had remarked that "[w]hen legislative power is united with executive power in a single person or in a single body of the magistracy, there is no liberty," identifying their fusion with despotism.[13] For Lenin, however, as for Marx and Engels, division was, in the form of the class struggle, a trauma lying at the very origins of the state. In the words of *The State and Revolution*: "The state is a product and a manifestation of the *irreconcilability* of class antagonisms. The state arises, where, when and insofar as class antagonisms objectively *cannot* be reconciled. And conversely, the existence of the state proves that the class antagonisms are irreconcilable" (emphases in the original).[14]

Hence, the "separation of powers" celebrated by Enlightenment liberalism as a bulwark against arbitrary authority and as guarantee of "rule of law" was, on the one hand, viewed as a distraction from the decisive role of force as something coterminous with the very existence of a state; and on the other, as a sign of the alienating powers of the historical state, that is, its tendency to replicate its own quasi-theological "rise" above its subjects' individual wills with the production of "institutions divorced from the people and set against the people" ("Dual" 39)—with bureaucracy (*SR* 388, 392). Given the drastic difference in points of departure (the irrelevance, for Lenin, of contractual relations or assumptions based on a hypothetical "state of nature"), Montesquieu's sign of despotic arbitrariness changed meaning in the context of proletarian democracy, for it was now a means of attenuating the effects of bureaucratization that subtended the alienation of sovereign power from the toiling majority: hence, the demand, stated in "The Dual Power" and repeated numerous times in *The State and Revolution* and elsewhere, for a democracy where elected officials would, as in the Paris Commune, be "subject to recall" by the people and where they would be paid no more than "the ordinary pay of a competent worker" ("Dual" 39). "The bureaucracy" will be "replaced by the direct rule of the people themselves" or at least subjected to their immediate control. *The State and Revolution* explicitly envisions the abolition of parliamentarianism (i.e. a system of representation based on greed and deceit),[15] and thereby the abolition of the "division of labor between the legislative and the executive" as well: "the parliamentarians themselves have to work, have to execute their own laws, have themselves to test the results achieved in reality, and to account directly to their constituents" (*SR* 424).

Such directives for the radical simplification[16] of the tasks of government may be taken as important clues as to the relative paucity of concern with the theory of internal sovereignty after the brief interlude of April 1917. *The State and Revolution* reveals that the desired fusion of legislative and executive powers is conceptually predicated not simply on proletarian aversion to bureaucracy and to parliamentary parasitism and deception but also on a prior division within the nature of state functions in Lenin's own theory—one which neutralizes, at least in Lenin's mind, the potentially autocratic effects of abolishing the "separation of powers". On the one hand, the state is an organ of force, exercised by the ruling class (bourgeoisie or proletariat), through its specialized delegates in the judicial system, army and police or through the direct action of the "armed people" respectively; on the other, the state also involves the more neutral and benign function of coordinating production and distribution, of "control and accounting" (*SR* 470, 473) as tasks that can, under proletarian rule, be learned by all, therefore transforming everyone (and thereby also no one) into a "bureaucrat" (*SR* 472–3, 481, 487–9). To recall Engels, as Lenin himself does: The state is simply "government of persons" (through pure coercion), on the one hand, and "administration of things" on the other.[17] The element of coercive force would have to be preserved in the transitional period of the "dictatorship of the proletariat," though its class direction would be reversed in ways Lenin hoped would gradually decrease both its extent and its ferocity (*SR* 463–4); "control and accounting" will persist well beyond this phase, albeit in ever-more universalized, ever-more simplified and habituated forms (*SR* 420–1, 427). And between the two, between pure force and mere technical administration, the problem of sovereignty—the question of who holds the "absolute and perpetual power of the commonwealth,"[18] what its relationship to civil society is or what its true "marks" are—seems to disappear altogether, notwithstanding the resonance of the revolutionary slogan "All power to the Soviets" (*vsya vlast' sovetam*). Lenin's use of this slogan turns out to embody a concrete "resolution" to the dilemmas of dual power addressed in April rather than any attempt to prescribe the specific institutions of rule in a proletarian republic.[19] Ever a tactical thinker, Lenin could remain remarkably vague about questions he did not wish to settle in definitive form.

There was, however, a price to be paid for such vagueness, particularly after *The State and Revolution* and its insistence that "proletarian democracy," which Lenin identified both with the "dictatorship of the proletariat" and with the Paris Commune, "is no longer the state proper" (*SR* 419) or is only a "semi-state" (*SR* 397) and "a transitional state" (*SR* 463), one on the path to its self-cancellation and disappearance. The idea, almost obsessively repeated in that text, that the goal of proletarian democracy could only be to "crush, smash to atoms" the "bourgeois, even the republican bourgeois, state machine" (*SR* 477) implies not only a belief in the imminent disappearance of the political grounds of sovereignty but, by extension, a complete evasion of the question of the stabilization of socialist power and of its organs. Yet, and at the same time, this projection of an effectively anarchist abolition of state power presupposes the means of a power that is absolute, "untrammeled by any laws, absolutely unrestricted by any rules whatever"—in other words sovereign in the most absolutist of senses.[20]

In "The Dual Power," Lenin would assure his audience that "[w]e are not Blancists, we do not stand for the seizure of power by a minority" ("Dual" 40). *The State and Revolution* likewise envisioned proletarian democracy as a democracy of the "oppressed classes" (SR 420), the social *majority*. But such pronouncements are by no means the final word on the subject: Lenin had also asserted, in 1906, that the "dictatorship of the revolutionary people" is not one of the "whole people" but of a vanguard which would "*enlist* the *whole* people [. . .] in organizing the *state*" ("Cadets" 247; first and last emphases added), while, in October of 1917, he would state that "the Party cannot be guided by the temper of the masses because it [the temper] was changeable and incalculable."[21] Likewise, though his "Proposed Amendments" to the RSDLP (Bolshevik) Party Program referred to "the sovereignty of the people" and specified that "supreme power in the state must be vested entirely in the people's representatives," he does not seem to have objected to these sentences being struck out entirely from the revision of April 1917.[22] Finally, and as Ghița Ionescu rightly observed, the first Constitution of the "Russian Socialist Federated Soviet Republic," adopted in July 1918, resolved the tension between the "withering state" ideal of the Commune and the exigencies of state power in favor of the latter, for its very ratification implied the existence of "a state with territorial sovereignty and power of coercion."[23] As for the specifics regarding the locus of sovereign power in that founding document, it is worth noting that though it declares that "[a]ll the central and local power belongs to [the] Soviets" and refers to the "All-Russian Congress of Soviets" as "the supreme power" of the Republic, it also nominates a *second* organ of power, the "All-Russian Central Executive Committee," as the "supreme legislative, executive, and controlling organ of the Russian Federated Soviet Republic."[24]

With the Civil War drastically curtailing a number of freedoms enshrined in the 1917 Party Program,[25] the call for direct control of the affairs of state by the armed and organized workers and peasants would soon be replaced by the installation of a new bureaucracy, centered on the apparatus of an oppositionless Party, whose use of repression soon extended to dissenting workers themselves. In the post-Leninist era, discussion of popular sovereignty seems to disappear altogether, except in conjunction with the question of national self-determination, itself part of Lenin's legacy. There, "sovereignty" was free of the severe constraints imposed by an earlier preoccupation with the "withering away" of the state as the sole guarantee of freedom from coercion; but it was not free of the tensions that attended to the dialectic of unity and division, "bourgeois right" and the attempt at imagining its revolutionary negation, during the spring of 1917 and its immediate aftermath.[26]

Notes

1   V. I. Lenin, "The Dual Power," April 9, 1917. In *Collected Works* (henceforth *LCW*), vol. 24, ed. Bernard Isaacs (Moscow: Progress Publishers, 1964), 38–9, 41. Henceforth abbreviated parenthetically as "Dual."

2   V. I. Lenin, "The Tasks of the Proletariat in Our Revolution: Draft Platform for the Proletarian Party," September 1917, *LCW*, vol. 24, 61. Henceforth abbreviated parenthetically as "Tasks."

3   See Neil Faulkner, "Dual Power," in *A People's History of the Russian Revolution* (London: Pluto Press, 2017), 137–8.

4   Carl Schmitt, *Political Theology: Four Chapters on the Concept of Sovereignty*, trans. George Schwab (Chicago: University of Chicago Press, 2005), 6.

5   See Evgenii Pashukanis, *Selected Writings in Marxism and Law*, trans. Peter B. Maggs (New York: Academic Press, 1980), 133, 138, 142, 144; Andrew Levine, *The General Will: Rousseau, Marx, Communism* (Cambridge: Cambridge University Press, 1993), 103–4; and Naveen Kanalu, "Law, Absolute Will, and the 'Withering of the State': Sovereignty at the Limits of Lenin's 'Dictatorship of the Proletariat," in *The Russian Revolution as Ideal and Practice: Failures, Legacies and the Future of Revolution*, ed. Thomas Telios et al. (London: Palgrave Macmillan, 2020), 85.

6   The Russian "dual power" (*dvoevlastie*) is, as Trotsky was to note, also translatable as "Dual" or "double" *sovereignty*, "because the stem, *vlast*, means *sovereignty* as well as power." See Leon Trotsky, *History of the Russian Revolution*, trans. Max Eastman (New York: Pathfinder, 2005), 223.

7   Kanalu thus notes that "Lenin does not privilege the political concept of sovereignty in general as a means to understanding the state" (86).

8   "Letters on Tactics," *LCW*, vol. 24, 46.

9   See the chapters on Bodin, Hobbes, and Rousseau in this volume.

10 On the significance of a Hobbesian conception of the presumed will of a class as "absolute will," see Kanalu 87–9.

11 See Lucio Colletti, *From Rousseau to Lenin: Studies in Ideology and Society*, trans. John Merrington and Judith White (New York: Monthly Review Press, 1972), 181.

12 See Levine, 105.

13 (Charles de) Montesquieu, *The Spirit of the Laws*, trans. Anne M. Cohler, Basia C. Miller and Harold S. Stone (Cambridge: Cambridge University Press, 1989), 157.

14 V. I. Lenin, *The State and Revolution. LCW*, vol. 25, ed. Stepan Apresyan and Jim Riordan, 387. Hereafter cited as *SR*.

15 Though not without, Lenin insists in that work, "representative institutions and the elective principle" (*SR*, 423).

16 Envisioning socialist state administration as increasingly "simple" is a repeated aspect of *State and Revolution*, connected to the expectation of a "withering away" of the state. It is important, in this regard, to bear in mind Antonio Gramsci's remarks on the difference in relations between state and civil society in Russia and western democracies in *Selections from the Prison Notebooks*, trans. Quintin Hoare and Geoffrey Nowell Smith (New York: International Publishers, 1971), 238.

17 See Lenin, *SR*, 396; and Frederick Engels, *Anti-Dühring*, in *Marx and Engels: Collected Works*, vol. 25 (London: Lawrence & Wishart, 1987), 268.

18 Bodin, *Of Sovereignty*, trans. Julian H. Franklin (Cambridge: Cambridge University Press, 1992), 1.

19 See Lenin, "All Power to the Soviets!," 3 July, 1917, *LCW*, vol. 25, 153–4.

20 V. I. Lenin, "The Victory of the Cadets and the tasks of the Workers' Party," April 1906. *LCW*, vol. 10, ed. Andrew Rothstein, 246. Henceforth parenthetically cited as "Cadets."

21 "Meeting of the Central Committee of the R.S.D.I.P. (B.)," October 16, 1917. *LCW*, vol. 26, ed. George Hanna, 191. And see Rosa Luxemburg's penetrating critique of this line of argument in *The Russian Revolution* (pub. 1922), in *Rosa Luxemburg Speaks*, ed. Mary-Alice Waters (New York: Pathfinder, 2004), 509–11.

22 See "Materials Relating to the Revision of the Party Programme," April–May 1917. *LCW*, vol. 24, 461, 472. Henceforth abbreviated as "MRPP."

23 Ghiţa Ionescu, "Lenin, the Commune and the State: Thoughts for a Centenary," *Government and Opposition* 5, no. 2 (April 1970): 131–65 (161).

24 See *The Russian Constitution* (*The Nation*, January 4, 1919), 4, 8, 9. Henceforth cited parenthetically as *RC*.

25 See "MRPP," esp. 472, on the "inviolability of person" and on "unrestricted freedom of conscience, speech, the press, assembly, strikes and association."

26 See, indicatively, V. I. Lenin, "The Discussion of Self-Determination Summed Up" (July 1916). *LCW*, vol. 22, ed. George Hanna, 320–60; and Robert A. Jones, *The Soviet Concept of "Limited Sovereignty" from Lenin to Gorbachev* (London: Palgrave Macmillan, 1990), esp. 1–44.

19

Carl Schmitt and the Sovereignty of Decision

Mika Ojakangas

Sovereign is he who decides on the state of exception.[1]

In a democracy, the people are sovereign. [. . .] The people are the highest judge, just as they are the highest legislator.[2]

I

Carl Schmitt's theories of sovereignty must be understood in the context of his political alignments. Right after World War I, which brought to an end the authoritarian regime of the German Empire, Schmitt came out as a fierce critic of constitutional liberalism and parliamentary democracy. Like many contemporary right-wing conservatives, he believed that constitutional liberalism together with a parliamentary system of government paved the way to the fragmentation of society and ultimately, to civil strife. The rule of law, the separation of powers, inalienable basic rights, the idea of parliamentary discussion, and party politics, he argued, undermine the power and authority of the state, leaving the state vulnerable to the attacks of its "enemies."

Schmitt's response to this "crisis" of authority was the rehabilitation of the authority of the state (with a special emphasis on executive power) and the concept of sovereignty in particular. Yet instead of endeavoring to figure out an alternative to the liberal democratic system of government at this point of his career, Schmitt aimed at revealing the alleged inconsistencies of political liberalism and to show that in the final analysis liberal democratic constitutions are also based on certain authoritarian principles, notably on the principle of sovereignty. Without sovereignty, so Schmitt's argument goes, there is no legal order and to the extent that he conceived every order as legal order, no order tout court.

When it comes to legal theory, Schmitt's concept of sovereignty in *Political Theology* was a critical response to the liberal rule-of-law tendencies in legal positivism, the then prevailing paradigm in German jurisprudence. Legal positivism, which had become a general doctrine and method in the German science of law since 1848, arose as a critical response to the tradition of natural law. The natural law tradition had sought the foundation of positive law in human nature. In the eyes of the new generation of legal scholars, however, such an approach was not scientifically tenable. In the modern post-metaphysical world, they argued, scientific research of law cannot be based on philosophical speculations about the alleged universality of human nature. It must be based on an objective inquiry into the legal norms valid in a given political system.

Although Schmitt criticized certain aspects of legal positivism, he did not do it from the perspective of natural law. Like most of his contemporaries, he believed that the tradition of natural law was over. In Schmitt's view, however, legal positivism threw the baby out with the bathwater by abandoning the quest for the origins and thereby, the legitimacy of law. In legal positivism, Schmitt argued, law is identified with legal norms, whereupon the mere objective existence of a norm becomes the criterion of its validity and legality becomes the only form of legitimacy.

In Schmitt's view, this tendency came to its logical end in the work of Hans Kelsen. Kelsen, whose aim was to develop a pure science of law, identified the state with the legal order and the legal order with the hierarchical system of valid norms. As pantheism made possible the true knowledge of nature, Kelsen argued, the knowledge that the state is a system of valid legal rules and norms makes possible the true science of law. In his view, all non-normative concepts and conceptions, all considerations concerning, for instance, the political sources of law, have to be set aside— including the concept of the people and the personified concept of the sovereign. The concept of sovereignty can be retained but only on the condition that sovereignty refers to nothing but the unity of the system of legal norms.[3]

Schmitt's response to these tendencies in legal positivism was to outline a "decisionist" theory of law. Criticizing Kelsen in particular—but also dismissing his endeavor to develop a pure science of law independent of social sciences and moral philosophy—Schmitt argued that legal life cannot be exhausted in the system of norms. In his view, we cannot understand law without taking into account those concrete persons and empirical positions of power which are involved in the process of legislation and the administration of justice. And to the extent that concrete persons are included in the process, Schmitt argued, there opens up a gap between norms and the manner in which they gain realization. A judge, for example, is not a machine that mechanically applies legal norms. Norms do not determinate legal decisions, judges do: "Law is concretized only in a judgment, not in a norm."[4]

In Schmitt's view, a similar logic prevails in the legal order as a whole. The existing system of legal norms cannot be a sovereign, for the system of norms as such is null and void. For Schmitt, the sovereignty of law "means only the sovereignty of men who draw up and administer the law."[5] In *Political Theology*, however, Schmitt does not define the sovereign as a supreme judge, not even as the highest authority. Instead the sovereign is he who decides on the "state of exception" (*Ausnahmezustand*).

What is the state of exception? The state of exception, Schmitt explains, is not chaos or anarchy but a means to overcome chaos and anarchy. It is a means to govern in a situation when the everyday frame of life is critically disturbed and the very existence of legal order is in peril. In such a situation— during a civil war for instance—normally valid legal norms become inert and inapplicable, because the validity and applicability of norms, Schmitt argues, presupposes a concrete normal situation. It presupposes an everyday frame of life to which norms can factually be applied: "There exists no norm that is applicable to chaos" (PT 15). Hence, norms cannot prevent the escalation of the crisis at hand. Therefore, there must be a person or an organ in the state that is able to decide not only whether the state of exception prevails but also what should be done in order to prevent the collapse of the entire political system. This person or organ is the sovereign.

Why a state of exception? Why does Schmitt not define sovereignty in the traditional manner as the absolute and perpetual power of the state? Compared to his predecessors' formulations, the sovereign's power appears limited in Schmitt's theory. If the sovereign decides on the state of exception alone, what is his function in normal times? Is sovereignty normally dormant?

It is—and it is not. Firstly, Schmitt believes that the traditional formulation of sovereignty as the highest, legally independent, and underived power is too abstract and therefore, does not have much practical meaning.[6] The state of exception endows sovereignty with the *concreteness* it traditionally lacks. Secondly, to the extent that the sovereigns decide on the state of exception, they *also* decide on whether a normal situation exists. Although the sovereign interferes in the affairs of the state only during crisis, when the very existence of the legal order is at stake, this order is nonetheless based on its decision *not* to interfere. Hence, sovereignty is not normally dormant but always present in the mode of a potentiality. For this reason Schmitt can conclude that the sovereign's decision does not concern the state of exception alone but "produces and guarantees the situation in its totality" (PT 13).

In Schmitt's view, thirdly, the *essence of law* comes to the fore in the state of exception. As already said, the state of exception is not chaos but remains within the framework of order, not only in the political sense—"the state remains, whereas law recedes" (PT 12)—but also in the juristic sense. This follows from the fact that Schmitt's concept of legal order includes two basic form-elements, the legal norm and the decision. The state of exception suspends the normative element of legal order and reveals the element of decision (*Entscheidung*) in its absolute purity. As a juristic form-element, however, the decision is not equal to the normative element. It is the constitutive form of law as such. The state of exception reveals the original existential and non-normative character of law and legal order: "Every legal order is based on a decision" (PT 10).

Finally, it should be noted that although Schmitt constantly emphasizes concrete persons over against legal norms, he also insists that the sovereign can be *whoever* decides on the state of exception. He accuses legal positivism of impersonalism and nihilism but at the same time he himself leaves open the question of who is authorized to decide on the state of exception. Indeed, for Schmitt, the question is not about authorization at all but about *capacity*. The sovereign is not a pre-given instance authorized to decide on the state of exception but anyone who is capable of deciding on the state of exception at a particular moment of history: "The sovereign is not a legitimate monarch or a competent instance but precisely the one who decides in a sovereign way."[7] In this way, Schmitt is able to distance himself from the traditional theory of legitimate sovereignty and to leave the door ajar for illegitimate dictatorship. This is the meaning of Schmitt's famous formulation in *Political Theology*: "Authority proves that to produce law it need not be based on law" (PT 13).[8]

II

In *Political Theology*, Schmitt does not address the question of popular sovereignty. Yet he had done it in his extensive study on the history and the essence of dictatorship (*Dictatorship*) published a year before the publication of *Political Theology* in 1921. At the end of the book, in the chapter on sovereign dictatorship, he argued that the fundamental principle of democracy is the constituent power (*verfassungsgebende Gewalt*) of the people. This unlimited power lays down the foundations of the constitution—without becoming subject to the constitution once it is established:

> From the infinite, incomprehensible abyss of the force of the *pouvoir constituant*, new forms emerge incessantly, which it can destroy at any time and in which its power is never limited for good.[9]

In a democracy, as Schmitt continues his reflection on the same subject in his *Constitutional Theory* (1928), only the people (*das Volk*) may decide on the type and the form of their political organization. In themselves, however, the people have no form or organization. They are the unformed and unorganized origin of all forms and organizations, the unrepresented foundation of all representations. As long as the people exist, "their life force and energy is inexhaustible and always capable of finding new forms of political existence" (CT 131).

In a sense, the constituent power of the people and the sovereignty that decides on the state of exception converge. They both constitute the foundation of legal order. Yet while the sovereign who decides on the state of exception decides on the normal situation indirectly, the constituent power does it directly. Every democratic constitution rests directly on the constituent power or, on the "existential total-decision" (*Totalentscheidung*) of the people. The total-decision of the people is not a decision on the state of exception but on the production (*Herstellung*) of the constitution (CT 241). The ground of the Weimar Constitution, for instance, cannot be found in any article of the constitutional law. According to Schmitt, it is found in the political existence and will of the German people. The Weimar Constitution and, thereby, the form of government of the German democratic state, is an existential total-decision of the German people.

The idea of the people as the constituent power of the nation was not new. It can be traced back to the conceptual distinction between *pouvoir constituant* and *pouvoir constitué* first made by a French theorist of the Revolution, Emmanuel Sieyès. Like Schmitt, Sieyès attributes constituent power to the nation, whose will is the origin of all legality. For him, constituent power is power which is not defined by a constitution but which is presupposed by it. But we must notice that Schmitt uses Sieyès' distinction for his own purposes, specifically abolishing the limits that Sieyès sets on constituent power. According to the latter, constituent power is limited by natural law, which stands prior to and above the nation.[10] For Schmitt, nothing stands prior to and above the constituent power of the people. It precedes natural law and transcends it as it precedes the constitution and is above it.

Yet although Schmitt says that the people are the unorganized origin of all organizations, as a political unity, the people is not without certain attributes. The people as a unity capable of political action is not a random collection of private individuals. Firstly, the existence of the people presupposes *homogeneity* and, thereby, identification and exclusion of the enemy: "Democracy requires first homogeneity and second—if the need arises—elimination or eradication of heterogeneity."[11] This is how Schmitt reads Rousseau's principle of democratic identity, namely the identity of those who rule and those who are ruled.[12] According to Schmitt, this identity does not entail the "abstract" equality of all people. Such equality, Schmitt claims, is characteristic of the liberal worldview but not of the democratic one. Democratic equality entails the equality of those who share similar physical or moral qualities—and consequently, an exclusion of those who are different.

Secondly, Schmitt argues, the democratic people exists only in the sphere of *publicity*. For this reason, Schmitt does not hesitate to denounce even an individual and secret ballot as an anti-democratic institution. The secret ballot is not a democratic but, again, a liberal idea—and in Schmitt's view, it contradicts the whole concept of the people. The individual and secret ballot transforms a citizen into a private man of the private sphere, who by voting expresses only his individual opinion. Rather than elections, Schmitt argues, the normal expression of the people's will is *acclamation* by an assembled multitude. After the people have decided on the type and form of constitution, they can only say yes or no to a question posed to them by those who have political authority (CT 131–2). This is why Schmitt is able to maintain that even dictatorial and Caesaristic methods are not necessarily antidemocratic. Not only can they evoke acclamation, but they can also be "a direct expression of democratic substance and power."[13]

Thirdly, although democracy is based on the principle of identity of those who rule and those who are ruled, absolute identity is impossible, for the masses are, as Schmitt maintains, sociologically and psychologically heterogeneous. Therefore, he argues, the principle of identity has to be supplemented with the principle of *identification*. The people become conscious of its political existence as a political unity and homogeneous nation only by identifying itself with a representation that is given to them from above. Indeed, Schmitt holds that representation is a necessary element of every theory of the state, including a democratic state: "No democratic state can renounce absolutely all representation" (CT 240). Yet the necessity of representation in democracy does not entail the necessity of parliamentary democracy. In Schmitt's view, even one person can express the people's will as well as a group of secretly elected parliamentary representatives. Reflecting on the Weimar Constitution, Schmitt in fact came to the conclusion that the president (*Reichspräsident*)—rather than the parliamentary representatives— represents "the political total will of the German nation."[14]

III

Schmitt's concept of sovereignty was a conservative reaction to the democratization of the German nation-state. The theory of the sovereign deciding on the state of exception was a right-wing anti-parliamentary intervention into the academic and political discussion on the foundations of the modern state and the Weimar Republic in particular. Although the development of the modern state from the absolutist state towards the rule-of-law state (*Rechtsstaat*) had downplayed the role of a personal sovereign in theory, the modern state, Schmitt argued, cannot dispense with sovereignty: even the rule-of-law state is ultimately based on the sovereign decision. Hence, dictatorship is not, so Schmitt's argument goes, antithetical to the modern rule-of-law state. In the final analysis, every state is a dictatorship. And to the extent that the sovereign is anyone capable of deciding in a sovereign way, every state is a dictatorship based on one's sheer capacity to declare a state of exception and to bring it to an end with the measures one sees fit.

Similarly, Schmitt's theory of the people as the constituent power of the nation, although radically democratic in principle, turns out to be, if correctly scrutinized, not only a critique of the fundamental principles of constitutional liberalism but also a defense of plebiscitary dictatorship. The people are the anarchic foundation of the constitution, but in order to become a people in the political sense of the word it must be represented by those who factually rule. Hence, the revolutionary force of an unorganized and unrepresented people is only virtual. Yet Schmitt had again a "good" authoritarian reason to emphasize the anarchic *archê* of the democratic state. If the foundation of the democratic state is not the written constitution but the will of the people, the person who represents this will is authorized to take any measures whatever if they are interpreted as the will of the people.

Finally, it must be mentioned that after Hitler's rise to power, Schmitt, who joined the Nazi party in May 1933, abandoned his decisionist theory of sovereignty and the state. Schmitt had identified the Italian fascist state with the traditional state-form compatible with his theory of sovereignty, democracy, and representation. The fascist state was still capable of producing acclamation and genuine representation. In Schmitt's view, however, the triumph of the national-socialist idea of the Leader and the Movement entailed the end of the state: "The state—as a specific order within the political unity—no longer has a monopoly on politics. It is nothing but an organ in the service of the Leader of the Movement."[15]

For Schmitt, however, the end of the state was not a catastrophe. On the contrary, adhering fully to the National Socialist idea of the Leader and the Movement, Schmitt became increasingly sarcastic toward the modern state, associating it with a long historical series of liberal neutralizations and depoliticizations. The same holds true with the concept of sovereignty. The Leader is not a sovereign dictator because his decisions are not indeterminate. Unlike in the decisionist theory of the state, they do not emanate from a normative nothingness: the Leader is bound to the racial homogeneity (*Artgleichheit*) of the German People. The Leader is the embodiment of this homogeneity and thus determined by it.[16] In National Socialist Germany, there was no longer a need for the theory of sovereignty or the state.

Notes

1   Carl Schmitt, *Political Theology: Four Chapters on the Concept of Sovereignty*, trans. George Schwab (Cambridge, MA: MIT Press, 1985), 5.

2   Carl Schmitt, *Constitutional Theory*, trans. Jeffrey Seitzer (Durham: Duke University Press, 2008), 300.

3   Hans Kelsen, *Problem der Souveränität und die Theorie des Völkerrecht* (Tübingen: J. C. B. Mohr, 1920), 330.

4   Carl Schmitt, *Der Wert des Staates und die Bedeutung des Einzelnen* (Munich: C. H. Beck, 1914), 79.

5 Carl Schmitt, *The Concept of the Political*, trans. George Schwab (Chicago: University of Chicago Press, 1996), 67.

6 On the other hand, Schmitt also emphasizes that the political tradition since Jean Bodin's classical formulation in the *Six Books of the Commonwealth* has—more or less—comprehended the significance of the emergency situation in the theory of sovereignty.

7 Carl Schmitt, *Über die Drei Arten des rechtswissenschaftlichen Denkens* (Berlin: Duncker & Humblot, 1993), 23. Translation mine.

8 In this sense, Schmitt was a true heir to Thomas Hobbes to whom the law was identical with the sovereign's command. One of Schmitt's favorite quotations was Hobbes's *auctoritas, non veritas, facit legem*—authority, not truth, makes the law.

9 Carl Schmitt, *Dictatorship*, trans. Michael Hoelzland and Graham Ward (Cambridge: Polity Press, 2013), 127.

10 See Emmanuel Sieyès, *Qu'est-ce que le tiers-état* (Paris: Flammarion, 1988), ch. 5.

11 Carl Schmitt, *The Crisis of Parliamentary Democracy*, trans. Ellen Kennedy (Cambridge, MA: MIT Press, 1996), 10.

12 In a democracy, the sovereign and the subject are "identical correlatives." Jean-Jacques Rousseau, *The Social Contract* (London: Penguin Books 1980), 138. For a discussion of Rousseau's theory of sovereignty, see the relevant chapter in the present volume.

13 Schmitt, *The Crisis*, 17.

14 Carl Schmitt, *Der Hüter der Verfassung* (Tübingen: J. C. B. Mohr, 1931), 159. In this regard, Schmitt's position was not far from that of Max Weber, who had argued that the Weimer Republic needs a strong presidency directly elected by plebiscite, equipped with suspensory veto and the power of dissolving the parliament.

15 Schmitt, *Über die Drei Arten*, 44.

16 For a detailed analysis of Schmitt's theory of Nazism, see Ville Suuronen, "Carl Schmitt as a Theorist of the 1933 Nazi Revolution: 'The Difficult Task of Rethinking and Cultivating Traditional Concepts'," *Contemporary Political Theory* (2020): 1–23 (Online First Article).

20

Arendt on Sovereignty

Shmuel Lederman

Under human conditions [. . .] freedom and sovereignty are so little identical that they cannot even exist simultaneously. Where men wish to be sovereign, as individuals or as organized groups, they must submit to the oppression of the will, be this the individual will with which I force myself, or the "general will" of an organized group. If men wish to be free, it is precisely sovereignty they must renounce.[1]

Hannah Arendt's work can be seen to a large extent as a concentrated attack on the concept of sovereignty. It could hardly have been otherwise, as the basic lens through which Arendt looked at the world and tried to understand it was human plurality. Once human plurality is taken seriously, there is no place for the idea that we, as individuals or collectives, can or should be independent of the perspectives, judgments and actions of others in our shared world. A radical critique of the idea(l) of sovereignty was called for from early on in Arendt's intellectual development and it became increasingly rich and multilayered through her political and philosophical interventions.

Let us start where it is easiest: with the sovereignty of the state. Already in an early essay from 1945, "Approaches to the 'German Problem'," Arendt notes that "the national State, once the very symbol of the sovereignty of the people, no longer represented the people, becoming incapable of safeguarding either its external or internal security."[2] Here we need to distinguish between the two parts of the term Arendt uses in this statement: the "national state." Arendt's critique of nationalism and the nation-state is well known: she understood it as the takeover of the state by the nation, which naturally meant that those who are not part of the nation, namely national and ethnic minorities as well as refugees from other ethnic and national groups, would often be discriminated against, persecuted, or simply would not be allowed into the state. Moreover, once the state represents a specific nation, whatever serves the nation or constitutes its supposed "general will" becomes the basis of the state's foreign policy, often dismissing any moral inhibitions. The most extreme case, of course, was Nazi Germany, but it is worth noting how Arendt, in a symposium in 1964, links the evil Nazi Germany perpetrated with the kind of policies that were part and parcel of the logic of all nation-states:

> Those whom the Nazis had declared to be outlaws in their own territory became outlaws everywhere. Antisemitism was neither the only nor the decisive reason for this development; the political structure of the European nation-state was unable to assimilate large groups of foreigners, and its legal system was unable to cope with statelessness. However, the simple fact that all refugees from Nazi territories had been "undesirable" by definition was of considerable importance as a psychological preparation for the Holocaust.[3]

The nation-state, due to the imperative of keeping its population as homogenous as possible and granting a special political status to the ethnic group it purports to represent, is unable to address the growing problem of stateless persons. Most of those rejected by their own country, like the Jews, became refugees no country wanted. Thus, the sovereign nation-state, by its inherent tendencies, was inclined to create a large number of "superfluous" people who all too often found themselves locked up in detention and concentration camps as an undesirable population.

Moreover, if World War II proved anything, it is that most nation-states were not protected from the savage attacks of the more powerful ones. In a rapidly integrating world, the very idea of the total independence of the nation-state in determining its foreign and domestic politics as well as its economic policy was bound to clash with reality. For all these reasons, Arendt rejected the sovereign nation-state as unsuitable for the modern world and as having pernicious effects on the possibility of the co-existence of different ethnic populations.

However, it is often overlooked that Arendt's critique was aimed not only at the nation-state, but also at the modern state as such. Arendt understood the basic tendency of the modern state to be the centralization of power. "The modern state was," Arendt writes in 1946, "a 'strong state' which through its growing tendency towards centralization monopolized the whole of political life."[4] This left few opportunities for political participation and responsibility for the vast majority of citizens, and was one of the main factors leading to the atomization, alienation and loneliness on which the totalitarian movements built.[5] This is why, from early on, Arendt supported the federalization of the state into multiple local units that would allow every citizen who wished to do so to participate in politics. This vision was expressed in her discussion of the French Resistance:

> The cardinal principle of French resistance was *libérer et fédérer*; and by federation was meant a federated structure of the Fourth Republic [. . .] integrated in a European Federation. It is in almost identical terms that the French, Czech, Italian, Norwegian, and Dutch underground papers insist on this as the primary condition of a lasting peace—although [. . .] only the French underground has gone as far as to state that a federative structure of Europe must be based on *similarly federated structures in the constituent states.*[6]

Such de-centralization of the state, explains Arendt, would allow far more political responsibility and the kind of forgotten happiness only action and speech in the public sphere can grant.[7] In Germany in particular, she notes in another essay from 1950, mechanisms of local self-government at the expense of the centralized state, such as giving extensive power to the sub-states (*Länders*) and similarly to local communities, would diminish the centralization of power and would "teach grass-roots democracy in the field of communal or local affairs."[8] Rarely do these comments receive attention by scholars. The key to understanding what she had in mind is her suggestion, in an essay from 1948 on the Jewish–Arab conflict in Palestine, to establish local Jewish–Arab councils everywhere in Palestine, at the city and village level, which "would mean that the Jewish-Arab conflict would be resolved on the lowest and most promising level of proximity and neighborliness."[9] By the de-centralization of the state, then, Arendt meant the creation of a participatory democracy, in which citizens can take part in political decision making through local councils. This vision, which she would later present as the "lost treasure" of modern revolutions and as a "people's utopia," was inspired by the socialist movements of the late nineteenth and early twentieth century, and was shared, among other groups, by the French Resistance.[10]

Yet Arendt understood this vision in her own terms. For her, its attractiveness came not from being a useful tool for workers' self-management or for a socialist revolution, but rather from its promise to allow every citizen to take part in politics and thus enjoy the experience of freedom, which for Arendt meant the ability to act and speak in the public sphere together with one's fellow citizens. Arendt's problem with the principle of sovereignty, then, was not just the aspiration of *national* sovereignty through the state, but also the very idea that there should be a sovereign state, namely a state that centralizes power in order to rule its citizens effectively, and thus deprives them from exercising their own potential political power. It is in this fundamental sense that sovereignty and freedom, as Arendt insists in my opening quote, are inherently opposed to each other.

This critique of the centralized state and the vision of domestic and international federalization remained constant in Arendt's thought, and it was meant to divide power among individuals as well as groups, including ethnic groups, within the state. As she states in 1963, "there can only be real democracy [. . .] where the centralization of power in the nation-state has been broken, and replaced with a diffusion of power into the many power centers of a federal system." This is since individuals and collectives are "almost always powerless against the monopoly of a centrally organized state apparatus, and the powerlessness of the citizen, even when all his rights are protected, stands in basic opposition to democracy in all its forms."[11]

The sovereignty of the state had detrimental consequences, in Arendt's view, also in the international arena. In "On Violence," she goes as far as to suggest that the main cause for wars was the simple fact that there was no arbiter in international affairs above the nation-state, and this is bound to remain so as long as "national independence, namely, freedom from foreign rule, and the sovereignty of the state, namely, the claim to unchecked and unlimited power in foreign affairs, are identified."[12] The sovereignty of the state had to be at the very least significantly limited if the prospects of war were to be diminished. The development of international law, designating appropriate powers to an international court, was one solution Arendt supported, but this was hardly enough. In a 1970 interview, she explains further that between sovereign states there can be no last resort except war, and therefore anyone who wishes to see an end to the phenomenon of war between states has to envision a new kind of state, based on a "federal system, whose advantage is that power moves neither from above nor from below, but is horizontally directed so that the federated units mutually check and control their powers." Such a state, based on citizen councils, "to which the principle of sovereignty would be wholly alien, would be admirably suited to federations of the most various kinds, especially because in it power would be constituted horizontally and not vertically."[13]

In this insistence on the division of power within the state as a way to check the power of each unit Arendt draws on Montesquieu, whom she invokes explicitly when she discusses the division of power in the United States.[14] However, as mentioned above, she also follows a long socialist tradition which pointed to the same need, albeit for different reasons. Unfortunately, Arendt does not specify how exactly such a state would function either on the domestic or on the international level. She was more interested in explicating the guiding principles and the political advantages of such a state rather than its practical complexities. What most clearly emerges from her writings on the subject is that such a new form of government would be wholly alien to the principle of sovereignty, which means also alien to the very notion of a "general will" that could somehow apply to a plurality of individuals and groups. For Arendt, the basic assumptions behind the principle of sovereignty were diametrically opposed to the guiding thread of her entire corpus: the recognition of human plurality.

* * *

A particularly challenging aspect of Arendt's writings on sovereignty is her reflections on what may be called the sovereignty of the individual, which can be roughly divided into two main themes. First, Arendt makes clear that our understanding of the world is almost entirely dependent on the extent of our engagement with the perspectives of others. We *always* see the world from a limited viewpoint, from our specific position in it. Therefore, our only way to get a fuller grasp of the common world is to try to see it from the point of view of others. This is particularly true when it comes to the public sphere, where our willingness to consider the perspectives of others is crucial for our ability to judge and orient ourselves. As Arendt puts it:

> That the capacity to judge is a specifically political ability in exactly the sense denoted by Kant, namely, the ability to see things not only from one's own point of view but in the perspective of all those who happen to be present; even that judgment may be one of the fundamental abilities of man as a political being insofar as it enables him to orient himself in the political realm, in the common world—these are insights that are virtually as old as articulated political experience. The Greeks called this ability *phronesis*, or insight, and they considered it the principal virtue or excellence of the statesman in distinction from the wisdom of the philosopher.[15]

Contrary to the interpretation of many commentators,[16] I believe that while the ability to imagine what we would experience and think if we were in the place of others was certainly important for Arendt, she always saw this capacity as emerging from actual encounters with our fellow citizens, rather than something that can take place in our heads alone in a kind of "representative thinking." In other words, we are never sovereign in our understanding of the very world we live in; our comprehension of it is always already shaped by the shared experience of our society and those close to us. Furthermore, if we wish to get a better understanding of the world and have a richer sense of reality, it is our supposed sovereignty that we need to renounce.

The second and even more challenging aspect of Arendt's reflections on individual sovereignty is our very understanding of the Self. Especially in her most important work in political theory, *The Human Condition*, Arendt suggests that our inner self tends to be fluctuating and unstable, to the extent that it is perhaps more accurate to speak about multiple inner "selves." Yet somehow, out of this inner plurality emerges a unique identity, disclosed only in the company of others. This unique identity is disclosed only when we act and speak in the public realm with our fellow citizens. Arendt insists that we cannot disclose who we are intentionally, among other reasons because we *do not know* our own unique identity. She uses the Greek idea of *daimon*, which accompanies each person throughout his life—"always looking over his shoulder from behind and thus visible only to those he encounters"[17]—to suggest that others can see *who* we are, our unique identity, better than ourselves. Thus, it is somehow revealed to those who see and hear us when we act or speak, so that our own understanding of who we are depends on others to reflect it to us. We find in Arendt, then, a radically intersubjective understanding of the Self and its relation to the world, which both borrows and departs from Heidegger.[18] This concept of the Self presents a critique of sovereignty which combines ethical, existential and political implications: we discover ourselves and the world by speaking and acting with others, and the extent to which we are able to do so depends on the political spaces available to us.

Yet, there seems to be more tension and complexity in the Arendtian Self than commentators are prepared to grant. In most accounts one finds the notion that in Arendt there is no unified Self prior to speech and action in the public sphere. As one authoritative commentator has put it,

> Arendt's agonistic conception [. . .] is based on the rejection of anything like an expressivist conception of the self [. . .] The expressivist conception assumes a core self, a basic or essential unity of innate capacities that are expressed, actualized, or concretized in the world of appearances [. . .] In contrast, the performance model deployed by Arendt [. . .] seeks to unmask this "fiction" [. . .] From Arendt's point of view the self that precedes action, the biological or psychological self, is an essentially dispersed, fragmented, and plural self [. . .] Arendt challenges the assumption that a single, unified subject resides behind action.[19]

However, Arendt is explicit that our unique identity is disclosed rather than *created* in the public sphere. She is also quite clear that this identity is stable over time. In one statement, for example, she argues that "[t]his unchangeable identity of the person, though disclosing itself intangibly in act and speech, becomes tangible only in the story of the actor's and speaker's life; but as such it can be known, that is, grasped as a palpable entity only after it has come to its end."[20] There is, then, an *unchangeable* identity of the person. Yet, this identity remains intangible even after our action and speech in the public sphere. It seems to be stable and in constant flux at the same time; and it is knowable in full only to others, especially those who tell the story about the person after she passes away and thus, in a way, *determine* the kind of identity that she leaves behind. Arendt's precise concept of the Self, then, remains somewhat mysterious. What is clear is that it is radically non-sovereign. We depend on others for the recognition of our unique identity and for our understanding of reality. One can even speak of the Arendtian challenge of letting ourselves be "undone by each other."[21] One can see how profound and resistant to any notion of sovereignty the acceptance of the human condition of plurality was for Arendt.

To conclude, there is an important reason why, in the opening quote, Arendt contrasts sovereignty with freedom. Arguably, Arendt presents us with a unique concept of freedom. It is neither freedom of the will; nor freedom from the interference of others or the state, as in the liberal tradition; nor, finally, freedom from domination, as in the republican tradition. For Arendt, freedom is always political; it "appears" only when we act and speak together in the public sphere. In other words: it is a unique human potential that can be experienced only in the company of our fellow citizens. Therefore, the division of the state into multiple public realms in which the citizens can actively participate through speech and action is a necessary condition for the very experience of freedom, as far as "ordinary" citizens are concerned. This is also why Arendt urges us to see how fundamentally dependent we are on others in our very experience of the world and of ourselves. It is on this radical level—politically and philosophically—that Arendt believed freedom and sovereignty "cannot even exist simultaneously" and why "if men wish to be free, it is precisely sovereignty they must renounce."

Notes

1 Hannah Arendt, "What is Freedom?," in *Between Past and Future: Eight Exercises in Political Thought* (New York: Penguin Books, 2006), 163.

2 Hannah Arendt, "Approaches to the 'German Problem'," in Hannah Arendt, *Essays in Understanding, 1930–1954: Formation, Exile, and Totalitarianism*, ed. Jerome Kohn (New York: Schocken Books, 1994), 111–2.

3 Hannah Arendt, "The Destruction of Six Million: A Jewish World Symposium," in Hannah Arendt, *The Jewish Writings*, ed. Jerome Kohn and Ron H. Feldman (New York: Schocken Books, 2007), 490–1.

4 Hannah Arendt, "The Nation," in *Essays in Understanding*, 209.

5 See Jennifer Gaffney, "Another Origin of Totalitarianism: Arendt on the Loneliness of Liberal Citizens," *Journal of the British Society for Phenomenology* 47, no. 1 (2016): 1–17.

6 Arendt, "Approaches," 114, emphasis added.

7 Ibid., 114.

8 Hannah Arendt, "The Aftermath of Nazi Rule: Report from Germany," in *Essays in Understanding*, 267.

9 Hannah Arendt, "To Save the Jewish Homeland," in *The Jewish Writings*, 400.

10 See Shmuel Lederman, *Hannah Arendt and Participatory Democracy: A People's Utopia* (New York: Palgrave Macmillan, 2019), ch. 2. On Blücher's influence on this vision, see my "Hannah Arendt and Heinrich Blücher: Reflections on Philosophy, Politics and Democracy," *Arendt Studies* 1 (2017): 87–100.

11 Hannah Arendt, "Nation-State and Democracy," in *Thinking Without a Banister*, ed. Jerome Kohn (New York: Schocken Books, 2018), 261.

12 Hannah Arendt, "On Violence," in *Crises of the Republic* (New York: Harcourt Brace Jovanovich, Inc., 1972), 107.

13 Hannah Arendt, "Thoughts on Politics and Revolution," in *Crises of the Republic*, 230; 233.

14 Hannah Arendt, *On Revolution* (New York: Penguin Books, 2006), 143.

15 Hannah Arendt, "The Crisis in Culture," in *Between Past and Future*, 217–8.

16 See, for example, Nancy Fraser, "Communication, Transformation, and Consciousness-Raising," in *Hannah Arendt and the Meaning of Politics*, ed. Craig Calhoun and John McGowan (Minneapolis: University of Minnesota Press, 1997), 171; Rosine Kelz, *The Non-Sovereign Self, Responsibility, and Otherness: Hannah Arendt, Judith Butler, and Stanley Cavell on Moral Philosophy and Political Agency* (New York: Palgrave Macmillan, 2016), 42.

17 Hannah Arendt, *The Human Condition* (Chicago: The University of Chicago Press, 1998), 179–80.

18 Lewis P. Hinchman and Sandra K. Hinchman, "Existentialism Politicized," in *Hannah Arendt: Critical Essays*, eds. Lewis P. Hinchman and Sandra K. Hinchman, 143–78 (New York: State University of New York Press, 1994); Dana R. Villa, *Arendt and Heidegger: The Fate of the Political* (New Jersey: Princeton University Press, 1996).

19 Villa, *Arendt and Heidegger*, 90.

20 Arendt, *The Human Condition*, 193.

21 Judith Butler, *Precarious Life: The Powers of Mourning and Violence* (London and New York: Verso, 2004), 23.

21

Foucault and Agamben on Sovereignty

Taking Life, Letting Live, or Making Survive

Carlo Salzani

Beneath that great absolute power, beneath the dramatic and somber absolute power that was the power of sovereignty, and which consisted in the power to take life, we now have the emergence, with this technology of biopower, of this technology of power over "the" population as such, over men insofar as they are living beings. It is continuous, scientific, and it is the power to make live. Sovereignty took life and let live. And now we have the emergence of a power that I would call the power of regularization, and it, in contrast, consists in making live and letting die.[1]

[A] third formula can be said to insinuate itself between the other two, a formula that defines the most specific trait of twentieth-century biopolitics: no longer either to make die or to make live, but to make survive. The decisive activity of biopower in our time consists in the production not of life or death, but rather of a mutable and virtually infinite survival. In every case, it is a matter of dividing animal life from organic life, the human from the inhuman,

the witness from the Muselmann, *conscious life from vegetative life maintained functional through resuscitation techniques, until a threshold is reached: an essentially mobile threshold that, like the borders of geopolitics, moves according to the progress of scientific and political technologies. Biopower's supreme ambition is to produce, in a human body, the absolute separation of the living being and the speaking being,* zoē *and* bios, *the inhuman and the human—survival.*[2]

Two of the most outstanding figures of late twentieth-century political philosophy, Michel Foucault and Giorgio Agamben, are linked by a sort of "filiation bond," whereby Agamben claimed to take up and develop Foucault's "biopolitical" project, transforming it, two decades after its subdued inception, into a central and inescapable issue for contemporary philosophical-political debate. From early on, however, critics have emphasized how the two projects differ in scope and intention, and one of the fundamental differences is precisely their understanding of biopower in relation to sovereignty: whereas Foucault saw the two modes of power as historically distinct and (at times, though not consistently) as mutually exclusive, Agamben came to conflate them into one single meta-structure which spells out the very essential trait of Western metaphysics. Both construe their political project in fundamental opposition to sovereignty, but, just like the ways of understanding it, also the modes of this opposition differ to the point of taking opposite routes.

* * *

Sovereignty was the "counterconcept"[3] of Foucault's political philosophy, both in the sense that it constituted the antagonist of his political project, and that he elaborated his analyses of power in contrast to traditional theories based on the concept of sovereign power. In a June 1976 interview with Alessandro Fontana and Pasquale Pasquino, he famously said that "We need to cut off the King's head" in political theory,[4] which echoed the claim he made a few months earlier, in the January 14, 1976 session of the lecture course at the Collège de France *Society Must Be Defended*, that "We have to study power outside the model of Leviathan, outside the field delineated by juridical sovereignty and the institution of the State" (*SMBD* 34). To understand the workings of power in modern societies, he argued, we need to look beyond the state and the law and traditional political theories. This intention is clearly at work in the early 1970s in his writings and in his teaching at the Collège de France, which basically focus on and elaborate a series of theories on "disciplinary power"—from *Penal Theories and Institutions* (1971–72), to *The Punitive Society* (1972–73), *Psychiatric*

Power (1973–74) and *The Abnormal* (1974–74), culminating in 1975 in the publication of *Discipline and Punish: The Birth of The Prison*. In the 1975–76 course *Society Must Be Defended*, he identified a further type of power, also pitched against traditional sovereign power, that he named "biopower."

In this lecture course Foucault gave his famous definition of sovereignty: in the session of March 17, 1976, he identified the main attribute of sovereign power as "the right of life and death." It is a strange right, he commented; it is dissymmetrical, since it is exercised only when the sovereign decides to kill, and is therefore always "tipped in favor of death." Its essence is thus the right to kill: "It is essentially the right of the sword," that is, "the right to take life or let live" (*SMBD* 240–1). The last chapter of the first volume of his *History of Sexuality*, published a few months later, is indeed entitled "Right of Death and Power over Life" and refines this definition: sovereign power—or the juridico-institutional power, as he also calls it—was "exercised mainly as a means of deduction (*prélèvement*), a subtraction mechanism [. . .]. Power in this instance was essentially a right of seizure: of things, time, bodies, and ultimately life itself; it culminated in the privilege to seize hold of life in order to suppress it."[5] Although the law is the sovereign's main means of ruling, its symbol is the sword. This is therefore basically a negative power, based on prohibition and punishment—just like the law which upholds it.

From the end of the sixteenth century, this power was progressively integrated, and then superseded (though Foucault is not consistent on this point), by what he called "disciplinary power," a power exercised not, like sovereign power, over land and territory, but over bodies and what they do, and alien to the discourse of the law. Rather than through prohibition and punishment, it works through "normalization," through the regulation and discipline of individual bodies. Finally, the end of the eighteenth century saw a further technology of power emerge, no longer focused on the management of individual bodies but aimed at entire populations: no longer an "anatomo-politics of the human body" (i.e. disciplinary politics), but a "biopolitics of the human race" (*SMBD* 243). This new technology focuses on the ratio of births to deaths, the rate of reproduction, the fertility of a population, and so on. If the right of sovereignty was the right to take life or let live, then this new power is characterized by the "right to make live and to let die" (*SMBD* 241). As such, it is no longer a negative power based on subtraction, but rather a positive power based on *production*: "It exerts a positive influence on life, endeavors to administer, optimize, and multiply it"; its balance is not tipped in favor of death, but, to the contrary, in favor of life, with a consequent "disqualification of death" (*SE1* 137–8):

> death becomes, insofar as it is the end of life, the term, the limit, or the end of power too. Death is outside the power relationship. Death is beyond the reach of power . . . In the right of sovereignty, death was the moment of the most obvious and most spectacular manifestation of

the absolute power of the sovereign; death now becomes, in contrast, the moment when the individual escapes all power, falls back on himself and retreats, so to speak, into his own privacy. (*SMBD* 248)

A further consequence is a progressive "juridical regression," whereby the law (prohibition and punishment symbolized by sword and death) is substituted by the productive action of the "norm," which takes charge of life's needs with continuous regulatory and corrective mechanisms (*SE1* 144).

Foucault was not consistent in regard to the historical determination of these three forms of power. If in *Society Must Be Defended* and *The History of Sexuality* he saw them as "increasingly in conflict" and incompatible (*SMBD* 39), so that the power of death was finally "supplanted" by the management of life (*SE1* 139–40), in the following lecture course, *Security, Territory, Population* (1977–78; he gave no lecture course in 1976–77), he saw them as coexisting at different levels in a sort of triangular structure.[6] Ultimately, as Roberto Esposito writes, he could not decide between discontinuity and continuity and kept running "simultaneously in both directions."[7]

*   *   *

At the very beginning of his seminal work *Homo Sacer* (1995, the first of nine books divided into four volumes and composing the homonymous project), Agamben purports to "complete" the biopolitical project that Foucault's untimely death interrupted (a disputable claim, since biopower ultimately played a little and transitory part in Foucault's writings and teachings, and was abandoned long before his death)[8] by focusing on the "hidden point of intersection between the juridico-institutional and the biopolitical models of power." *Contra* Foucault, Agamben's thesis is that

the two analyses cannot be separated, and that the inclusion of bare life in the political realm constitutes the original—if concealed—nucleus of sovereign power. *It can even be said that the production of a biopolitical body is the original activity of sovereign power.* In this sense, biopolitics is at least as old as the sovereign exception.[9]

This means, in the end, that *there is no intersection at all*, since the two powers ultimately *coincide*,[10] and the explicit focus on life that Foucault identified as the main trait of modern politics merely brings to light the secret and immemorial bond holding together sovereignty and life.

To sustain this claim Agamben grafts on Foucault's biopolitics Carl Schmitt's theory of sovereignty, according to which sovereign is he who decides on the exception. What defines the sovereign is not the right of life and death, but the power of declaring a state of emergency or exception, thereby suspending the law. This right, Agamben argues, places the sovereign simultaneously inside and outside the law, and provides the paradigm for the main structure that characterizes, in general, Western metaphysics: the sovereign exception, or inclusive exclusion, which includes something by excluding it. This is the very structure that determines the relation between law and life: the human polity is construed through the separation of biological life (*zoè*) from public, proper political life (*bios*), whereby the former is deemed impolitical and relegated to the private space of the home. This very exclusion, however, simultaneously includes *zoè* as excluded, producing thereby the paradigm of political exclusion, which Agamben names "bare life." What epitomizes this excluded life is an (until Agamben's adoption of it) obscure figure of Roman law, *homo sacer*, the "sacred man" who is banned and may be killed by anybody but may not be sacrificed in a religious ritual. Hence, life is *always* the main object of power's technologies: politics is *always* biopolitics. What changes in modernity is merely that the exception becomes the rule and the *arcanum imperii* is revealed out in the open.

This "development" of Foucault's theory entails not only the conflation and reduction of all forms of power to a single, all-encompassing model, but also a fundamental *ontologization* of politics that replaces Foucault's historical or genealogical inquiries with a conceptual, generalizing theory of Western politics as a monolithic, ahistorical structure. Politics ultimately turns out to be only one instance of a more essential—metaphysical and negative—structure, the inclusionary exclusion, which allegedly characterizes all systems and apparatuses of the West, from language to subjectivity, from humanity itself to anthropogenesis. Politics, therefore, is logically secondary to sovereignty.[11] Sovereign, disciplinary and bio-power are not historically specific or contingent forms, but expressions of one single, overarching structure of Western metaphysics; they do not differ in being exercised over territory, individual body or population, but in the level at which they disclose the *arcanum imperii*, power's hold on every individual body. From a conception of sovereignty as legitimation or authorization of power, we move thus to a notion of sovereignty as pure power, as power as such. Moreover, the law is here not distinguished from disciplinary or biopolitical norm, but is rather equated to *normativity as such*—"the entire text of tradition in its regulative form, whether the Jewish Torah or the Islamic Shariah, Christian dogma or the profane *nomos*" (*HS* 51)—and made into the main instrument of sovereignty.

Within this totalizing logic, no active or strategic resistance is possible, as it was instead in Foucault, for whom all power relations are contingent and ultimately reversible. Agamben's vision is much more drastic and bleaker, since sovereignty's hold on life for him is always negative, repressive, deadly: biopolitics always tips towards "thanatopolitics" (the politics of death). For Agamben, the only way out from the deadly grip of sovereignty is an equally totalizing countermove, that is, the complete shutdown of the metaphysical machinery of the West.

*   *   *

Foucault coined the term "thanatopolitics" to define the "reverse of biopolitics."[12] The "disqualification of death" in biopolitics does not mean in fact that power has ceased to kill—to the contrary, in modernity "massacres have become vital" and "genocide is ... the dream of modern powers" (*SE1* 137). But given that biopower's objective is essentially to make live, he wonders, how can it let die? The answer he gives is: through racism. Through racism power can introduce a break between what must live and what must die and can continue to exercise the sovereign right to kill: "In a normalizing society, race or racism is the precondition that makes killing acceptable" (*SMBD* 255). This point smooths out the difference between sovereignty and biopolitics, since Foucault freely admits that with biopower "racism is inscribed as the basic mechanism of power, as it is exercised in modern States. As a result, the modern State can scarcely function without becoming involved with racism at some point" (*SMBD* 254). The extreme example, where this apparent contradiction was taken to a "paroxysmal point," was the Nazi state, "which has generalized biopower in an absolute sense, but which has also generalized the sovereign right to kill," so that the two mechanisms *coincide exactly*:

> The Nazi State makes the field of the life it manages, protects, guarantees, and cultivates in biological terms absolutely coextensive with the sovereign right to kill anyone, meaning not only other people, but also its own people. There was, in Nazism, a coincidence between a generalized biopower and a dictatorship that was at once absolute and retransmitted throughout the entire social body by this fantastic extension of the right to kill and of exposure to death. (*SMBD* 260)

This coincidence, for Agamben, inheres to sovereign power *as such*, and the Nazi state merely realized its logic in full and brought it to light with paradigmatic violence. The Nazi state, and especially the Nazi death camp, constitute for Agamben the paradigmatic instance of sovereign (bio)power insofar as "its inhabitants were stripped of every political status and wholly reduced to bare life." In the camp, "power confronts nothing but pure life, without mediation." That is why "the camp is the very paradigm of political space at the point at which politics becomes biopolitics and *homo sacer* is virtually confused with the citizen" (*HS* 171). Not the *polis*, but rather the camp is the "*nomos*," the paradigm, of the modern, as the title of *Homo Sacer*'s last chapter states.

Agamben devoted a whole book, *Remnants of Auschwitz* (1998), to the exploration of this paradigmatic extreme where biopolitics coincides immediately with thanatopolitics. This coincidence leads him to correct Foucault's alternative between making die and letting live (sovereignty), and making live and letting die (biopower); there is a third option, Agamben writes, and it is precisely this that reveals the "secret cypher," the *arcanum*, the very essence of sovereign (bio)power: to make survive. Survival is the "absolute biopolitical substance" because it shows in its "purity," as it were, the capture of life by sovereign power. It is the end product of the sovereign's most intimate activity; it is "bare life" as the biopolitical body, *homo sacer* (*RA* 156). In the Nazi death camp, the embodiment of *homo sacer* was the *Muselmann*, the last stage of dehumanization in which all traces of a qualified, meaningful life have been stripped away. In its total bareness, the *Muselmann* shows the sovereign (bio)power's supreme ambition: the absolute separation of life from all human forms and predicates.

* * *

From the late 2000s, Agamben has been progressively toning down his use of the vocabulary of sovereignty, which could appear as a moving away from sovereignty toward a (more Foucauldian) analysis of the practices of government, as in *The Kingdom and the Glory* (2007). It is indisputable that this book seriously engages with Foucault's concept of "governmentality," which the latter developed in the 1977–78 lecture course *Security, Territory, Population* (first published in French in 2004) precisely as an alternative to sovereignty. However, Agamben's overall approach, intention, and conceptual frame remains consistent up to the completion of the project *Homo Sacer* in 2015, with the publication of *The Use of Bodies*: perhaps he does not call it "sovereignty" anymore, but power's deadly capture of life remains the metaphysical, totalizing structure that his philosophical project calls on to overcome.

Notes

1   Michel Foucault, *Society Must Be Defended: Lectures at the Collège the France, 1975–76*, trans. David Macey (New York: Picador, 2003), 247. Hereafter parenthetically in the text as *SMBD*.

2   Giorgio Agamben, *Remnants of Auschwitz: The Witness and the Archive*, trans. Daniel Heller-Roazen (New York: Zone Books, 1999), 155–6. Hereafter parenthetically in the text as *RA*.

3   Banu Bargu, "Sovereignty," in *The Cambridge Foucault Lexicon*, ed. Leonard Lawlor and John Nale (Cambridge: Cambridge University Press, 2014), 456.

4   Michel Foucault, "Truth and Power," in *Power/Knowledge: Selected Interviews and Other Writings 1972–1977*, ed. Colin Gordon (New York: Pantheon, 1980), 121.

5   Michel Foucault, *The History of Sexuality, Volume 1: An Introduction*, trans. Robert Hurley (New York: Pantheon, 1978), 136. Hereafter parenthetically in the text as *SE1*.

6   Michel Foucault, *Security, Territory, Population: Lectures at the Collège de France, 1977–1978*, trans. Graham Burchell (Basingstoke: Palgrave Macmillan, 2007), 107–8.

7   Roberto Esposito, *Bios: Biopolitics and Philosophy*, trans. Timothy Campbell (Minneapolis, MN: University of Minnesota Press, 2008), 43.

8   Paul Patton, "Agamben and Foucault on Biopower and Biopolitics," in *Giorgio Agamben: Sovereignty and Life*, ed. Matthew Calarco and Steven DeCaroli (Stanford, CA: Stanford University Press, 2007), 206.

9   Giorgio Agamben, *Homo Sacer: Sovereign Power and Bare Life*, trans. Daniel Heller-Roazen (Stanford, CA: Stanford University Press, 1998), 6, emphasis in the original. Hereafter parenthetically in the text as *HS*.

10 Tom Frost, "Agamben's Sovereign Legalization of Foucault," *Oxford Journal of Legal Studies* 30.3 (2010): 549.

11 Claire Colebrook and Jason Maxwell, *Agamben* (Cambridge: Polity Press, 2016), 61–2.

12 Michel Foucault, "The Political Technology of Individuals," in *Power: Essential Works of Foucault, 1954–1984*, ed. James Faubion, vol. 3 (New York: The New Press, 2000), 416.

22

Derrida on the "Slow and Differentiated" Deconstruction of Sovereignty

James Martel

[W]hat I am looking for would be, then a slow and differentiated deconstruction of this logic and the dominant, classic concept of nation-state sovereignty (which is a reference for Schmitt), without ending up with a de-politicization, but an other politicization, a re-politicization that does not fall into the same ruts of the "dishonest fiction," without ending up, then, in a de-politicization but another politicization, a re-politicization and therefore another concept of the political.
[. . .] it cannot be a matter, under the pretext of deconstruction, of purely and simply, frontally, opposing sovereignty. There is not SOVEREIGNTY or THE sovereign. There is not THE beast and THE sovereign. There are different and sometimes antagonistic forms of sovereignty, and it is always in the name of one that one attacks another: for example [. . .] it is in the name of a sovereignty of man, or even of the personal subject, of his autonomy (for autonomy and liberty are also sovereignty, and one cannot without warning and without threatening by the same token all liberty, purely and simply attack the motifs or the rallying cries of independence, autonomy, and even nation-state sovereignty, in the name of which some weak peoples are struggling against the colonial and imperial hegemony of more powerful states).

*In a certain sense, there is no contrary of sovereignty, even if there
are things other than sovereignty. Even in politics (and the question
remains of knowing if the concept of sovereignty is political
through and through)—even in politics, the choice is not between
sovereignty and nonsovereignty, but among several forms of
partings, partitions, divisions, conditions that come along to broach
a sovereignty that is always supposed to be indivisible and
unconditional. Whence the difficulty, awkwardness, aporia even,
and the slowness, the always unequal development of such a
deconstruction. This is less than ever the equivalent of a destruction.
But recognizing that sovereignty is divisible, that it divides and
partitions, even where there is any sovereignty left, is already
to begin to deconstruct a pure concept of sovereignty that
presupposes indivisibility. A divisible sovereignty is no longer a
sovereignty, a sovereignty worthy of the name, i.e. pure
and unconditional.*[1]

The passage I have selected for my discussion of sovereignty in Jacques
Derrida's work reveals the tremendous ambivalence that attends his
discussions of sovereignty more generally. In so much of his writing,
sovereignty is a terrible thing. In *The Politics of Friendship* he reveals how
sovereignty is connected to murder and fratricide; even as it purports to be
the solution to violence, for Derrida, sovereignty is more often the source of
rather than the solution to bloodshed.[2] In *Rogues*, Derrida worries about
the "rogue" state that lurks behind even the most benign façade of sovereign
authority.[3] In *Specters of Marx*, he sees sovereignty as being part and parcel
of western hegemony, leading to exploitation, violence and inequality in the
world.[4] In these and other writings we can see that Derrida has no illusions
about sovereignty. At the same time, he seems drawn to the concept of
sovereignty, which he continually revisits. In doing so, he also appears to feel
the draw of sovereign power. There are even times when Derrida actually
fears its elimination lest it be replaced by something worse.[5]

These questions demarcate the terrain of Derrida's ambivalent attitude
towards sovereignty. For all of his concerns about sovereignty's illicit source
of authority and its violence, as the second paragraph of the passage above
indicates, Derrida worries about the recklessness inherent in attempting a
full-on repudiation of sovereign authority. Even if sovereignty functions as a
kind of empty—and hence violent—signifier, he tells us that "one cannot
without warning and without threatening all liberty, purely and simply
attack the motifs or the rallying cries of independence, autonomy and even

nation-state sovereignty, in the name of which some weak peoples are struggling against the colonial and imperial hegemony of more powerful states."

In other words, Derrida is suggesting that somehow sovereignty remains cathected to all of the claims that have been associated with its name, so that a notion such as liberty is somehow caught up with a sovereign form of authority regardless of how pernicious and bloody (and opposed to actual liberty) the latter always seems to be. Even if sovereignty in its present form is in some ways the antithesis of what he seeks from political life, Derrida is telling us here that the path to goals like liberty and justice does not lie in the wholesale destruction of sovereignty per se.

Perhaps most critically of all, as the above-cited passage also demonstrates, Derrida recognizes that sovereignty cannot be gotten rid of in any event; he worries that the notion of being free of sovereignty once and for all is a chimera. Insofar as he tells us that "it cannot be a matter, under the pretext of deconstruction, of purely and simply opposing sovereignty," Derrida further claims that "there is no contrary of sovereignty, even if there are things other than sovereignty."

Rather than try to get rid of sovereignty then, Derrida says that he would instead subject it to deconstruction (which, he is careful to tell us, is quite different from sovereignty's destruction). Thus he states that "recognizing that sovereignty is divisible, that it divides and partitions, even where there is any sovereignty left, is already to begin to deconstruct a pure concept of sovereignty that presupposes indivisibility."

This demonstrates Derrida's strategy in *The Beast and the Sovereign*, a two-volume book that began as a lecture series between December 2001 and March 2003. These lectures represented an attempt, if not to reconcile (since there could be no true reconciliation with such a force), at least to make a kind of co-existence with the concept of sovereignty possible. Derrida seeks a way to learn to live with it such that it in turn allows others their own life as well.

Much of *The Beast and the Sovereign* is taken up by Derrida's attempt to dig deep into sovereignty, what it is and how it works. Shortly after the passage above, Derrida reiterates a point that he makes repeatedly across both volumes, that sovereignty is a kind of "fiction" (even if it is a "dishonest" one, since fiction can have both constructive and destructive qualities for Derrida);[6] he also calls it a "prosthesis."[7] In terms of that latter claim, for Derrida, sovereignty constitutes an artificial state which supplements nature with law and a particular political order. He calls this a prosthesis because it claims to be an extension of nature (as a prosthetic limb might be). In fact, rather than serving as an extension of nature, sovereignty here works to make nature into an extension of itself.

Derrida's key insight is not that sovereignty's fictional and prosthetic nature renders it weak; on the contrary, it is the source of its greatest power. Indeed, for Derrida fictions are the basis of politics and the effects they have on human subjects are profound (but critically not inalterable). Furthermore, in its prosthetic form, sovereignty is perhaps the greatest fiction of them all.

The very title of the book(s), *The Beast and the Sovereign,* speaks volumes about the ambivalence inherent in Derrida's concept of sovereignty more generally. These two images, often conjured up in the same sentence, seem to be opposites, with the beast being understood as "outside" of the law and beneath the level of politics and the sovereign being somehow both above the law and politics. Here again sovereignty's prosthetic nature allows it to join natural and artificial and human-made things together.

For Derrida, however, the relationship between the beast and the sovereign is more complicated than a simple opposition. As he suggests, sovereignty is never quite free of the beast insofar as, without the fear or threat of the savage beneath the façade, sovereignty would be ineffective. Indeed, this is a key part of how its fictional nature serves sovereignty so well; despite the fact that the beast and the sovereign must have nothing to do with one another, as a fiction and as a prosthetic device, sovereignty can be connected to the beast nonetheless. Sovereignty is, after all, marked by a savage bestiality that never quite goes away. A beast cannot govern or even establish a state (although the founding of states seems to nearly always involve a beast nonetheless; witness the wolf that suckled Romulus and Remus, for example). It seems as though, if the beast is entirely gone, the state too must disappear.

This conundrum is the basis of Derrida's ambivalence. The state always threatens to turn into—or perhaps more accurately reveal—the beast that lays beneath the smooth surface of sovereign authority. Sovereignty is in some sense nothing more than a mask over that beast's face; but how powerful is that mask! The mask seems to tame or change the beast, to draw it into its own fictions so that it acts in an "unbeastly" manner, so that it allows, at least in theory, for things like democracy and justice (although for Derrida these things always remain "to come").[8]

This is where deconstruction comes into play. Recall once again Derrida's statement that "recognizing that sovereignty is divisible, that it divides and partitions, even where there is any sovereignty left, is already to begin to deconstruct a pure concept of sovereignty that presupposes indivisibility." Because a sense of its indivisibility and its unchallengeable power are at the heart and soul of what makes the fiction of sovereignty effective, Derrida's move to recognize the ways that sovereignty is never one and is thus always, to some extent, at odds with itself, comes across as extremely subversive and directly hostile to sovereign power. It seems to threaten sovereignty at its very core, to rip off the mask once and for all and show the world what sovereignty is underneath (a beast and an unnatural one at that).

But this is not quite what Derrida is trying to do. Such a move would smack of precisely the kind of positivism and ipseity—that is to say its own self-promotion as being unproblematically real and true—that his notion of deconstruction sets out to, well, deconstruct. Furthermore, even if he did want to so expose the sovereign, Derrida's own theory militates against such an outcome. It is critical to note that, for Derrida, the "beast" beneath the sovereign is no more "true" and authentic to sovereignty than the prosthesis of sovereignty itself. It is the fiction and the relationship that it both disguises and makes possible that serves to render sovereignty the power that it is. Accordingly, if there is no prosthesis, there is no beast either. Both elements are required to constitute and sustain the fiction of sovereign authority.

This does not mean that Derrida is not opposing sovereignty (he is) or that he is willing to leave sovereignty essentially intact (he isn't). It is rather that, as already noted, for Derrida deconstruction is neither a form of exposure nor of destruction but something entirely different. It might be tempting at this point to say that through deconstruction, Derrida could find a form of sovereignty (suitably altered) that he would prefer. But I think that it is a mistake to think this way. If deconstruction were merely a gauntlet that sovereignty had to pass through in order to shed its more unsavory elements, then it would be more a matter of reforming a system than radically subverting it. Deconstruction is less a way to fix something that is broken and more a way to recognize—and to some extent to benefit from— its brokenness. Deconstruction, I would say, is more an attitude of resistance than amelioration. In this way, deconstruction is opposed to authority in one sense but is itself a form of authority—indeed, as Derrida tells us elsewhere, a form of justice.[9]

To think further about deconstruction as a form of authority (however paradoxical that might seem) as well as the kinds of effects it has on sovereignty, it is helpful to think about what Derrida is resisting in his own turn to deconstruction. As we see in my opening passage, Derrida's great opponent here is Carl Schmitt, a thinker who, in Derrida's view, gives the clearest voice for what sovereignty is *supposed to be.* As Schmitt famously states, "Sovereign is he who decides upon the exception."[10] He further offers us the friend/enemy distinction as the basis of both politics and sovereign authority.

In challenging this viewpoint, Derrida tells us quite clearly in those opening lines of the passage that his goal is not a "de-politicization" but a "re-politicization" or the production of "another politicization," that is to say, another way to think about politics and sovereignty. In his view, sovereignty can and does survive the failure of its great and principle fiction (that of its purity and indivisibility). While it may be reckless to get rid of sovereignty altogether it is not so reckless to get rid of or at least expose that part of the fiction (that aspect which for Derrida is "dishonest," leading us to assume that there are other, "honest" fictions within sovereignty that deconstruction helps to reveal to us). This is once again not to suggest that deconstruction produces a "good" form of sovereignty. It rather means that a deconstructed sovereignty is less resilient against the kinds of resistance that deconstruction instantiates; it allows those anarchic elements that are suppressed by sovereignty to emerge and better (co-) exist with sovereignty itself.

The question of "honest" vs. "dishonest" sovereign fictions also helps to explain why for Derrida we can't have something like liberty if we try to get rid of sovereignty altogether. This is because the "fictions" of sovereignty are bound up inextricably with politics, which is similarly caught up with such fictions, including what it promises (liberty, equality, etc.). Even were we to suppose that Derrida could do away with sovereignty, he is certainly not willing to do away with politics altogether. We see in the very tenacity that is a hallmark of the fiction of sovereignty a similar tenacity in terms of its relationship to political life as a whole.

Accordingly, in the above passage, we can begin to discern something of an alternative definition of sovereignty to Schmitt's. For Derrida, sovereignty is not based on an exception but indeed on a fiction, a fiction that is not dissolved by deconstruction but rather viewed differently and indeed altered in terms of its sustaining fiction(s). Here, some of the more beneficial narratives of collective and creative potential associated with sovereignty could perhaps (with "perhaps" being a complicated word for Derrida) come to pass, or at least become less impossible.

In this way, deconstruction becomes critical to the program of re-politicizing sovereignty. Derrida tells us at the very beginning of the passage cited above that he seeks "a *slow and differentiated* deconstruction of this logic and the dominant, classic concept of nation-state sovereignty." But why must it be "*slow and differentiated*"? In a sense, thinking of deconstruction in this way reflects the job of deconstruction in general in terms of the way that it disaggregates what is not meant to be disaggregated and requires some time to mark and understand the effects of that disaggregation. Or perhaps more accurately, it seems that in deconstructing sovereignty in particular, deconstruction is revealing something about itself as well: the fact that it itself resembles what it demonstrates about sovereignty, the fact that it is not unitary and smooth but variated and uneven, with many actions and aspects within itself co-existing under one name.

This can be seen more clearly when Derrida speaks further on in the passage of "partings, partitions, divisions, conditions that come along to broach a sovereignty that is always supposed to be indivisible and unconditional." This series of articulations constitutes the very nature of deconstruction. Although sovereignty may be a fiction, it is a fiction with many parts and those parts often work at cross purposes. Using parts of the fiction to defeat a kind of ultimate—and dishonest—fiction (that sovereignty is pure and indivisible) shows deconstruction in action. This may happen, once again, in a particularly revealing way—that is to say, particularly revealing not only of sovereignty but of deconstruction itself as well.

For Derrida, this deconstructive move is not purely negative because it allows the component parts of the sovereign fiction to emerge, as it were, in their own right. This, not in the sense that they are revealed as the "authentic" face of sovereignty, but rather simply insofar as these components are all key parts of how sovereignty operates; their separate realities and unrealities are no greater or lesser (i.e. no more or less fictional) than the whole package of sovereign power.

Derrida also speaks of "the difficulty, awkwardness, aporia even, and a slowness, the always unequal development of such a deconstruction," referring now back again to the idea of a "*slow and differentiated*" form of deconstruction. Here, Derrida is recognizing that deconstruction is neither easy nor a given. This is not a matter of a surefire way to engage with sovereignty but rather a steady but uneven set of approaches that is itself as varied as the sovereign fictions that deconstruction acts upon. It is not only that sovereignty resists this deconstruction by its (false) insistence on its purity and indivisibility. It is also that the uneven terrain of sovereignty does not allow for a smooth deconstruction either (precisely because sovereignty is neither pure nor indivisible).

The passage comes full circle when Derrida tells us that sovereignty, when it is taken into its component and varied parts (i.e. deconstructed), "is no longer a sovereignty, a sovereignty worthy of the name, i.e. pure and unconditional." This is not, once again, to say that sovereignty no longer exists but rather that it is not the same kind of sovereignty as before. It is less connected to its originary violence, to determination and hierarchy. Here we begin to see a bit more clearly what Derrida means by a "re-politicization" and "another politics." In a sense, deconstruction has not added anything new to the political scene that it encounters; rather, by disaggregating sovereignty at least partially, it makes more options for politics both visible and possible.

A different kind of thinker might be far more tempted to argue for another politics that was not tied up, as Derrida insists, with the name of sovereignty.[11] To his credit, Derrida is not afraid to face the awful and bloody baggage that the name sovereignty brings with it. Furthermore, he is, by the same token, not willing to jettison this name, in part because he fears that whatever comes in its wake would be far worse and also because he seems to genuinely think that there is something about sovereignty that *works*. For all of his condemnation of sovereignty's bloodthirsty nature, *The Beast and the Sovereign* is as much an acknowledgment of sovereignty's ability to create something (political authority) out of nothing as it is a condemnation of what it does with the power that it accrues. It may be for this reason that Derrida thinks that it might be possible to keep the baby (a good and effective form of politics) *and* the bathwater (the name of sovereignty) in a way that is helpful for the human beings who live under this name.

Notes

1   Jacques Derrida, *The Beast and the Sovereign, Vol. 1*, ed. Michel Lisse, Marie-Louise Mallet, and Ginette Michaud, trans. Geoffrey Bennington (Chicago: University of Chicago Press, 2009), 75–7.

2   Jacques Derrida, *The Politics of Friendship*, trans. George Collins (New York: Verso Press, 2005). See, for example, 135, 181–2, 236.

3   Jacques Derrida, *Rogues: Two Essays on Reason*, trans. Pascale-Anne Brault and Michael Naas (Stanford, CA: Stanford University Press, 2004), 102.

4   Jacques Derrida, *Specters of Marx: The State of the Debt, the Work of Mourning and the New International*, trans. Peggy Kamuf, intro. Berndt Magnus and Stephen Cullenberg (New York: Routledge, 1994), 83–4.

5   See for example *Rogues*, 104.

6   *The Beast and the Sovereign, Vol. 1,* 77.

7   Ibid.

8   Jacques Derrida, "Force of Law: The 'Mystical Foundation of Authority'," in *Deconstruction and the Possibility of Justice*, ed. Drucilla Cornell, Michel Rosenfeld, and David Gray Carlson (New York: Routledge, 1992), 2–67 (27).

9   Ibid., p. 15.

10 Carl Schmitt, *Political Theology: Four Chapters on the Concept of Sovereignty*, trans. George Schwab (Cambridge, MA: MIT Press, 1985), 1.

11 Wendy Brown calls this Derrida's "sovereign hesitations." See her essay in *Derrida and the Time of the Political*, ed. Suzanne Guerlac and Pheng Cheah (Durham, NC: Duke University Press, 2009), 114–34.

FURTHER READING

Chapter 1

Goldin, Paul R., ed., *Dao Companion to the Philosophy of Han Fei* (Dordrecht: Springer, 2013).

Pines, Yuri, *Envisioning Eternal Empire: Chinese Political Thought of the Warring States Era* (Honolulu: University of Hawaii Press, 2009).

Pines, Yuri, trans. and ed., *The Book of Lord Shang: Apologetics of State Power in Early China* (New York: Columbia University Press, 2017).

Liu Zehua's articles on China's ideology of monarchism collected in a special issue of *Contemporary Chinese Thought* 45.2–3 (2013–14).

Chapter 2

Bourbon, Marion, Valéry Laurent, and Thornton Lockwood, eds., *Polis: The Journal for Ancient Greek and Roman Political Thought* 36, no. 1 (2019).

Frank, Jill, *A Democracy of Distinction: Aristotle and the Work of Politics* (Chicago: The University of Chicago Press, 2005).

Schofield, Malcolm, *Saving the City: Philosopher-Kings and Other Classical Paradigms* (London: Routledge, 1999).

Tessitore, Aristide, ed., *Aristotle and Modern Politics: The Persistence of Political Philosophy* (Notre Dame, IN: University of Notre Dame Press, 2002).

Chapter 3

Atkins, Jed W., *Roman Political Thought* (Cambridge: Cambridge University Press, 2018), Ch. 1.

Fritz, K. von, *The Theory of the Mixed Constitution in Antiquity: A Critical Analysis of Polybius' Ideas* (New York: Columbia University Press, 1954).

Hahm, David, "Polybius' Applied Political Theory," in *Justice and Generosity*, ed. A. Laks and M. Schofield (Cambridge: Cambridge University Press, 1995), 7–47.

Straumann, Benjamin, *Crisis and Constitutionalism: Roman Political Thought from the Fall of the Republic to the Age of Revolution* (Oxford: Oxford University Press, 2016), Ch. 4.

Walbank, F. W., "Polybius on the Roman Constitution," *The Classical Quarterly* 37, no. 3/4 (1943): 73–89.

Chapter 4

Bauman, Richard A., *The Crimen Maiestatis in the Roman Republic and Augustan Principate* (Johannesburg: Witwatersrand University Press, 1967).

Fears, J. Rufus, "The Cult of Jupiter and Roman Imperial Ideology," in *Aufstieg und Niedergang der römischen Welt*, ed. Wolfgang Haase (Berlin: Gruyter, 1981), 7–141.

Ferrary, Jean-Louis, "Les origines de la loi de majesté à Rome," *Comptes rendus des séances de l'Académie des Inscriptions et Belles-Lettres* (1983): 556–72.

Hammer, Dean, "Between sovereignty and non-sovereignty: *Maiestas populi Romani* and foundational authority in the Roman Republic," in *Proceedings of the British Academy*, ed. Christopher Smith (London: British Academy; forthcoming).

Nicolet, Claude, *Space, Geography, and Politics in the Early Roman Empire* (Ann Arbor: University of Michigan Press, 1991).

Chapter 5

Campanini, Massimo, *La politica nell'Islam. Una interpretazione* (Bologna: Il Mulino, 2019).

Galston, Miriam, *Politics and Excellence: The Political Philosophy of Alfarabi* (Princeton: Princeton University Press, 1990).

Mahdi, Muhsin, *Alfarabi and the Foundation of Islamic Political Philosophy* (Chicago: University of Chicago Press, 2001).

Chapter 6

Gewirth, Alan, *Marsilius of Padua and Medieval Political Philosophy* [= Marsilius of Padua, *The Defender of Peace*, vol. 1] (New York: Columbia University Press, 1951).

Nederman, Cary J., *Community and Consent: The Secular Political Theory of Marsiglio of Padua's Defensor Pacis* (Lanham, MD: Rowman & Littlefield, 1995).

Syros, Vasileios, *Marsilius of Padua at the Intersection of Ancient and Medieval Traditions of Political Thought* (Toronto: University of Toronto Press, 2012).

Chapter 7

Forhan, Kate Langdon, *The Political Theory of Christine de Pizan* (Aldershot: Ashgate 2002).

Pizan, Christine de, *The Book of the City of Ladies and Other Writings*, trans. Ineke Hardy, ed. Sophie Bourgault and Rebecca Kingston (Indianapolis, IN: Hackett Publishing, 2018).

Willard, Charity Cannon, *Christine de Pizan: Her Life and Works* (New York: Persea Books, 1984).

Chapter 8

Bodin, Jean, *The Six Bookes of a Commonweale. A Facsimile Reprint of the English Translation of 1606, Corrected and Supplemented in the Light of a New Comparison with the French and Latin Texts*, ed. Kenneth D. McRae (Cambridge, MA: Harvard University Press, 1962).

Foisneau, Luc, "Sovereignty and Reason of State: Bodin, Botero, Richelieu and Hobbes," in *The Reception of Bodin*, ed. Howell A. Lloyd (Leiden and Boston: Brill, 2013), 323–42.

Lloyd, Howell A., *Jean Bodin, "This Pre-eminent Man of France": An Intellectual Biography* (Oxford: Oxford University Press, 2017).

The Bodin Project: Aids to the study of Jean Bodin [website curated by a group of Bodin scholars] https://projects.iq.harvard.edu/bodinproject/biography-bodin

Chapter 9

Borschberg, Peter, *Hugo Grotius "Commentarius in Theses XI"* (Bern: Pieterlen, 1994).

Grotius, Hugo, *The Rights of War and Peace*, ed. Richard Tuck (Indianapolis, IN: Liberty Fund, 2005).

Nifterik, Gustaaf van, "A Reply to Grotius's Critics. On Constitutional Law," *Grotiana* 39 (2018): 77–95.

Barducci, Marco, *Hugo Grotius and the Century of Revolution, 1613–1718* (Oxford: Oxford University Press, 2017).

Baumgold, Deborah, *Contract Theory in Historical Context. Essays on Grotius Hobbes and Locke* (Leiden: Brill, 2010).

Chapter 10

Armitage, David, Conal Condren, and Andrew Fitzmaurice, eds., *Shakespeare and Early Modern Political Thought* (Cambridge: Cambridge University Press, 2009).

Gil, Daniel Juan, *Shakespeare's Anti-Politics: Sovereign Power and the Life of the Flesh* (Houndmills and New York: Palgrave Macmillan, 2013).

Hadfield, Andrew, *Shakespeare and Republicanism* (Cambridge: Cambridge University Press, 2005).

Haverkamp, Anselm, *Shakespearean Genealogies of Power: A Whispering of Nothing in* Hamlet, Richard II, Julius Caesar, Macbeth, The Merchant of Venice, *and* The Winter's Tale (New York: Routledge, 2010).

Lupton, Julia Reinhard, *Citizen-Saints: Shakespeare and Political Theology* (Chicago: University of Chicago Press, 2005).

Chapter 11

Como, David, *Radical Parliamentarians and the English Civil War* (Oxford: Oxford University Press, 2018).

Lee, Daniel, *Popular Sovereignty in Early Modern Constitutional Thought* (Oxford: Oxford University Press, 2016).

Mendle, Michael, *Dangerous Positions: Mixed Government, the Estates of the Realm, and the Answer to the XIX Propositions* (University, AL: University of Alabama Press, 1985).

Mendle, Michael, *Henry Parker and the English Civil War: The Political Thought of the Public's "Privado"* (Cambridge: Cambridge University Press, 1995).

Chapter 12

Burgess, Glenn, *British Political Thought 1500–1660: The Politics of the Post-Reformation* (London: Palgrave Macmillan, 2009).

Malcolm, Noel, *Aspects of Hobbes* (Oxford: Clarendon Press, 2002).

Martinich, A. P. and Kinch Hoekstra, eds., *The Oxford Handbook of Hobbes* (New York: Oxford University Press, 2016).

Skinner, Quentin, *Hobbes and Republican Liberty* (Cambridge: Cambridge University Press, 2008).

Springborg, Patricia, ed., *The Cambridge Companion to Hobbes's Leviathan* (Cambridge: Cambridge University Press, 2007).

Chapter 13

Corbett, Ross J., *The Lockean Commonwealth* (Albany: State University of New York Press, 2009).

Davis, Michael, "Locke's Political Society," *Journal of Moral Philosophy*, 11:2 (2014), 209–31.

Locke, John, *Two Treatises of Government*, ed. Peter Laslett (Cambridge: Cambridge University Press, 1988).

Locke, John, "First Tract on Government" and "Second Tract on Government," in John Locke, *Political Essays*, ed. Mark Goldie (Cambridge: Cambridge University Press, 2007), 3–133.

Chapter 14

Bertram, Christopher, *Routledge Philosophy GuideBook to Rousseau and "The Social Contract"* (London: Routledge, 2003), ch. 6.

Douglass, Robin, "Rousseau's Critique of Representative Sovereignty: Principled or Pragmatic," *American Journal of Political Science* 57, no. 2 (July 2013): 735–47.

Putterman, Ethan, *Rousseau, Law, and the Sovereignty of the People* (Cambridge: Cambridge University Press, 2016).

Tuck, Richard, *The Sleeping Sovereign: The Invention of Modern Democracy* (Cambridge: Cambridge University Press, 2016), ch. 3.

Urbanati, Nadia, "Rousseau on the Risks of Representing the Sovereign," *Politische Vierteljahresschrift* 53, no. 4 (2012): 646–67.

Chapter 15

Blackstone, William, *Commentaries on the Laws of England* (1765; Chicago: University of Chicago Press, 1979).

Hamilton, Alexander, John Jay, and James Madison, *The Federalist Papers*, ed. George W. Carey and James McClellan (1788; Indianapolis: The Liberty Fund, 2001).

McDonald, Forrest, *States' Rights and the Union: Imperium in Imperio, 1776–1876* (Lawrence: University Press of Kansas, 2000).

Onuf, Peter and Nicholas Onuf, *Federal Union, Modern World: The Law of Nations in an Age of Revolutions, 1776–1814* (Madison, WI: Madison House, 1993).

Vattel, Emer de, *The Law of Nations* (Indianapolis, IN: Liberty Fund, 2008).

Chapter 16

Claeys, Gregory, *Thomas Paine: Social and Political Thought* (Boston: Unwin Hyman, 1989).

Foner, Eric, *Tom Paine and Revolutionary America* (New York: Oxford University Press, 1976).

Lounissi, Carine, *La Pensée politique de Thomas Paine en contexte: Théorie et pratique* (Paris: Champion, 2012).

Lounissi, Carine, *Thomas Paine and the French Revolution* (Basingstoke: Palgrave-Macmillan, 2018).

Paine, Thomas, *Rights of Man, Common Sense and Other Political Writings*, ed. Mark Philp (Oxford: Oxford University Press, 1995).

Paine, Thomas, *The Writings of Thomas Paine*, coll. and ed. Moncure Daniel Conway (New York: G.P. Putnam's Sons, 1894).

Paine, Thomas, *The Complete Writings of Thomas Paine*, ed. Philip S. Foner (New York: The Citadel Press, 1945).

Chapter 17

Dimova-Cookson, Maria, *Green's Moral and Political Philosophy: A Phenomenological Perspective* (Houndsmills: Palgrave, 2001).

Morrow, John, ed., *T. H. Green* (Aldershot: Ashgate, 2007).

Nicholson, Peter P., *The Political Philosophy of the British Idealists: Selected Studies* (Cambridge: Cambridge University Press, 1990).

Thomas, Geoffrey, *The Moral Philosophy of T. H. Green* (Oxford: Clarendon Press, 1987).

Tyler, Colin, *Civil Society, Capitalism and the State. Part 2 of The Liberal Socialism of Thomas Hill Green* (Exeter: Imprint-Academic, 2012).

Chapter 18

Badiou, Alain, "One Divides Itself into Two," in *Lenin Reloaded: Toward a Politics of Truth*, ed. Sebastian Budgen, Stathis Kouvelakis and Slavoj Žižek (Durham: Duke University Press, 2007), 7–17.

Brie, Michael, *Rediscovering Lenin: Dialectics of Revolution and Metaphysics of Domination* (New York: Palgrave Macmillan, 2019).

Losurdo, Domenico, *War and Revolution: Rethinking the 20th Century*, trans. Gregory Elliott (London: Verso, 2015).

Qinian, An, "A Few Questions Concerning Lenin's Conception of the Dictatorship of the Proletariat," in *The Palgrave Handbook of Leninist Political Philosophy*, ed. Tom Rockmore and Norman Levine (New York: Palgrave Macmillan, 2018), 381–400.

Toscano, Alberto, "Dual Power Revisited: From Civil War to Biopolitical Islam," *Soft Targets* 2, no. 1 (2006): 150–5.

Chapter 19

Caldwell, Peter C., *Popular Sovereignty and the Crisis of German Constitutional Law: The Theory and Practice of Weimar Constitutionalism* (Durham: Duke University Press, 1997).

Kalyvas, Andreas, *Democracy and the Politics of the Extraordinary: Max Weber, Carl Schmitt, and Hannah Arendt* (Cambridge: Cambridge University Press, 2008).

Kervégan, Jean-François, *Hegel, Carl Schmitt: Le politique entre spéculation et positivité* (Paris: Presses Universitaires de France, 1992).

Scheuerman, William E., *Carl Schmitt: The End of Law* (Lanham: Rowman & Littlefield, 1999).

Chapter 20

Birmingham, Peg, *Hannah Arendt and Human Rights: The Predicament of Common Responsibility* (Bloomington: Indiana University Press, 2006).

Buckler, Steve, *Hannah Arendt and Political Theory: Challenging the Tradition* (Edinburgh: Edinburgh University Press, 2011).

Gündogdu, Ayten, *Rightlessness in an Age of Rights: Hannah Arendt and the Contemporary Struggles of Migrants* (New York: Oxford University Press, 2015).

Lederman, Shmuel, *Hannah Arendt and Participatory Democracy: A People's Utopia* (New York: Palgrave Macmillan, 2019).

Young-Bruehl, Elizabeth, *Hannah Arendt: For Love of the World* (New Haven: Yale University Press, 2004).

Chapter 21

Agamben, Giorgio, *Homo Sacer: Sovereign Power and Bare Life*, trans. Daniel Heller-Roazen (Stanford, CA: Stanford University Press, 1998).

Agamben, Giorgio, *Remnants of Auschwitz: The Witness and the Archive*, trans. Daniel Heller-Roazen (New York: Zone Books, 1999).

Foucault, Michel, *The History of Sexuality, Volume 1: An Introduction*, trans. Robert Hurley (New York: Pantheon, 1978).

Foucault, Michel, *Security, Territory, Population: Lectures at the Collège de France, 1977–1978*, trans. Graham Burchell (Basingstoke: Palgrave Macmillan, 2007).

Foucault, Michel, *Society Must Be Defended: Lectures at the Collège the France, 1975–76*, trans. David Macey (New York: Picador, 2003).

Chapter 22

Derrida, Jacques, *Rogues* (Stanford, CA: Stanford University Press, 2002).

Derrida, Jacques, *Politics of Friendship* (New York: Verso, 1994).

Honig, Bonnie, "Declarations of Independence: Arendt and Derrida on the Problem of Founding a Republic," *The American Political Science Review* 85, no. 1 (March, 1991): 97–113.

Patton, Paul, "Deconstruction and the Problem of Sovereignty," *Derrida Today* 19, issue 1 (2017): 1–20.

Ville, Jacques de, "Sovereignty without Sovereignty: Derrida's Declarations of Independence," *Law and Critique* 19 (2008): 87–114.

INDEX

www.ingramcontent.com/pod-product-compliance
Ingram Content Group UK Ltd.
Pitfield, Milton Keynes, MK11 3LW, UK
UKHW020701280225
455688UK00004B/198

9 781350 099692